Turbo Pascal®
Memory Management
Techniques

Turbo Pascal®
Memory Management
Techniques

Len Dorfman
Marc J. Neuberger

Windcrest®/McGraw-Hill

FIRST EDITION
FIRST PRINTING

Library of Congress Cataloging-in-Publication Data

Dorfman, Len.
    Turbo Pascal memory management techniques / by Len Dorfman and
Marc J. Neuberger.
        p.   cm.
    Includes index.
    ISBN 0-8306-4059-2 (pbk.)
    1. Pascal (Computer program language) 2. Turbo Pascal (Computer
file) 3. Memory management (Computer science) I. Neuberger, Marc
J. II. Title.
QA76.73.P2D67   1993
005.265—dc20
                                              92-36638
                                                 CIP

Acquisitions Editor: Brad Schepp
Supervising Editor: Robert E. Ostrander
Book Editor: David M. McCandless
Production: Katherine G. Brown
Book Design: Jaclyn J. Boone
Cover: Sandra Blair Design and Brent Blair
   Photography, Harrisburg, Pa.

Contents

To Barbara and Rachel, for their love and spirited humor.
To Stephen Moore, for his eagle's eye.

Len

To Leah, Joe, and Miriam for their love, support, and friendship.

Marc

How to use this book

In order to benefit most from this book, you should have at least beginner's knowledge of the Pascal programming language and its basic object-oriented features. The programs in this book were developed and tested using Borland's Turbo Pascal 6.0.

Although the assembly bindings were assembled using TASM, knowledge of assembly programming is not required to use the memory management functions presented in the book.

Introduction

This practical, how-to book has been designed with the intent of providing object-oriented Pascal programmers with the practical tools required for seamless dynamic integration of high memory (Expanded Memory, Extended Memory, and the hard disk) into application programs. This book provides the tools required for Extended Memory, Expanded Memory and Virtual Memory management in the 8086/8088 real mode.

EMS and XMS memory management functions provide the building blocks used to support the Virtual Memory Manager system presented in Chapter 6. The full source for the VMM system is presented along with the EMS and XMS interface. A comprehensive memory management library is also provided on disk.

When you finish this book, you will understand the workings of EMS, XMS and a Virtual Memory Management system. This understanding will allow you to take full advantage of EMS, XMS and hard disk memory in your application programs. You'll have at your disposal a set of simple-to-use virtual dynamic memory allocation functions which will permit your program access to memory areas in the multiple-megabyte range.

The book begins with a straightforward discussion of a PC's memory management scheme. Once the memory management overview is completed, Chapter 2 introduces the Memory Arena (as it's called by Microsoft) or the Memory Control Block (MCB—as is known by much of the industry). A full blown Memory Control Block display program is presented.

Chapter 3 presents an explanation of the EMS 3.0 and 3.2 functions. The chapter's demonstration programs are designed to exercise many EMS 3.0 and 3.2 functions. The source code and function prototype for each EMS function is presented along with the demonstration programs' source code.

Once you have a handle on using EMS 3.0 and 3.2 functions, Chapter 4 continues the EMS discussion by exploring the EMS version 4.0 expanded memory standard. Taking the lead from Chapter 3, most of the EMS 4.0 functions are prototyped and the source for the functions is presented. The sources for several EMS 4.0 demonstration programs are also presented in Chapter 4.

Chapter 5 introduces the Extended Memory Specification (XMS) version 2.0. As with the EMS chapters, the full source for each function is presented along with XMS demonstration programs.

Chapter 6 presents the source code to a Virtual Memory Manager that enables you, for example, to open up a two-megabyte area of memory for use in your application program. This dynamically allocated memory may be opened, written to, read from, and freed as with standard dynamically allocated memory. The VMM interface functions are prototyped and two VMM demonstration programs are also presented. We've taken great care in constructing the source code comments in this chapter. This was done to help facilitate your understanding of the VMM's complex inner workings.

1
Memory management overview

Although many programmers feel that the segment-offset architecture of the 80x86 series of CPUs is byzantine, the CPUs work just fine. In the vernacular, "They get the job done!"

Let's draw a thumbnail sketch of the 80x86 memory architecture. The 80x86 series of processors has three modes of operation. The least common denominator is *real mode*—available to all 80x86 processors—in which the CPU acts like an 8086/8088, with addresses composed of a 16-bit segment and a 16-bit offset. These two words are combined to form a 20-bit physical address by shifting the segment left by 4 bits and adding the offset. This gives an address space of 1M.

In *16-bit protected mode*—available on 80286's and up—an address is comprised of a 16-bit selector and a 16-bit offset. Rather than being used directly to compute the physical address, the selector denotes a descriptor in a descriptor table. Among other things, the descriptor contains a 24-bit base address to be used in address computation. The offset is added to this base address. Thus 16M of memory can be addressed.

In *32-bit protected mode*—available on 80386's and up—an address is made up of a 16-bit selector and a 32-bit offset. Again, the selector denotes a descriptor, which now contains a 32-bit base address. The offset is added to this base address. This allows access to 4G of physical memory. In addition, the 32-bit offsets allow memory to be configured into a 4G linear address space, accessible through just an offset.

Most existing MS-DOS and PC-DOS programs run in real mode. This book deals with memory management in real mode.

When programming in the real mode, as opposed to the 80286-80386-80486 protected mode, the CPU cannot address memory above 1M. Memory below 1M can be divided into two sections: memory from 0K to 640K can be called the *Low Memory Area* and the memory from 640K to 1024K (1M) can be called the *Upper Memory Area.* Memory above 1M can be called the *Extended Memory Area.*

Memory Range	Name
0K to 640K	Low Memory Area
640K to 1M	Upper Memory Area
Above 1M	Extended Memory Area

The Low Memory Area is used for things like the PC BIOS's data area, DOS, interrupt vectors, device drivers, and TSRs. What remains for program use is called the Transient Program Area (TPA).

The Upper Memory Area is reserved for BIOS code and hardware devices. Video display adapters require various amounts of upper memory for access to their screen refresh buffers. The system BIOS (Basic Input Output System), which provides low-level hardware access, resides in upper memory. Disk controllers also occupy some upper memory for their interface to the operating system.

The Extended Memory Area is available to anyone with the know-how to exploit the EMS and/or XMS specifications.

Low memory is divided up into blocks of memory. Each of these blocks is described by a Memory Control Block (MCB) structure. These control blocks contain information indicating the size of the memory block and whether the memory block is free or owned by a program.

With all of the various needs which must be filled by the lower memory area, space can run out. Pre-DOS 5.0 users could find themselves with 450K (or less!) for their application program's use (the TPA).

Although DOS 5.0 and commercial memory management utility programs improve the memory management situation considerably by allowing users to load TSRs, device drivers and DOS into upper and Extended Memory, you're still limited by the paltry 640K boundary for the TPA.

Why the description of "paltry" for the 640K limit? Suppose you need to dynamically allocate 1M of memory for a program's use. Simply stated, 640K "won't get the job done." As the programs that software designers write become larger and increasingly complex, there is a crying need for ways to access more than 640K of memory.

Prior to the advent of EMS and XMS, one solution was to use disk storage as a substitute for RAM. Although this situation did work, using hard disk storage as a substitute for RAM proved very cumbersome. Disk access is a perceptible order of magnitude slower than RAM access. Programs that used the hard disk as a work-around the 640K limit were painfully slow. And, as they say, "time is money."

Hardware designers, however, proved up to the challenge of breaking the 640K boundary, bringing Expanded Memory (EMS) into being. EMS provided a clever page flipping scheme where chunks of Extended

Memory could be mapped to an address in Upper Memory. Programs called Expanded Memory Managers (EMM) were designed to support this page-flipping memory management scheme, either through the use of hardware page mapping, or the 80286/80386 paging capabilities.

This arrangement proved quite workable because Lotus, Intel, and Microsoft (LIM) together created the EMS standard. Having a standard for EMS proved essential for developing well behaved programs which would not corrupt other programs' EMS-based data. Although page flipping was not as elegant as a linear addressing scheme might have proved, it certainly beat using the hard disk!

The 80286 chip's hitting the market heralded the arrival of protected mode programming by now allowing the CPU to access memory above the 1M boundary. Memory above 1M became known as Extended Memory. DOS, however, is not a protected mode operating system and does not have the means to access the area of memory above 1M. For a time, using Extended Memory in your programs proved risky business because there wasn't a specification standard regulating Extended Memory usage.

In the late 1980's, however, the Extended Memory (XMS) specification v2.0 appeared. The emergence of this XMS standard along with Microsoft's HIMEM.SYS XMS device driver allowed programmers to have access to Extended Memory in an orderly fashion.

DOS memory manager utility programs now allow inexpensive Extended Memory (XMS) to be reconfigured to function as Expanded Memory (EMS). This proves an economical solution. Many new-age 80x86 motherboards allow for installation of many megabytes of Extended Memory. Memory manager utility programs allow this Extended Memory to be divided up into various combinations of XMS and EMS.

At the time of this writing, real mode programmers currently have three distinct ways of breaking the 640K boundary for dynamic memory allocation uses. They are

- using EMS page flipping scheme.
- using Extended Memory.
- using the hard disk drive as substitute RAM.

Using Expanded Memory for dynamic memory allocation

An EMM program allocates a 64K area of the address space between 640K and 1024K for use as what is called the *page frame* area. Four 16K blocks of RAM from above 1M may then be mapped to this page frame area by making calls to the EMM program.

This 64K page frame is composed of four 16K physical pages. The four physical pages are taken (really mapped) from a large collection of what are called *logical pages* (those of you familiar with operating systems will note that this terminology is somewhat backwards: here the program references physical pages that get mapped to logical pages instead of the other way around). Let's try to visualize the relationship between 16K logical pages, 16K physical pages, and 64K page frames. Figure 1-1 shows one way of viewing the EMS physical and logical page relationship.

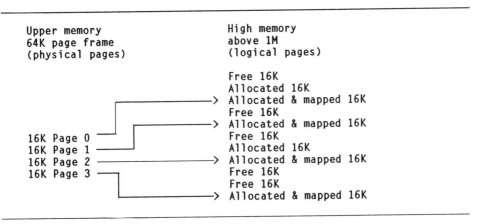

1-1 The EMS physical and logical page relationship.

The EMS page mapping process may be thought of as follows:

1. Map up to four different 16K logical pages to the four different 16K physical pages using your EMM.
2. Read from or write to physical pages.
3. Map new 16K logical pages to physical pages.
4. Go to 2.

Table 1-1 presents a summary listing of the functions associated with EMS 3.0, 3.2, and 4.0.

Table 1-1 The EMS 3.0, 3.2, and 4.0 specification listing.

Ver.	Funct.	Sub.	Description
3.0	40h		Get EMS status
3.0	41h		Get EMS page frame address
3.0	42h		Get number of EMS 16K pages
3.0	43h		Allocate EMS handle and 16K pages
3.0	44h		Map EMS logical pages to physical pages
3.0	45h		Free EMS handle and logical pages
3.0	46h		Get EMS version installed
3.0	57H		Save EMS page map
3.0	48h		Restore EMS page map

Table 1-1 Continued.

Ver.	Funct.	Sub.	Description
3.0	49h		(Reserved for future use)
3.0	4Ah		(Reserved for future use)
3.0	4Bh		Get EMS handle count
3.0	4Ch		Get EMS handle pages
3.0	4Dh		Get all EMS pages for all handles
3.2	4Eh	00h	Save EMS page map
3.2	4Eh	01h	Restore EMS page map
3.2	4Eh	02h	Save and restore EMS page map
3.2	4Eh	03h	Get size of EMS page map information
4.0	4Fh	00h	Save partial EMS page map
4.0	4Fh	01h	Restore partial EMS page map
4.0	4Fh	02h	Get size of partial EMS page map information
4.0	50h	00h	Map multiple EMS pages by number
4.0	50h	01h	Map multiple EMS pages by address
4.0	51h		Reallocate EMS pages for handle
4.0	52h	00h	Get EMS handle attribute
4.0	52h	01h	Set EMS handle attribute
4.0	52h	02h	Get EMS attribute capability
4.0	53h	00h	Get EMS handle name
4.0	53h	01h	Set EMS handle name
4.0	54h	00h	Get all EMS handle names
4.0	54h	01h	Search for EMS handle names
4.0	54h	02h	Get total EMS handles
4.0	55h	00h	Map EMS pages by number and JMP
4.0	55h	01h	Map EMS pages by address and JMP
4.0	56h	00h	Map EMS pages by number and CALL
4.0	56h	01h	Map EMS pages by address and CALL
4.0	56h	02h	Get space for EMS map page and CALL
4.0	57h	00h	Move memory region
4.0	57h	01h	Exchange memory regions
4.0	58h	00h	Get addresses of mappable EMS pages
4.0	58h	01h	Get number of mappable EMS pages
4.0	59h	00h	Get hardware configuration
4.0	59h	01h	Get number of raw 16K pages
4.0	5Ah	00h	Allocate handle and standard EMS pages
4.0	5Ah	01h	Allocate handle and raw 16K pages
4.0	5Bh	00h	Get alternate EMS map registers
4.0	5Bh	01h	Set alternate EMS map registers
4.0	5Ch		Prep EMM for warm boot
4.0	5Dh	00h	Disable EMM operating system functions
4.0	5Dh	01h	Enable EMM operating system functions
4.0	5Dh	02h	Release EMS access key

We recommend that EMS be the first place a programmer look in order to break the 640K memory boundary limit for dynamic memory allocation.

Using Extended Memory
for dynamic memory allocation

We rate using XMS for Extended Memory usage as a second choice to EMS for the following reasons:

1. EMS allows mapping pages into addressable memory while XMS requires data to be transferred to and from Extended Memory. Mapping is a much faster operation than transferring 16K of data.
2. EMS provides a richer set of functionality than XMS does.

Table 1-2 presents a listing of the XMS v2.0 specification.

Table 1-2 The XMS 2.0 specification list.

Ver.	Funct.	Description
2.0	00h	Get XMS Version Number
2.0	01h	Request High Memory Area
2.0	02h	Release High Memory Area
2.0	03h	Global Enable A20
2.0	04h	Global Disable A20
2.0	05h	Local Enable A20
2.0	06h	Local Disable A20
2.0	07h	Query A20
2.0	08h	Query Free Extended Memory
2.0	09h	Allocate Extended Memory Block
2.0	0Ah	Free Extended Memory Block
2.0	0Bh	Move Extended Memory Block
2.0	0Ch	Lock Extended Memory Block
2.0	0Dh	Unlock Extended Memory Block
2.0	0Eh	Get Handle Information
2.0	0Fh	Reallocate Extended Memory Block
2.0	10h	Request Upper Memory Block
2.0	11h	Release Upper Memory Block

Using the hard disk
for dynamic memory allocation

Using file I/O in Pascal is a relatively straightforward task. Building extended level memory management functions using DOS-based file I/O functions provides a useful backup method for Extended Memory usage when the host computer doesn't have EMS or XMS memory available.

We deem the disk dynamic memory allocation management option as "backup" because it is painfully slow compared to RAM-based methods.

Summary

DOS is a real mode operating system and allows no more than 640K for a program's use. The memory available for a program's use is called the TPA (Transient Program Area).

Many programs require far more memory than the 640K limit, and various memory management strategies come to the fore.

Using EMS for dynamic memory allocation proves both reliable and fast. The reliability of EMS was fostered by the emergence of the standard. Programming standards ensure well-behaved programs. EMS is our first choice for dynamic memory allocation because of the functionality associated with the EMS 3.0, 3.2, and 4.0 specifications, and the speed of mapping as opposed to the speed of data transfer.

Using XMS for dynamic memory allocation also proves fast and reliable. We rate using XMS for dynamic memory allocation second to using EMS because the XMS v2.0 specification has less functionality than the EMS specifications.

For these reasons, the following memory management rating list naturally follows:

1. EMS (Expanded Memory)
2. XMS (Extended Memory)
3. Hard disk drive

2
Understanding memory control blocks

A complete understanding of memory management must include a description on how DOS handles memory allocation in low memory. Simply stated, DOS divides the 640K of low memory into a series of contiguous memory blocks. These memory blocks are sized in multiples of 16-byte memory "paragraphs," which makes sense because the segment selector registers (DS,CS,ES,SS) work in paragraph boundaries and not single-byte boundaries (recall that in forming an address, the segment is shifted left by 4, or equivalently, multiplied by 16).

DOS creates a one-paragraph (16-byte) section of memory that describes certain attributes of the block of memory associated with it. In this book, the one-paragraph memory block descriptor is called the MCB, or Memory Control Block. Other industry sources have referred to it at the Memory Arena and Arena Header.

Your PC's low memory has many memory blocks that describe memory held by programs, device drivers, and free memory. As there is an MCB for each block of memory, these multiple MCBs have come to be known collectively as the *MCB chain*.

In memory, the MCB is immediately followed by the block of memory that it describes. Let's have a look at the MCB structure as it seemed to behave in pre-DOS 4.0 days. Note that I use the term "seem to behave" because in early Microsoft documentation the contents of the MCB were not delineated. In fact, the DOS call to locate the address of the first MCB is still an undocumented DOS service.

Pre-DOS 4.0 MCB

```
MCB__Mcb = record
            chain__status:  Char;
            owner__psp:     Word;
```

```
size_paragraphs:   Word;
dummy:             array[1..3] of Byte;
reserved:          array[0..7] of Char;
end;
```

The first element of the MCB structure is an 8-bit value that holds the status of the memory chain. If it holds an ASCII 'M', this means that there are more memory blocks in the memory block chain. If it holds an ASCII 'Z', then this MCB is the last MCB in the chain.

The second element in the MCB holds the segment value of the PSP (Program Segment Prefix) of the program that owns the block of memory described by the MCB. DOS creates this 256-byte PSP when a program is loaded. In this chapter, we will use the following information from a program's PSP:

PSP segment value is used as program owner ID
PSP:[0x2C] holds segment of program environment
PSP:[0x80] holds program command line length
PSP:[0x81] holds ASCII command line start

The third element in the MCB structure contains a 16-bit integer that contains the size, in paragraphs, of the memory block associated with the MCB. To calculate the size of the memory block in bytes, simply take the number of paragraphs and multiply that value by 16. (Of course, to assembly coders, shifting 4 bits left is a little slicker than multiplying by 16.)

Once you know the length of the memory block described by the MCB, it's very easy to find the next memory block in the chain. All you need to do is to take the MCB's segment, add the size in paragraphs of the memory block to that segment, and then add 1 (for the MCB itself). Lo and behold, you'll then have the segment for the next MCB in the MCB chain.

Programs like MAPMEM, MEM, TDMEM, and PROG2-3.PAS (a memory display utility program is presented in FIG. 2-3) work by getting the segment of the first MCB, displaying some information, getting the next MCB, displaying more information, and continuing with that process until the end of the MCB chain is reached. Once you have access to the MCB, PSP and program's environment there are many things about the memory block owner that you can report.

In DOS 4.0 and later, the 8-byte fifth element holds the name (without extension) of the program that owns that MCB's memory block. This eases the task of finding the MCB's owner program name because you no longer need to search the owner program's environment for the owner name.

Next is the MCB structure for the DOS 4.0 and later MCB.

Post-DOS 4.0 MCB

```
MCB_Mcb = record
            chain_status:  Char;
            owner_psp:     Word;
```

```
size_paragraphs:    Word;
dummy:              array[1..3] of Byte;
file_name:          array[0..7] of Char;
end;
```

Now that we've introduced the MCB and its structure, let's write some code!

Preparatory memory management routines

Figure 2-1 presents the source code listing to __MCB.PAS. __MCB.PAS contains a collection of definitions that will prove useful in displaying information about the MCB chain.

Take a moment to review the source code to __MCB.PAS. All that is defined there are the MCB layout and two functions that are really just Pascal wrappers for DOS services.

2-1 The source code listing to __MCB.PAS.

```
(* * * * * * * * * * * * * * * * * *
 *
 * _mcb.pas
 *
 * Unit file for the MCB functions
 *
 * * * * * * * * * * * * * * * * * * *)

unit    _mcb;

INTERFACE

uses    _globals;


(* * * * * * * * * * * * * * * * * *
 *
 * Memory Control Block Structure
 *
 * * * * * * * * * * * * * * * * * * *)


type
    MCB_Mcb = record
        chain_status:       Char;
        owner_psp:          Word;
        size_paragraphs:    Word;
        dummy:              array[1..3] of Byte;
        file_name:          array[0..7] of Char;
        end;

    MCB_McbPtr = ^MCB_Mcb;
```

2-1 Continued.

```
function    getMcbPointer
                :   MCB_McbPtr;
function    getVecPointer(
                vecNum: Byte)
                :   DWord;


IMPLEMENTATION

uses    dos;

function    getMcbPointer: MCB_McbPtr;

var
    regs:                   Registers;
    firstMCBSeg:            Word;

begin

    (*
     *  Use int21 subcode $52 to look up the vector
     *)
    regs.AH:- $52;
    MsDos(regs);
    firstMCBSeg:- WordPtr(Ptr(regs.ES, regs.BX-2))^;
    getMcbPointer:- Ptr(firstMCBSeg, 0);

end;

function    getVecPointer(vecNum: Byte): DWord;

var
    regs:                   Registers;

begin

    (*
     *  Use int21 subcode $35 to look up the vector
     *)
    regs.AL:- vecNum;
    regs.AH:- $35;
    MsDos(regs);
    getVecPointer:- DWord(Ptr(regs.ES, regs.BX));

end;

end.
```

Writing a memory chain display utility program

Quite a few fine memory display utility programs are on the market today. The purpose of the demonstration programs presented in this chapter is to clearly demonstrate how the information contained in the

MCB and PSP may be obtained. We believe that a programming example is worth more than 1024 words.

Figure 2-2 presents the source code listing to PROG2-1.PAS. This program steps through the MCB memory chain and displays the MCB status, MCB segment value, PSP segment value and the size of the memory block in 16-byte paragraphs.

2-2 The source code listing to PROG2-1.PAS.

```
(* * * * * * * * * * * * * * * * *
 *
 * prog2-1.pas
 *
 * Demonstration of
 *    getMcbPointer(...)
 *
 * * * * * * * * * * * * * * * * * *)

program prog2_1;

uses    _globals,
        _mcb;

var
    mcbPtr:              MCB_McbPtr;

begin

    (*
     * fill Mem Cntl
     * block with info
     *)
    mcbPtr:= getMcbPointer;

    (*
     * print header
     *)
    writeln;
    writeln;
    writeln('Box Boy"s Memory Display Program  (Rev .1) ');
    writeln;
    writeln('CHAIN   MCB      PSP     PARAGRAPHS ');
    writeln('-------------------------------------');

    (*
     * loop and print MCB
     * information
     *)
    while True do begin
        (*
         * format buffer to print
         * primitive information
         *)
        writeln(mcbPtr^.chain_status, '        ',
                hex(Seg(mcbPtr^), 4), '     ',
                hex(mcbPtr^.owner_psp, 4), '     ',
                mcbPtr^.size_paragraphs:6);
```

```
            (*
             * if the 'Z' is reached
             * then break
             *)
            if mcbPtr^.chain_status - 'Z' then begin
                Exit;
                end

            (*
             * otherwise add
             * paragraph size to
             * pointer segment
             * and add 1 to cover mcb
             *)
            else begin
                mcbPtr:- Ptr(Seg(mcbPtr^)+mcbPtr^.size_paragraphs+1, 0);
                end;
            end;
end.
```

Let's compile PROG2-1.PAS. From the command line, type

    tpc /v /m prog2-1

and press Enter. TPC is the name of the Turbo Pascal compiler. The /v switch tells the compiler to include debugging information in the executable. This is useful if you want to debug the program to better understand how it works. The /m switch is the "make" option. It builds modules used by the program if their source has been modified since they were last compiled. So, for example, if you have changed __MCB.PAS, it will be recompiled because PROG2-1 uses __MCB. All of the sample programs in this book can be compiled using this command.

Now let's run PROG2-1.EXE. Figure 2-3 presents the screen output of PROG2-1.EXE as reported by my computer.

```
Box Boy's Memory Display Program  (Rev .1)

CHAIN   MCB     PSP     PARAGRAPHS
____    ____    ____    _____
M       025B    0008    1721
M       0915    0008       4
M       091A    091B     148
M       09AF    0000       4
M       09B4    091B      63
M       09F4    0000       4
M       09F9    09FA     936
M       0DA2    0ECF      37
M       0DC8    0000       2
M       0DCB    0DCC     258
Z       0ECE    0ECF   37169
```

2-3 The screen output for PROG2-1.EXE.

Figure 2-4 presents the source code listing to PROG2-2.PAS. This program removes the MCB segment report from PROG2-1's display, calculates the memory block size in bytes, and prints the owner program's name.

2-4 The source code listing to PROG2-2.PAS.

```
(* * * * * * * * * * * * * * * * * *
 *
 * prog2-2.pas
 *
 * Further demonstration of
 *    getMcbPointer(...)
 *
 * * * * * * * * * * * * * * * * * * *)

program prog2_2;

uses    _globals,
        _mcb;


var
    mcbPtr:             MCB_McbPtr;
    env:                CharPtr;
    envSeg:             Word;
    temp:               WordPtr;
    i:                  Word;

begin

    (*
     * Get pointer to the first MCB
     *)
    mcbPtr:= getMcbPointer;

    (*
     * Print the header
     *)
    writeln;
    writeln('Box Boy''s Memory Display Program (Rev .2)');
    writeln;
    writeln(' PSP   SIZE      PROGRAM   ');
    writeln(' ---   ------    ---------- ');


    (*
     * Loop over the MCB's printing out the info
     *)
    while True do begin

        (*
         * Print the easy stuff
         *)
        write(hex(mcbPtr^.owner_psp, 4), '  ',
            (DWord(mcbPtr^.size_paragraphs) shl 4):6, '    ');
```

```
(*
 *  If the PSP for this MCB is 0, then it represents
 *  free memory
 *)
if mcbPtr^.owner_psp - 0 then begin
    write('(free mem)');
    end

(*
 *  If the PSP is 8 then print config
 *)
else if mcbPtr^.owner_psp - $08 then begin
        write('config');
        end

(*
 *  Otherwise it's a program, so print the program name
 *)
else begin
    (*
     *  Get environment segment pointer
     *)
    temp:- WordPtr(Ptr(mcbPtr^.owner_psp, $2c));

    (*
     *  Get program environment segment
     *)
    envseg:- temp^;

    (*
     *  Set pointer to environment
     *)
    env:- Ptr(envseg,0);

    (*
     *  Search environment for the program name
     *
     *  Scan to the double delimiter.
     *)
    while (env^ <> Chr(0)) or (CharPtr(DWord(env)+1)^ <> Chr(0)) do begin
        env:- CharPtr(DWord(env)+1);
        end;

    (*
     *  Skip the double delimiter:
     *)
    env:- CharPtr(DWord(env)+2);

    (*
     *  Search for executable filename.
     *)
    while env^ <> '.' do begin
        env:- CharPtr(DWord(env)+1);
        end;
```

```
            (*
            *  Backspace to backslash that precedes the
            *  executable filename
            *)
            while env^ <> '\' do begin
                env:= CharPtr(DWord(env)-1);
                end;


            (*
            *  Point to the first letter of the filename
            *)
            env:= CharPtr(DWord(env)+1);

            (*
            *  Print the text up to the dot
            *)
            i:= 0;
            while (i < 12) and (env^ <> '.') do begin
                write(env^);
                env:= CharPtr(DWord(env)+1);
                i:= i + 1;
                end;

            (*
            *  Print out the extension.
            *)
            if i < 12 then begin
                for i:= 0 to 3 do begin
                    write(env^);
                    env:= CharPtr(DWord(env)+1);
                    end;
                end;
            end;
    (*
    *  Put out a Carriage return here
    *)
    writeln;

    (*
    *  See if we've reached the 'Z', the last MCB
    *)
    if mcbPtr^.chain_status = 'Z' then begin
        Exit;
        end;

    (*
    *  Add paragraph size to pointer segment and
    *  add 1 to cover length of mcb itself
    *)
    mcbPtr:= Ptr(Seg(mcbPtr^)+mcbPtr^.size_paragraphs+1,0);
    end;

end.
```

Figure 2-5 presents the program listing output for PROG2-2 on one of our computers.

```
Box Boy's Memory Display Program (Rev .2)

PSP    SIZE     PROGRAM

0008   27536    config
0008      64    config
091B    2368    command.com
0000      64    (free mem)
091B    1008    command.com
0000      64    (free mem)
09FA   14976    MOUSE.COM
0ECF     592    PROG2-2.EXE
0000      32    (free mem)
0DCC    4128    PROG2-2.EXE
0ECF  594704    PROG2-2.EXE
```

2-5 The screen output for PROG2-2.EXE.

Figure 2-6 presents the source code listing to PROG2-3.PAS. This long program presents a more polished, comprehensive version of PROG2-1 and PROG2-2.

2-6 The source code listing to PROG2-3.PAS.

```
(* * * * * * * * * * * * * * * * *
 *
 * prog2-3.pas
 *
 * A slightly more comprehensive
 * Memory Display Utility
 *
 * * * * * * * * * * * * * * * * * *)

program prog2_3;

uses    dos,
        crt,
        _globals,
        _mcb;



(*
 *
 *  Define a function to get the PSP
 *)
function get_prog_psp: WORD;

var
    regs:                   registers;
```

2-6 Continued.

```
begin

    regs.AH:- $51;

    MsDos(regs);

    get_prog_psp:- regs.BX;
end;


(*
 * Define a function to get the DOS version
 *)

procedure getDosVersion(var maj_rev: WORD; var min_rev: WORD);

var
    regs:                 registers;
begin
    regs.AL:- $01;
    regs.AH:- $30;
    MsDos(regs);

    maj_rev:- regs.AL;
    min_rev:- regs.AH;

end;

(*
 * isFNameChar tells whether a character is a "reasonable" filename
 * character. Filenames can have any character, but we exercise some
 * judgement over what characters are acceptable.
 *)
function isFNameChar(c: Char) : Boolean;

begin
    isFNameChar:- ((c >- 'a') and (c <- 'z')) or
                  ((c >- 'A') and (c <- 'Z')) or
                  ((c >- '0') and (c <- '9')) or
                  (c - '_') or
                  (c - '-') or
                  (c - '$');
end;

(* * * * * * * * * * *
 * declare MCB
 * structures
 * * * * * * * * * * * *)
var
    mcbPtr:               MCB_McbPtr;
    ownerMcbPtr:          MCB_McbPtr;

    maj_rev:              Word;
    min_rev:              Word;

    help:                 Boolean;

    tmpStr:               String;

    f2e:                  BytePtr;
    seg2e:                Word;
```

Writing a memory chain display utility program **19**

2-6 Continued.

```
prog_psp:            Word;

i:                   Word;

temp:                WordPtr;
envseg:              Word;
env:                 CharPtr;

charCount:           Word;

command:             String;
expectCommand:       Boolean;
done:                Boolean;

vectorsPrinted:      Word;
vecSeg:              Word;
remainder:           Word;

begin
    (*
     *  Check help flag and set on '/h' command line
     *  parameter
     *)
    tmpStr:= paramStr(1);
    help:= (paramCount <> 0) and
                    (tmpStr[1] - '/') and
                    ((tmpStr[2] - 'H') or
                        (tmpStr[2] - 'h') or
                        (tmpStr[2] - '?')));

    (*
     *  Get DOS version
     *)
    getDosVersion(maj_rev, min_rev);

    (*
     *  Get pointer to int 2eh (points into command com code).
     *  We'll use this to figure out whether a vector is hooked by
     *  COMMAND.COM
     *)
    f2e:= BytePtr(getVecPointer($2e));
    seg2e:= Seg(f2e^) + (Ofs(f2e^) shr 4);

    (*
     * get program psp
     *)
    prog_psp:= get_prog_psp;

    (*
     * fill Mem Cntl
     * block with info
     *)
    mcbPtr:= getMcbPointer;

    (*
     *  Put out first header line:
     *)
    TextBackground(Cyan);
    TextColor(Black);
    write(
    '          Clementine''s Memory Display Program V2.0    DOS Rev ',
    maj_rev:2, '.', min_rev:1,
    '                 ');
```

```
(*
 *  Reset the attributes to normal:
 *)
TextBackground(Black);
TextColor(White);

if help then begin

    (*
     * place the cursor
    writeln;
    writeln;

    (*
     *  Print help messages
     *)
    writeln('Program Syntax: prog2-3 [option]');
    writeln;
    writeln('Options:');
    writeln('   /H  -> Help information');
    writeln('   /?  -> Help information');

    (*
     * place the cursor
     *)
    writeln;
    writeln;

    (*
     * exit to DOS
     *)
    Halt;
    end;

(*
 *  Put out second header line:
 *)
TextBackground(LightGray);
TextColor(Black);
write(
'PSP   SIZE  PROGRAM   COMMAND  LINE           HOOKED  VECTORS     ');
(*
 *  Reset attributes.
 *)
TextBackground(Black);
TextColor(White);
(*
 *  Loop and print MCB information
 *)
repeat
    (*
     *  Get the owner's MCB address.
     *)
    ownerMcbPtr:= Ptr(mcbPtr^.owner_psp - 1, 0);
    (*
     *  Print out the basic information
     *)
    write(hex(mcbPtr^.owner_psp, 4),'3',
          (DWord(mcbPtr^.size_paragraphs) shl 4):6, '3');
```

```
    expectCommand:- True;

    (*
     *  If vector 2eh points within this block then
     *  it's COMMAND.COM
     *)
    if (seg2e >- Seg(mcbPtr^)) and
            (seg2e <- Seg(mcbPtr^) + (mcbPtr^.size_paragraphs)) or
            (seg2e >- Seg(ownerMcbPtr^)) and
            (seg2e <- Seg(ownerMcbPtr^)) then begin
        write('COMMAND ');
        expectCommand:- False;
        end

    (*
     *  If PSP is 0 then it's free
     *)
    else if mcbPtr^.owner_psp - 0 then begin
        write('(FREE)  ');
        expectCommand:- False;
        end

    (*
     *  If PSP is 8 then it's config
     *)
    else if mcbPtr^.owner_psp - $08 then begin

        write('(SYSTEM)');
        expectCommand:- False;
        end

    (*
     *  If we're running DOS 4.0 or better, then we can
     *  look in the owner's MCB structure for program name
     *)
    else if maj_rev >- 4 then begin
        i:- 0;
        while (i < 8) and isFNameChar(ownerMcbPtr^.file_name[i]) do begin
            write(ownerMcbPtr^.file_name[i]);
            i:- i + 1;
            end;
        if i - 0 then begin
            write('(N/A)   ');
            end
        else begin
            while i < 8 do begin
                write(' ');
                i:- i + 1;
                end;
            end;
        end

    (*
     *  Otherwise print the program name from the owner psp
     *)
    else begin

        (*
         *  Get environment segment pointer
         *)
        temp:- WordPtr(Ptr(mcbPtr^.owner_psp, $2c));
```

```
(*
 *  Get program environment segment
 *)
envseg:= temp^;

(*
 *  Set pointer to environment
 *)
env:= Ptr(envseg,0);

(*
 *  Search environment for the program name
 *
 *  Scan to the double delimiter.
 *)
while (env^ <> Chr(0)) or (CharPtr(DWord(env)+1)^ <> Chr(0)) do begin
    env:= CharPtr(DWord(env)+1);
    end;

(*
 *  Skip the double delimiter:
 *)
env:= CharPtr(DWord(env)+2);

(*
 *  Search for executable filename.
 *)
while env^ <> '.' do begin
    env:= CharPtr(DWord(env)+1);
    end;

(*
 *  Backspace to backslash that precedes the
 *  executable filename
 *)
while env^ <> '\' do begin
    env:= CharPtr(DWord(env)-1);
    end;


(*
 *  Point to the first letter of the filename
 *)
env:= CharPtr(DWord(env)+1);

(*
 *  Print the text up to the dot
 *)
charCount:= 0;
while env^ <> '.' do begin
    write(env^);
    env:= CharPtr(DWord(env)+1);
    charCount:= charCount + 1;
    end;

for i:= charCount+1 to 8 do begin
    write(' ');
    end;
end;
```

2-6 Continued.

```
    write('3');

    if expectCommand then begin
        (*
         *  Copy the command line.
         *)
        command:= StrPtr(Ptr(mcbPtr^.owner_psp, $80))^;

        (*
         *  Shorten the command line to 20 if necessary
         *)
        if Ord(command[0]) > 20 then begin
            command[0]:= Chr(20);
            end;

        (*
         *  Print it out
         *)
        write(command);

        (*
         *  Pad with spaces
         *)
        for i:= Ord(command[0])+1 to 20 do begin
            write(' ');
            end;
        end
    else begin
        write('                    ');
        end;


    write('3 ');


    (*
     *  Now let's see if we have hooked vectors:
     *)
    vectorsPrinted:= 0;
    for i:= 0 to 255 do begin
        vecSeg:= Seg(BytePtr(getVecPointer(i))^);
        if (vecSeg >= Seg(mcbPtr^)) and
                (vecSeg <= Seg(mcbPtr^) + mcbPtr^.size_paragraphs) then begin
            (*
             *  See if we've filled the line:
             *)
            if (vectorsPrinted > 0) and
                    (vectorsPrinted mod 12 = 0) then begin
                write(' ');
                write('    |    |       |            | ');
                end;
            write(hex(i,2), ' ');
            vectorsPrinted:= vectorsPrinted + 1;
            end;
        end;

    (*
     *  Clear the rest of the line and advance to next line
     *)
    if vectorsPrinted = 0 then begin
        remainder:= 37;
        end
```

2-6 Continued.

```
    else begin
        remainder:= 37 - 3 * (((vectorsPrinted + 11) mod 12) + 1);
        end;
    for i:= 1 to remainder do begin
        write(' ');
        end;


    (*
     *  If we've reached the 'Z', we're at the end.
     *  Otherwise go to the next block
     *)
    if mcbPtr^.chain_status = 'Z' then begin
        done:= True;
        end
    else begin
        mcbPtr:= Ptr(Seg(mcbPtr^) + mcbPtr^.size_paragraphs + 1, 0);
        done:= False;
        end;

until done;

writeln(
'_____|_____|_____|_____|_____');

end.
```

Many instructive programming techniques are used in this highly documented source file. The comments have been carefully written to aid in your understanding.

Summary

Low memory is organized into a sequence of memory blocks, each headed by a 16-byte Memory Control Block (MCB). The memory blocks follow one after another contiguously in memory. Thus, it is easy to go from one MCB to the next.

By looking at these MCBs, we can find out the owner program's PSP, whether the memory block is the last in the chain, the size of the memory block referred to by the MCB, the location of the next MCB in the chain, the owner program's command line, and the owner program's name.

Understanding how MCBs operate will lay a firm foundation for understanding low memory management.

Figure 2-7 presents the source code listing to PROG2-4.PAS. This program uses the standard library "Exec" function to invoke PROG 2-3.EXE. Running the parent PROG2-4.EXE program will allow you to see the memory used both by PROG2-4 and by PROG2-3.

2-7 The source code listing to PROG2-4.PAS.

```
(* * * * * * * * * * *
 *
 * prog2-4.pas
 *
 * test prog2-3 from
 * system call showing
 * how command.com
 * is invoked
 *
 * * * * * * * * * * * *)

(*
 * Because this program invokes another, we need to explicitly
 * set the stack and heap sizes.
 * We use 8192 for stack size, 0 for minimum heap, and 8192 for
 * maximum heap.
 *)
{$M 8192,0,8192}
program prog2_4;

uses    dos,
        crt;

var
    c:                  Char;
    i:                  Word;

begin

    (*
     * Print parameter 1 to the screen
     *)
    for i:= 1 to ParamCount do begin
        write(paramStr(i), ' ');
        end;
    writeln;
    writeln;
    writeln('Press any key to continue...');
    writeln;

    (*
     * Wait for key press
     *)
    c:= readKey;

    (*
     * Invoke the memory display program from within this
     * program.
     *)
    DosError:= 0;
    Exec('PROG2-3.EXE', '');
    if DosError <> 0 then begin
        writeln('Exec of PROG2-3 failed with DOS Error #', DosError);
        end;
end.
```

3
EMS 3.0 & 3.2

Chapter 3's content falls into two basic sections. The first portion of the chapter presents five EMS demonstration programs that show how several of the EMS 3.0 and 3.2 functions can be called from Turbo Pascal. The second section concentrates on presenting an EMS 3.0 and 3.2 programming interface. The EMS interface code is primarily implemented in assembly language. The associated function prototypes are presented in the text.

Peruse the sample programs before delving into the detailed description of the interface. You'll find that much of the interface is fairly intuitive.

EMS 3.0 demonstration programs

There are five demonstration programs presented in this section of Chapter 3. The first program, PROG3-1.PAS demonstrates the following EMS operations:

- testing for the presence of EMS
- getting the EMS status
- getting the EMS page frame address
- getting the EMS version number

Figure 3-1 presents the source code listing to PROG3-1.PAS.

3-1 The source code listing to PROG3-1.PAS.

```
(* * * * * * * * * * * * * * * * * */
 *
 * prog3-1.pas
 *
 *        Demonstrates
 *                - Testing for presence of EMS
 *                - Getting EMS status
 *                - Getting Page Frame Address
 *                - Getting EMS Version #
 *
 * * * * * * * * * * * * * * * * * *)

program prog3_1;

uses    _globals,
        _ems;

var
    version:            Word;
    pfa:                EMS_PageFrame;
    ems:                EMS_Ems;

begin

    (*
     * First check to see whether EMS is there:
     *)
    if ems.init then begin
        writeln('EMM is not present');
        Halt;
        end
    else begin
        writeln('EMM is present');
        end;

    (*
     * Now get the EMS status. This should be 0, indicating
     * no problem.
     *)
    if ems.getStatus then;
    writeln('EMS status is 0x', hex(errno, 2));

    (*
     * Now get the EMS version number and print it:
     *)
    if ems.getVersion(version) then begin
        ems_demoError('ems.getVersion');
        end;
    writeln('EMS version is ', (version shr 4) and $0F, '.',
                               (version) and $0F);

    (*
     * Now get the Page Frame Address:
     *)
    if ems.getPFA(pfa) then begin
        ems_demoError('ems.getPFA');
        end;
    writeln('Page Frame address is ', hex(Seg(pfa^), 4), ':',
                                      hex(Ofs(pfa^), 4));

end.
```

Figure 3-2 presents the source code listing to PROG3-2.PAS, a program that demonstrates the following EMS operations:

- allocating and freeing EMS pages
- getting the number of available EMS pages
- getting the number of pages allocated for each handle
- getting the number of active page handles

3-2 The source code listing to PROG3-2.PAS.

```
(* * * * * * * * * * * * * * * * * */
 *
 * prog3-2.pas
 *
 *       Demonstrates
 *          - Alloc/Free of EMS pages
 *          - Get # available EMS pages
 *          - Get # pages for each handle
 *          - Get # active handles
 *
 * * * * * * * * * * * * * * * * * *)

program prog3_2;

uses    crt,
        _globals,
        _ems;


var
     ems:                     EMS_Ems;


procedure displayActiveHandles;

type
     EMS_HandleInfoArrPtr= ^EMS_HandleInfoArr;


var
     handleInfoArray:    EMS_HandleInfoArrPtr;
     numActiveHandles:   Word;
     numActiveHandles2:  Word;

     i:                  Word;

begin
     (*
      * First find out how many active handles there are:
      *)
     if ems.getNumActiveHandles(numActiveHandles) then begin
          ems_demoError('EMS_Ems.getNumActiveHandles');
          end;

     (*
      * Now allocate a block of handleInfo packets big enough to
      * hold them.
      *)
     GetMem(handleInfoArray, numActiveHandles * sizeof(EMS_HandleInfo));
```

```
(*
 *  Now get the info.
 *)
if ems.getPagesAllHandles(handleInfoArray^, numActiveHandles2) then begin
    ems_demoError('EMS_Ems.getNumActiveHandles');
    end;

(*
 *  The following is a brief sanity clause (Everybody knows
 *  there ain't no sanity clause).
 *)
if numActiveHandles2 <> numActiveHandles then begin
    writeln('A most unusual situation has occurred...');
    Halt;
    end;

(*
 *  Finally, display it.
 *)
writeln('                                 └────────┼───────┴─────┘');

for i:= 0 to numActiveHandles - 1 do begin
    writeln(
                                          │    ',
        handleInfoArray^[i].handle:3,
        '    3   ',
        handleInfoArray^[i].numPages:3,
        '     3');

    if i+1 < numActiveHandles then begin
        writeln(
                                      ├───────┼──────┤');
        end;
    end;
writeln('═══════════════════════════════┴════════┴════┘');
(*
 *  Now free up the array.
 *)
FreeMem(handleInfoArray, numActiveHandles * sizeof(EMS_HandleInfo));
end;

procedure pause;

var
    c:                      char;

begin

    (*
     *  Display a little message:
     *)
    writeln('Hit <CR> to continue...');

    (*
     *  Wait for a <CR>
     *)
    c:= ReadKey;
    while c <> #13 do begin
        c:= ReadKey;
        end;

end;
```

```
var

    totalPages:        Word;
    freePages:         Word;
    handle1:           EMS_EmBlk;
    handle2:           EMS_EmBlk;

begin

    (*
     * First check for presence of EMS
     *)
    if ems.init then begin
        writeln('EMS is not present');
        Halt;
        end;

    (*
     * Get the number of free pages
     *)
    if ems.getFreeEM(totalPages, freePages) then begin
        ems_demoError('EMS_Ems.getFreeEM');
        end;

    (*
     * Print header:
     *)
    writeln('        Operation           Avail Pages       Active Handles');
    writeln('═══════════════════════════════════════════════════════════════╗ ');
    writeln('After initialization  |        ',
                 freePages:3,
             '       |  Handle    Pages  |');

    displayActiveHandles;
    pause;

    (*
     * Now allocate 5 pages.
     *)
    if handle1.allocEM(5) then begin
        ems_demoError('EMS_Ems.allocEM');
        end;

    (*
     * Get the number of free pages
     *)
    if ems.getFreeEM(totalPages, freePages) then begin
        ems_demoError('EMS_Ems.getFreeEM');
        end;

    (*
     * Print header:
     *)
    writeln('        Operation           Avail Pages       Active Handles');
    writeln('═══════════════════════════════════════════════════════════════╗ ');
    writeln('After 5 page allocate  |        ',
                 freePages:3,
             '       |  Handle    Pages  |');

    displayActiveHandles;
    pause;
```

```
(*
 *   Now allocate 7 pages.
 *)
if handle2.allocEM(7) then begin
    ems_demoError('EMS_EmBlk.allocEM');
    end;

(*
 *   Get the number of free pages
 *)
if ems.getFreeEM(totalPages, freePages) then begin
    ems_demoError('EMS_Ems.getFreeEM');
    end;

(*
 *   Print header:
 *)
writeln('        Operation          Avail Pages      Active Handles');
writeln('═══════════════════════════════════════════════════════════');
writeln('After 7 page allocate   |       ',
        freePages:3,
        '       |  Handle    Pages  |');

displayActiveHandles;
pause;

(*
 *   Now free the 5 page block.
 *)
if handle1.freeEM then begin
    ems_demoError('EMS_EmBlk.freeEM');
    end;

(*
 *   Get the number of free pages
 *)
if ems.getFreeEM(totalPages, freePages) then begin
    ems_demoError('EMS_Ems.getFreeEM');
    end;

(*
 *   Print header:
 *)
writeln('        Operation          Avail Pages      Active Handles');
writeln('═══════════════════════════════════════════════════════════');
writeln('After 5 page free       |       ',
        freePages:3,
        '       |  Handle    Pages  |');

displayActiveHandles;
pause;

(*
 *   Now free the 7 page block.
 *)
if handle2.freeEM then begin
    ems_demoError('EMS_EmBlk.freeEM');
    end;
```

3-2 Continued.

```
(*
 *  Get the number of free pages
 *)
if ems.getFreeEM(totalPages, freePages) then begin
    ems_demoError('EMS_Ems.getFreeEM');
    end;

(*
 *  Print header:
 *)
writeln('         Operation          Avail Pages     Active Handles');
writeln('═══════════════════════════════════════════════════════════════');
writeln('After 7 page free            |      ',
               freePages:3,
           '    |   Handle    Pages  |');

displayActiveHandles;
```

end.

Figure 3-3 presents the source code listing to PROG3-3.PAS, which demonstrates the following EMS operations:

- mapping of EMS pages
- transferring data to and from EMS

3-3 The source code listing to PROG3-3.PAS.

```
(* * * * * * * * * * * * * * * * * *
 *
 *  prog3-3.pas
 *
 *       Demonstrates
 *          - Mapping EMS pages
 *          - Transfer of memory from/to EMS
 *
 * * * * * * * * * * * * * * * * * *)

program prog3_3;

uses    _globals,
        _ems;

type
    BigArea-        array[0..65534] of Byte;
    BigPtr-         ^BigArea;

var
    ems:            EMS_Ems;
    pageFrame:      EMS_PageFrame;
    handle1:        EMS_EmBlk;
    handle2:        EMS_EmBlk;

    text:           String;

    i:              Word;

    three:          Word;
```

3-3 Continued.

```
begin
    three:- 3;

    (*
     *   First check for presence of EMS
     *)
    if ems.init then begin
        writeln('EMS is not present');
        Halt;
        end;

    (*
     *   Get the Page Frame Address.
     *)
    if ems.getPFA(pageFrame) then begin
        ems_demoError('EMS_Ems.getPFA');
        end;

    (*
     *   Get a couple of 4 page blocks of memory (64K each).
     *)
    if handle1.allocEM(4) then begin
        ems_demoError('EMS_EmBlk.allocEM');
        end;
    if handle2.allocEM(4) then begin
        ems_demoError('EMS_EmBlk.allocEM');
        end;

    (*
     *   Now let's map the first.
     *)
    for i:- 0 to 3 do begin
        if handle1.mapPage(i, i) then begin
            ems_demoError('EMS_EmBlk.mapPage');
            end;
        end;

    (*
     *   The memory is now mapped into the page frame. Let's
     *   move some text into random spots in it.
     *)
    StrPtr(@pageFrame^[0][400])^:-
        '       I took a speed reading course and I';

    StrPtr(@pageFrame^[1][801])^:-
        '       read "War and Peace".';

    StrPtr(@pageFrame^[2][4000])^:-
        '       It involves Russia.';

    StrPtr(@pageFrame^[three][2000])^:-
        '                       - Woody Allen'#13#10;

    (*
     *   Now print it back.
     *)
    writeln(StrPtr(@pageFrame^[0][400])^);
    writeln(StrPtr(@pageFrame^[1][801])^);
    writeln(StrPtr(@pageFrame^[2][4000])^);
    writeln(StrPtr(@pageFrame^[three][2000])^);
```

3-3 Continued.

```
(*
 *   Now let's map the second block
 *)
for i:- 0 to 3 do begin
    if handle2.mapPage(i, i) then begin
        ems_demoError('EMS_EmBlk.mapPage');
        end;
    end;

(*
 *   The memory is now mapped into the page frame. Let's
 *   move some text into random spots in it.
 *)
StrPtr(@pageFrame^[0][400])^:-
    '        Children make the most desirable opponents';

StrPtr(@pageFrame^[1][801])^:-
    '        in Scrabble as they are both easy to beat';

StrPtr(@pageFrame^[2][4000])^:-
    '        and fun to cheat.';

StrPtr(@pageFrame^[three][2000])^:-
    '                          - Fran Lebowitz'#13#10;

(*
 *   Now print it back.
 *)
writeln(StrPtr(@pageFrame^[0][400])^);
writeln(StrPtr(@pageFrame^[1][801])^);
writeln(StrPtr(@pageFrame^[2][4000])^);
writeln(StrPtr(@pageFrame^[three][2000])^);

(*
 *   Now let's map the first, backwards this time.
 *)
for i:- 0 to 3 do begin
    if handle1.mapPage(i, 3-i) then begin
        ems_demoError('EMS_EmBlk.mapPage');
        end;
    end;

(*
 *   Now print it back.
 *)
writeln(StrPtr(@pageFrame^[three][400])^);
writeln(StrPtr(@pageFrame^[2][801])^);
writeln(StrPtr(@pageFrame^[1][4000])^);
writeln(StrPtr(@pageFrame^[0][2000])^);

(*
 *   Now let's map the second block backwards.
 *)
for i:- 0 to 3 do begin
    if handle2.mapPage(i, 3-i) then begin
        ems_demoError('EMS_EmBlk.mapPage');
        end;
    end;
```

```
(*
 *  Now print it back. This time, we're going to calculate
 *  the offset from the beginning of the page frame area.
 *)
writeln(StrPtr(@BigPtr(pageFrame)^[3*EMS_STD_PAGE_SIZE + 400])^);
writeln(StrPtr(@BigPtr(pageFrame)^[2*EMS_STD_PAGE_SIZE + 801])^);
writeln(StrPtr(@BigPtr(pageFrame)^[1*EMS_STD_PAGE_SIZE + 4000])^);
writeln(StrPtr(@BigPtr(pageFrame)^[0*EMS_STD_PAGE_SIZE + 2000])^);

(*
 *  We're done. Free the memory we've allocated.
 *)
if handle1.freeEM then begin
    ems_demoError('EMS_EmBlk.freeEM');
    end;
if handle2.freeEM then begin
    ems_demoError('EMS_EmBlk.freeEM');
    end;
end.
```

Figure 3-4 presents the source code listing to PROG3-4.PAS, which demonstrates the following EMS operations:

- saving and restoring of the EMS page map

3-4 The source code listing to PROG3-4.PAS.

```
(* * * * * * * * * * * * * * * * * *
 *
 *  prog3-4.pas
 *
 *      Demonstrates
 *          - Save/Restore of the page map
 *
 * * * * * * * * * * * * * * * * * *)

program prog3_4;

uses    _globals,
        _ems;

var
    ems:            EMS_Ems;

    pageFrame:      EMS_PageFrame;
    handle1:        EMS_EmBlk;
    handle2:        EMS_EmBlk;

    text:           String;

    i:              Word;
    three:          Word;
```

3-4 Continued.

```
begin

    three:- 3;

    (*
     *  First check for presence of EMS
     *)
    if ems.init then begin
        writeln('EMS is not present');
        Halt;
        end;

    (*
     *  Get the Page Frame Address.
     *)
    if ems.getPFA(pageFrame) then begin
        ems_demoError('ems.getPFA');
        end;

    (*
     *  Get a couple of 4 page blocks of memory (64K each).
     *)
    if handle1.allocEM(4) then begin
        ems_demoError('EMS_EmBlk.allocEM');
        end;
    if handle2.allocEM(4) then begin
        ems_demoError('EMS_EmBlk.allocEM');
        end;

    (*
     *  Now let's map the first.
     *)
    for i:- 0 to 3 do begin
        if handle1.mapPage(i, i) then begin
            ems_demoError('EMS_EmBlk.mapPage');
            end;
        end;

    (*
     *  The memory is now mapped into the page frame. Let's
     *  move some text into random spots in it.
     *)
    StrPtr(@pageFrame^[0][400])^:-
        '        Be careful not to impart your wisdom to a guest';

    StrPtr(@pageFrame^[1][801])^:-
        '        whose background you do not know. You may be instructing';

    StrPtr(@pageFrame^[2][4000])^:-
        '        a Nobel Laureate in his own field';

    StrPtr(@pageFrame^[three][2000])^:-
        '                        - David Brown'#13#10;

    (*
     *  Now print it back.
     *)
    writeln(StrPtr(@pageFrame^[0][400])^);
    writeln(StrPtr(@pageFrame^[1][801])^);
    writeln(StrPtr(@pageFrame^[2][4000])^);
    writeln(StrPtr(@pageFrame^[three][2000])^);
```

3-4 Continued.

```
(*
 *  Save the map state. This will save the current map
 *  of the PFA and associate the saved state with handle1.
 *  We could as easily save it with handle2 as long as
 *  we restore it from the same place we saved it.
 *)
if handle1.savePageMap then begin
    ems_demoError('EMS_EmBlk.savePageMap');
    end;

(*
 *  Now let's map the second block
 *)
for i:= 0 to 3 do begin
    if handle2.mapPage(i, i) then begin
        ems_demoError('EMS_EmBlk.mapPage');
        end;
    end;

(*
 *  The memory is now mapped into the page frame. Let's
 *  move some text into random spots in it.
 *)
StrPtr(@pageFrame^[0][400])^:=
        '       I''m astounded by people who want to ''know''';

StrPtr(@pageFrame^[1][801])^:=
        '       the universe when it''s hard enough to find your';

StrPtr(@pageFrame^[2][4000])^:=
        '       way around Chinatown.';

StrPtr(@pageFrame^[three][2000])^:=
        '                            - Woody Allen'#13#10;

(*
 *  Now print it back.
 *)
writeln(StrPtr(@pageFrame^[0][400])^);
writeln(StrPtr(@pageFrame^[1][801])^);
writeln(StrPtr(@pageFrame^[2][4000])^);
writeln(StrPtr(@pageFrame^[three][2000])^);

(*
 *  Now let's restore the old map.
 *)
if handle1.restorePageMap then begin
    ems_demoError('EMS_EmBlk.restorePageMap');
    end;

(*
 *  Now when we print out, we should get the first set
 *  of lines.
 *)
writeln(StrPtr(@pageFrame^[0][400])^);
writeln(StrPtr(@pageFrame^[1][801])^);
writeln(StrPtr(@pageFrame^[2][4000])^);
writeln(StrPtr(@pageFrame^[three][2000])^);
```

3-4 Continued.

```
(*
 *  We're done. Free the memory we've allocated.
 *)
if handle1.freeEM then begin
   ems_demoError('EMS_EmBlk.freeEM');
   end;
if handle2.freeEM then begin
   ems_demoError('EMS_EmBlk.freeEM');
   end;
end.
```

Figure 3-5 presents the source code listing to PROG3-5.PAS, which demonstrates the following EMS operations:

- saving and restoring the EMS page map using EMS version 3.2 calls

3-5 The source code listing to PROG3-5.PAS.

```
(* * * * * * * * * * * * * * * * * *
 *
 * prog3-5.pas
 *
 *      Demonstrates
 *          - Save/Restore of the page map using 3.2 calls
 *
 * * * * * * * * * * * * * * * * * * *)

program prog3_5;

uses     _globals,
         _ems;


var
    ems:            EMS_Ems;

    pageFrame:      EMS_PageFrame;

    handle1:        EMS_EmBlk;
    handle2:        EMS_EmBlk;

    mapBuffer1:     ^DWord;
    mapBuffer2:     ^DWord;
    mapInfoSize:    Word;

    i:              Word;

    three:          Word;

begin

    three:= 3;
```

3-5 Continued.

```
(*
 *  First check for presence of EMS
 *)
if ems.init then begin
    writeln('EMS is not present');
    Halt;
    end;

(*
 *  Get the Page Frame Address.
 *)
if ems.getPFA(pageFrame) then begin
    ems_demoError('EMS_Ems.getPFA');
    end;

(*
 *  Get a couple of 4 page blocks of memory (64K each).
 *)
if handle1.allocEM(4) then begin
    ems_demoError('EMS_EmBlk.allocEM');
    end;
if handle2.allocEM(4) then begin
    ems_demoError('EMS_EmBlk.allocEM');
    end;

(*
 *  Now let's map the first.
 *)
for i:= 0 to 3 do begin
    if handle1.mapPage(i, i) then begin
        ems_demoError('EMS_EmBlk.mapPage');
        end;
    end;

(*
 *  The memory is now mapped into the page frame. Let's
 *  move some text into random spots in it.
 *)
StrPtr(@pageFrame^[0][400])^:=
    '       Neurotic means he is not as sensible as I am,';

StrPtr(@pageFrame^[1][801])^:=
    '       and psychotic means that he is even worse than';

StrPtr(@pageFrame^[2][4000])^:=
    '       my brother-in-law.';

StrPtr(@pageFrame^[three][2000])^:=
    '                          - Karl Menninger'#13#10;

(*
 *  Now print it back.
 *)
writeln(StrPtr(@pageFrame^[0][400])^);
writeln(StrPtr(@pageFrame^[1][801])^);
writeln(StrPtr(@pageFrame^[2][4000])^);
writeln(StrPtr(@pageFrame^[three][2000])^);

(*
 *  Save the map state. First we query as to how much
 *  memory is required, allocate the memory, then do
 *  the actual save.
 *)
```

```
if ems.getMapInfoSize32(mapInfoSize) then begin
    ems_demoError('EMS_Ems.mapInfoSize');
    end;
GetMem(mapBuffer1, mapInfoSize);
GetMem(mapBuffer2, mapInfoSize);

if ems.savePageMap32(mapBuffer1) then begin
    ems_demoError('EMS_Ems.savePageMap32');
    end;

(*
 *  Now let's map the second block
 *)
for i:= 0 to 3 do begin
    if handle2.mapPage(i, i) then begin
        ems_demoError('EMS_EmBlk.mapPage');
        end;
    end;

(*
 *  The memory is now mapped into the page frame. Let's
 *  move some text into random spots in it.
 *)
StrPtr(@pageFrame^[0][400])^:=
        'When I can no longer bear to think of the victims';

StrPtr(@pageFrame^[1][801])^:=
        ' of broken homes, I begin to think of the victims';

StrPtr(@pageFrame^[2][4000])^:=
        ' of intact ones.';

StrPtr(@pageFrame^[three][2000])^:=
        '                        - Peter De Vries'#13#10;

(*
 *  Now print it back.
 *)
writeln(StrPtr(@pageFrame^[0][400])^);
writeln(StrPtr(@pageFrame^[1][801])^);
writeln(StrPtr(@pageFrame^[2][4000])^);
writeln(StrPtr(@pageFrame^[three][2000])^);

(*
 *  Now let's swap maps, saving the current map into mapBuffer2,
 *  and loading the new map from mapBuffer1.
 *)
if ems.swapPageMap32(mapBuffer1, mapBuffer2) then begin
    ems_demoError('EMS_Ems.swapPageMap32');
    end;

(*
 *  Now when we print out, we should get the first set
 *  of lines.
 *)
writeln(StrPtr(@pageFrame^[0][400])^);
writeln(StrPtr(@pageFrame^[1][801])^);
writeln(StrPtr(@pageFrame^[2][4000])^);
writeln(StrPtr(@pageFrame^[three][2000])^);
```

```
(*
 *  Now let's finish by restoring the second page map.
 *)
if ems.restPageMap32(mapBuffer2) then begin
    ems_demoError('EMS_Ems.restPageMap32');
    end;

(*
 *  And print the contents:
 *)
writeln(StrPtr(@pageFrame^[0][400])^);
writeln(StrPtr(@pageFrame^[1][801])^);
writeln(StrPtr(@pageFrame^[2][4000])^);
writeln(StrPtr(@pageFrame^[three][2000])^);

(*
 *  We're done. Free the memory we've allocated.
 *)
if handle1.freeEM then begin
    ems_demoError('EMS_EmBlk.freeEM');
    end;
if handle2.freeEM then begin
    ems_demoError('EMS_EmBlk.freeEM');
    end;
end.
```

About the EMS 3.0 and 3.2 programmer's interface

The Turbo Pascal EMS interface described in this book is based on two object classes. The first, EMS_Ems, contains all of the functions that are not targeted at a specific EMS handle. An object of type EMS_Ems can be considered to be an "EMS system." The object is initialized through a call to EMS_Ems.init. Only one object of this type is required, because there's really only one EMS system.

The second object class is EMS_EmBlk. Objects of this type are blocks of EMS memory. An EMS block is denoted by a handle, so an object of this type contains an EMS handle. An EMS_EmBlk object is initialized via a call to EMS_EmBlk.allocEM, which allocates a specified amount of EMS memory, and associates the target object with that block of memory. Subsequent calls with that object as the target can map pages from the associated block, save the page map, get information about the block such as its size, etc.

All of the EMS related assembly files presented in Chapters 3 and 4 have been assembled and have had their resultant object modules included in _EMS.TPU (the compiled Turbo Pascal Unit).

Note that the assembly source file naming convention follows a consistent format. All EMS source names begin with the "EMS" prefix. This prefix is followed by two or three hexadecimal numbers. The first two numbers refer to the EMS Interrupt 67h function number. If there is a third number, it refers to the subfunction number. For example, the source file EMS5D2.ASM contains the source code to invoke interrupt 67h function 5Dh subfunction 2h. It's as simple as that.

Note that the naming convention for the EMS 4.0 interface is similar. For example, source file EMS5D2.ASM contains the code to function EMS__Ems.releaseAccessKey40(...). The numerical suffix refers to the EMS version number. In this case, function 5Dh subfunction 2h is supported only by EMS v4.0.

Finally, we have decided always to return the EMS function's error status via the errno variable defined in __GLOBALS.PAS. If a function takes an error, it returns the Boolean value True.

EMS function return status

False   Status OK, no error

True   Status NOT OK, error occurred, error code in the variable errno, defined in __GLOBALS.PAS

EMS functions that are required to return values to the calling function do so via "var" parameters in the function's definition.

Before presenting the EMS 3.0 and 3.2 programmer's interface code, we present two preparatory files. The first is a Turbo Pascal unit file for the EMS function calls and type definitions, and the second file is a defines file for use by the assembly language modules.

Figure 3-6 presents the source code listing to __EMS.PAS, which is a Turbo Pascal unit file containing EMS related objects that are composed of data elements, EMS, and utility functions.

3-6 The source code listing to __EMS.PAS.

```
(* * * * * * * * * * * * * * * * * *
 *
 * _ems.pas
 *
 * Ems and Emm related definitions,
 * structures and function prototypes
 *
 * * * * * * * * * * * * * * * * * * *)

unit _ems;

INTERFACE

uses _globals,
     dos;

const

    EMS_STD_PAGE_SIZE-   16384;
    EMS_PAGE_FRAME_SIZE- 4;
```

3-6 Continued.

```
(*
 * Define a couple of constants for the move and exchange operations.
 *)
    EMS_MOVE_CONV-        0;
    EMS_MOVE_EMS-         1;

(*
 * Define the EMS error codes.
 *)
    EMSErrOK-             $00;    { No error }
    EMSErrInternal-       $80;    { Internal EMM error }
    EMSErrHardware-       $81;    { EM Hardware error }
    EMSErrEMMBusy-        $82;    { EMM Busy }
    EMSErrHandInv-        $83;    { Handle Invalid }
    EMSErrUnimp-          $84;    { Undefined EMS function }
    EMSErrNoHandles-      $85;    { Handles Exhausted }
    EMSErrSaveRest-       $86;    { Error in save/restore of context }
    EMSErrReqGTPhys-      $87;    { Not enough physical EM for request }
    EMSErrReqGTAvail-     $88;    { Not enough available EM for request }
    EMSErrReqIsZero-      $89;    { Cannot allocate zero pages }
    EMSErrLogPgInv-       $8A;    { Invalid logical page number }
    EMSErrPhysPgInv-      $8B;    { Invalid physical page number }
    EMSErrSSAreaFull-     $8C;    { Mapping save area is full }
    EMSErrSaveFail-       $8D;    { Mapping save failed }
    EMSErrRestFail-       $8E;    { Mapping restore failed }
    EMSErrParameter-      $8F;    { Subfunction parameter not defined }
    EMSErrAttribute-      $90;    { Attribute type not defined }
    EMSErrUnsupported-    $91;    { Feature not supported }
    EMSErrOverlap-        $92;    { Source/dest of move overlap, move done }
    EMSErrLenInv-         $93;    { Length of move request invalid }
    EMSErrOverlapCE-      $94;    { Overlap of conventional and extended }
    EMSErrOffsetInv-      $95;    { Offset outside logical page }
    EMSErrRegionGT1MB-    $96;    { Region size > 1 megabyte }
    EMSErrOverlapFatal-   $97;    { Source/dest overlap prevented move }
    EMSErrMemTypeInv-     $98;    { Memory source/dest types invalid }
    EMSErrDMARegUnsupp-   $9A;    { Specified register set unsupported }
    EMSErrNoDMARegs-      $9B;    { No available alternate register sets }
    EMSErrAltRegsUnsupp-  $9C;    { Alternate registers unsupported }
    EMSErrDMARegUndef-    $9D;    { Specified register set undefined }
    EMSErrDMAChanUnsupp-  $9E;    { Dedicated DMA channels unsupported }
    EMSErrChanUnsupp-     $9F;    { Specified DMA channel unsupported }
    EMSErrNameNotFound-   $A0;    { No handle found for name }
    EMSErrNameExists-     $A1;    { Handle with same name already exists }
    EMSErrPointerInv-     $A3;    { Invalid pointer or source array bogus }
    EMSErrAccess-         $A4;    { Access denied by operating system }

type


    EMS_HandleName- array[0..7] of Char;

(* * * * * * * * * * * *
 *
 * structures
 *
 * * * * * * * * * * * *)

    EMS_MapByNumber - record
        logicalPage:        Word;   { Logical page }
        physicalPage:       Word;   { Physical page number }
        end;
```

```
EMS_MapByAddress- record
    logicalPage:        Word;   { Logical page }
    physicalSeg:        Word;   { Physical segment number }
    end;

EMS_HandleInfo- record
    handle:             Word;   { ems handle }
    numPages:           Word;   { ems pages associated with handle }
    end;
EMS_HandleInfoArr- array[0..0] of EMS_HandleInfo;

EMS_MappablePagesInfo- record
    pageSegment:        Word;   { Segment base address }
    physNumber:         Word;   { Physical page number }
    end;
EMS_MappablePagesInfoArr- array[0..0] of EMS_MappablePagesInfo;

EMS_HandleNameInfo- record
    handle:             Word;   { ems handle }
    name:               EMS_HandleName;
                                { ems name (version 4.0) }
    end;
EMS_HandleNameInfoArr- array[0..0] of EMS_HandleNameInfo;

EMS_MoveMemoryInfo- record
    length:             DWord;  { memory length }
    srcType:            Byte;   { 0-conventional,1-expanded }
    srcHandle:          Word;   { source handle }
    srcOffset:          Word;   { source offset }
    srcPage:            Word;   { source segment or logical page }
    destType:           Byte;   { 0-conventional,1-expanded }
    destHandle:         Word;   { destination handle }
    destOffset:         Word;   { destination offset }
    destPage:           Word;   { destination segment or logical page }
    end;

EMS_HardwareConfigInfo- record
    rawPgSize:          Word;   { size of raw pages in paragraphs }
    altRegSets:         Word;   { number of alternate reg sets }
    saveAreaSz:         Word;   { size of mapping save area in bytes }
    regsDma:            Word;   { num of regs can be assigned to dma }
    dmaType:            Word;   { 0-alt dma regs OK,1-one dma reg only }
    end;


EMS_Page- array[0..(EMS_STD_PAGE_SIZE-1)] of Byte;
EMS_PageFrameArea- array [0..2] of EMS_Page;
EMS_PageFrame- ^EMS_PageFrameArea;

(* * * * * * * * * * * *
 *
 *  function prototypes
 *)


EMS_Ems- object
    function        init
                        : Boolean;
    function        getStatus
                        : Boolean;
```

```
function        getPFA(
                    var page_frame: EMS_PageFrame)
                    : Boolean;
function        getFreeEM(
                    var total:      Word;
                    var free:       Word)
                    : Boolean;
function        getVersion(
                    var version:    Word)
                    : Boolean;
function        getNumActiveHandles(
                    var num_handles: Word)
                    : Boolean;
function        getPagesAllHandles(
                    var info:           EMS_HandleInfoArr;
                    var num_handles: Word)
                    : Boolean;


function        savePageMap32(
                    save_buffer:    Pointer)
                    : Boolean;
function        restPageMap32(
                    restore_buffer: Pointer)
                    : Boolean;
function        swapPageMap32(
                    rest_buffer:    Pointer;
                    save_buffer:    Pointer)
                    : Boolean;
function        getMapInfoSize32(
                    var size:       Word)
                    : Boolean;


function        savePartialMap40(
                    map:            Pointer;
                    buffer:         Pointer)
                    : Boolean;
function        restPartialMap40(
                    buffer:         Pointer)
                    : Boolean;
function        getPMapInfoSize40(
                    pages: Word;
                    var buffSize:   Word)
                    : Boolean;

function        getAttrCapability40(
                    var capability: Word)
                    : Boolean;

function        getAllHandleNames40(
                    var info_list:  EMS_HandleNameInfoArr)
                    : Boolean;
function        getTotalHandles40(
                    var handles:    Word)
                    : Boolean;

function        getStackNeeded40(
                    var stack_space: Word)
                    : Boolean;
```

3-6 Continued.

```
function       moveMemRegion40(
                   var buffer:      EMS_MoveMemoryInfo)
                   : Boolean;
function       swapMemRegions40(
                   var buffer:      EMS_MoveMemoryInfo)
                   : Boolean;

function       getAddrsMappable40(
                   var buffer:      EMS_MappablePagesInfoArr;
                   var num_entries: Word)
                   : Boolean;
function       getNumMappable40(
                   var mappablePages: Word)
                   : Boolean;

function       getHWConfig40(
                   var buffer:      EMS_HardwareConfigInfo)
                   : Boolean;

function       getNumRawPages40(
                   var total_pages: Word;
                   var free_pages: Word)
                   : Boolean;

function       getAltMapRegs40(
                   var active_map: Byte;
                   var regs_area:  Byte)
                   : Boolean;
function       setAltMapRegs40(
                   alt_set:        Byte;
                   var regs_area:  Byte)
                   : Boolean;
function       getAltMapRegSize40(
                   var buf_size:   Word)
                   : Boolean;
function       allocAltMapRegs40(
                   var alt_map:    Byte)
                   : Boolean;
function       releaseAltMapRegs40(
                   alt_map:        Byte)
                   : Boolean;

function       allocDMARegs40(
                   var regSet:     Byte)
                   : Boolean;
function       enableDMA40(
                   regSet:         Byte;
                   channel:        Byte)
                   : Boolean;
function       disableDMA40(
                   regSet:         Byte)
                   : Boolean;
function       releaseDMARegs40(
                   regSet:         Byte)
                   : Boolean;

function       prepEmmWarmBoot40
                   : Boolean;
```

```
function          enableEmmOSFuncs40(
                      a1:               Word;
                      a2:               Word;
                      var a3:           Word;
                      var a4:           Word)
                      : Boolean;
function          disableEmmOSFuncs40(
                      a1:               Word;
                      a2:               Word;
                      var a3:           Word;
                      var a4:           Word)
                      : Boolean;
function          releaseAccessKey40(
                      a1:               Word;
                      a2:               Word)
                      : Boolean;

function          errorText(
                      err:              Word)
                      : String;

end;


(*
 *
 *)
   Ems_EmBlk- object
       (*
        *  There's only one data element, the handle.
        *)
       handle:        Word;

       (*
        *  Now the methods:
        *)
       function          allocEM(
                             pages:            Word)
                             : Boolean;
       function          mapPage(
                             physical_page:    Word;
                             logical_page:     Word)
                             : Boolean;
       function          freeEM
                             : Boolean;
       function          savePageMap
                             : Boolean;
       function          restorePageMap
                             : Boolean;
       function          getPagesForHandle(
                             var num_pages:    Word)
                             : Boolean;
       function          mapPagesByNum40(
                             pages:            Word;
                             buffer:           Pointer)
                             : Boolean;
       function          mapPagesByAddr40(
                             pages:            Word;
                             buffer:           Pointer)
                             : Boolean;
       function          reallocHandPages40(
                             pages:            Word)
                             : Boolean;
```

3-6 Continued.

```
      function          getHandleAttr40(
                             var attribute:    Word)
                             : Boolean;
      function          setHandleAttr40(
                             attribute:        Word)
                             : Boolean;
      function          getHandleName40(
                             var handle_name: EMS_HandleName)
                             : Boolean;
      function          setHandleName40(
                             var handle_name: EMS_HandleName)
                             : Boolean;
      function          searchHandleName40(
                             var name:         EMS_HandleName)
                             : Boolean;
      function          mapPagesJumpNum40(
                             var buffer:       DWord)
                             : Boolean;
      function          mapPagesJumpSeg40(
                             var buffer:       DWord)
                             : Boolean;
      function          mapPagesCallNum40(
                             var buffer:       Word)
                             : Boolean;
      function          mapPagesCallSeg40(
                             var buffer:       Word)
                             : Boolean;
      function          allocHandleStd40(
                             pages:            Word)
                             : Boolean;
      function          allocHandleRaw40(
                             pages:            Word)
                             : Boolean;

    end;

  procedure          ems_demoError(
                             func: String);

IMPLEMENTATION

var
    ems:               EMS_Ems;

(*
 *  Load up the assembly language modules:
 *)

{$L EMS40}
{$L EMS41}
{$L EMS42}
{$L EMS43}
{$L EMS44}
{$L EMS45}
{$L EMS46}
{$L EMS47}
{$L EMS48}
{$L EMS4B}
{$L EMS4C}
```

3-6 Continued.

```
{$L EMS4D}
{$L EMS4E0}
{$L EMS4E1}
{$L EMS4E2}
{$L EMS4E3}
{$L EMS4F0}
{$L EMS4F1}
{$L EMS4F2}
{$L EMS500}
{$L EMS501}
{$L EMS51}
{$L EMS520}
{$L EMS521}
{$L EMS522}
{$L EMS530}
{$L EMS531}
{$L EMS540}
{$L EMS541}
{$L EMS542}
{$L EMS550}
{$L EMS551}
{$L EMS560}
{$L EMS561}
{$L EMS562}
{$L EMS570}
{$L EMS571}
{$L EMS580}
{$L EMS581}
{$L EMS590}
{$L EMS591}
{$L EMS5A0}
{$L EMS5A1}
{$L EMS5B0}
{$L EMS5B1}
{$L EMS5B2}
{$L EMS5B3}
{$L EMS5B4}
{$L EMS5B5}
{$L EMS5B6}
{$L EMS5B7}
{$L EMS5B8}
{$L EMS5C}
{$L EMS5D0}
{$L EMS5D1}
{$L EMS5D2}


function        EMS_Ems.getStatus
                    : Boolean;
                    external;
function        EMS_Ems.getPFA(
                    var page_frame: EMS_PageFrame)
                    : Boolean;
                    external;
function        EMS_Ems.getFreeEM(
                    var total:      Word;
                    var free:       Word)
                    : Boolean;
                    external;
```

3-6 Continued.

```
function        EMS_Ems.getVersion(
                    var version:    Word)
                    : Boolean;
                    external;
function        EMS_Ems.getNumActiveHandles(
                    var num_handles: Word)
                    : Boolean;
                    external;
function        EMS_Ems.getPagesAllHandles(
                    var info:           EMS_HandleInfoArr;
                    var num_handles: Word)
                    : Boolean;
                    external;


function        EMS_Ems.savePageMap32(
                    save_buffer:    Pointer)
                    : Boolean;
                    external;
function        EMS_Ems.restPageMap32(
                    restore_buffer: Pointer)
                    : Boolean;
                    external;
function        EMS_Ems.swapPageMap32(
                    rest_buffer:    Pointer;
                    save_buffer:    Pointer)
                    : Boolean;
                    external;
function        EMS_Ems.getMapInfoSize32(
                    var size:       Word)
                    : Boolean;
                    external;


function        EMS_Ems.savePartialMap40(
                    map:            Pointer;
                    buffer:         Pointer)
                    : Boolean;
                    external;
function        EMS_Ems.restPartialMap40(
                    buffer:         Pointer)
                    : Boolean;
                    external;
function        EMS_Ems.getPMapInfoSize40(
                    pages: Word;
                    var buffSize:   Word)
                    : Boolean;
                    external;


function        EMS_Ems.getAttrCapability40(
                    var capability: Word)
                    : Boolean;
                    external;


function        EMS_Ems.getAllHandleNames40(
                    var info_list:  EMS_HandleNameInfoArr)
                    : Boolean;
                    external;
```

3-6 Continued.

```
function          EMS_Ems.getTotalHandles40(
                      var handles:     Word)
                      : Boolean;
                      external;

function          EMS_Ems.getStackNeeded40(
                      var stack_space: Word)
                      : Boolean;
                      external;

function          EMS_Ems.moveMemRegion40(
                      var buffer:      EMS_MoveMemoryInfo)
                      : Boolean;
                      external;
function          EMS_Ems.swapMemRegions40(
                      var buffer:      EMS_MoveMemoryInfo)
                      : Boolean;
                      external;

function          EMS_Ems.getAddrsMappable40(
                      var buffer:      EMS_MappablePagesInfoArr;
                      var num_entries: Word)
                      : Boolean;
                      external;
function          EMS_Ems.getNumMappable40(
                      var mappablePages: Word)
                      : Boolean;
                      external;

function          EMS_Ems.getHWConfig40(
                      var buffer:      EMS_HardwareConfigInfo)
                      : Boolean;
                      external;

function          EMS_Ems.getNumRawPages40(
                      var total_pages: Word;
                      var free_pages: Word)
                      : Boolean;
                      external;

function          EMS_Ems.getAltMapRegs40(
                      var active_map: Byte;
                      var regs_area:  Byte)
                      : Boolean;
                      external;
function          EMS_Ems.setAltMapRegs40(
                      alt_set:         Byte;
                      var regs_area:  Byte)
                      : Boolean;
                      external;
function          EMS_Ems.getAltMapRegSize40(
                      var buf_size:   Word)
                      : Boolean;
                      external;
function          EMS_Ems.allocAltMapRegs40(
                      var alt_map:    Byte)
                      : Boolean;
                      external;
```

```
function        EMS_Ems.releaseAltMapRegs40(
                    alt_map:        Byte)
                    : Boolean;
                    external;
function        EMS_Ems.allocDMARegs40(
                    var regSet:     Byte)
                    : Boolean;
                    external;
function        EMS_Ems.enableDMA40(
                    regSet:         Byte;
                    channel:        Byte)
                    : Boolean;
                    external;
function        EMS_Ems.disableDMA40(
                    regSet:         Byte)
                    : Boolean;
                    external;
function        EMS_Ems.releaseDMARegs40(
                    regSet:         Byte)
                    : Boolean;
                    external;
function        EMS_Ems.prepEmmWarmBoot40
                    : Boolean;
                    external;
function        EMS_Ems.enableEmmOSFuncs40(
                    a1:             Word;
                    a2:             Word;
                    var a3:         Word;
                    var a4:         Word)
                    : Boolean;
                    external;
function        EMS_Ems.disableEmmOSFuncs40(
                    a1:             Word;
                    a2:             Word;
                    var a3:         Word;
                    var a4:         Word)
                    : Boolean;
                    external;
function        EMS_Ems.releaseAccessKey40(
                    a1:             Word;
                    a2:             Word)
                    : Boolean;
                    external;
function        EMS_EmBlk.allocEM(
                    pages:          Word)
                    : Boolean;
                    external;
function        EMS_EmBlk.mapPage(
                    physical_page:  Word;
                    logical_page:   Word)
                    : Boolean;
                    external;
function        EMS_EmBlk.freeEM
                    : Boolean;
                    external;
function        EMS_EmBlk.savePageMap
                    : Boolean;
                    external;
function        EMS_EmBlk.restorePageMap
                    : Boolean;
                    external;
```

```
function       EMS_EmBlk.getPagesForHandle(
                   var num_pages:    Word)
                   : Boolean;
                   external;
function       EMS_EmBlk.mapPagesByNum40(
                   pages:            Word;
                   buffer:           Pointer)
                   : Boolean;
                   external;
function       EMS_EmBlk.mapPagesByAddr40(
                   pages:            Word;
                   buffer:           Pointer)
                   : Boolean;
                   external;
function       EMS_EmBlk.reallocHandPages40(
                   pages:            Word)
                   : Boolean;
                   external;

function       EMS_EmBlk.getHandleAttr40(
                   var attribute:    Word)
                   : Boolean;
                   external;
function       EMS_EmBlk.setHandleAttr40(
                   attribute:        Word)
                   : Boolean;
                   external;
function       EMS_EmBlk.getHandleName40(
                   var handle_name: EMS_HandleName)
                   : Boolean;
                   external;
function       EMS_EmBlk.setHandleName40(
                   var handle_name: EMS_HandleName)
                   : Boolean;
                   external;
function       EMS_EmBlk.searchHandleName40(
                   var name:         EMS_HandleName)
                   : Boolean;
                   external;
function       EMS_EmBlk.mapPagesJumpNum40(
                   var buffer:       DWord)
                   : Boolean;
                   external;
function       EMS_EmBlk.mapPagesJumpSeg40(
                   var buffer:       DWord)
                   : Boolean;
                   external;
function       EMS_EmBlk.mapPagesCallNum40(
                   var buffer:       Word)
                   : Boolean;
                   external;
function       EMS_EmBlk.mapPagesCallSeg40(
                   var buffer:       Word)
                   : Boolean;
                   external;
function       EMS_EmBlk.allocHandleStd40(
                   pages:            Word)
                   : Boolean;
                   external;
function       EMS_EmBlk.allocHandleRaw40(
                   pages:            Word)
                   : Boolean;
                   external;
```

3-6 Continued.

```
function EMS_Ems.init: Boolean;
var
    emmxxxx0_name:      String;
    emmxxxx0_handle:    Word;

    regs:               Registers;

begin
    (*
     * Assume an error:
     *)
    errno:- EMSErrUnimp;

    (*
     * Initialize the name:
     *)
    emmxxxx0_name:- 'EMMXXXX0'#0;

    (*
     * Now try opening the device "EMMXXXX0"
     *)
    regs.DS:- Seg(emmxxxx0_name[1]);
    regs.DX:- Ofs(emmxxxx0_name[1]);
    regs.AL:- 0;                          { O_RDONLY }
    regs.AH:- $3D;                        { OPEN }
    regs.BX:- 0;
    regs.CX:- 0;
    regs.SI:- 0;
    regs.DI:- 0;
    MsDos(regs);

    if (regs.FLAGS and FCarry) <> 0 then begin
        (*
         * There was some kind of error. EMS must be unavailable.
         *)

        init:- True;
        exit;
        end;
    emmxxxx0_handle:- regs.AX;
    (*
     * Now we've got something. We need to make sure it's not
     * a file, but a device. ioctl() can give us this info.
     *)
    regs.AH:- $44;                        { IOCTL }
    regs.DS:- 0;
    regs.DX:- 0;
    regs.CX:- 0;
    regs.BX:- emmxxxx0_handle;
    regs.AL:- 0;
    MsDos(regs);
    if ((regs.FLAGS and FCarry) <> 0) or ((regs.DX and $80) - 0) then begin
        (*
         * Error occurred, or status was for a file. Close
         * handle, and return FALSE.
         *)
        regs.AH:- $3E;
        regs.BX:- emmxxxx0_handle;
        MsDos(regs);

        init:- True;
        exit;
        end;
```

```
      (*
       *   Finally, check the output status. If it's 0 that's bad.
       *)
      regs.AH:- $44;                        { IOCTL }
      regs.DS:- 0;
      regs.DX:- 0;
      regs.CX:- 0;
      regs.BX:- emmxxxx0_handle;
      regs.AL:- 7;
      MsDos(regs);
      if ((regs.FLAGS and FCarry) <> 0) or (regs.AL - 0) then begin
          (*
           *   Error occurred, or status was bad. Close
           *   handle, and return FALSE.
           *)
          regs.AH:- $3E;
          regs.BX:- emmxxxx0_handle;
          MsDos(regs);

          init:- True;
          exit;
          end;

      (*
       *   If we got here, we must be golden. Close the handle
       *   and return True.
       *)
      regs.AH:- $3E;
      regs.BX:- emmxxxx0_handle;
      MsDos(regs);

      (*
       *   No error:
       *)
      errno:- EMSErrOK;
      init:- False;
end;


function EMS_Ems.errorText(err: Word) : String;
begin

    case err of
        EMSErrOK:
            errorText:-    'No error';
        EMSErrInternal:
            errorText:-    'Internal EMM software error';
        EMSErrHardware:
            errorText:-    'EM Hardware error';
        EMSErrEMMBusy:
            errorText:-    'EMM Busy';
        EMSErrHandInv:
            errorText:-    'Handle Invalid';
        EMSErrUnimp:
            errorText:-    'Undefined EMS function';
        EMSErrNoHandles:
            errorText:-    'Handles Exhausted';
        EMSErrSaveRest:
            errorText:-    'Error in save/restore of context';
        EMSErrReqGTPhys:
            errorText:-    'Not enough physical EM for request';
```

3-6 Continued.

```
        EMSErrReqGTAvail:
            errorText:-  'Not enough available EM for request';
        EMSErrReqIsZero:
            errorText:-  'Cannot allocate zero pages';
        EMSErrLogPgInv:
            errorText:-  'Invalid logical page number';
        EMSErrPhysPgInv:
            errorText:-  'Invalid physical page number';
        EMSErrSSAreaFull:
            errorText:-  'Mapping save area is full';
        EMSErrSaveFail:
            errorText:-  'Handle already has a saved state associated with it';
        EMSErrRestFail:
            errorText:-  'Handle has no saved state associated with it';
        EMSErrParameter:
            errorText:-  'Subfunction parameter not defined';
        EMSErrAttribute:
            errorText:-  'Attribute type not defined';
        EMSErrUnsupported:
            errorText:-  'Feature not supported';
        EMSErrOverlap:
            errorText:-  'Source/dest of move overlap, move performed';
        EMSErrLenInv:
            errorText:-  'Length of move request invalid';
        EMSErrOverlapCE:
            errorText:-  'Overlap of conventional and extended memory';
        EMSErrOffsetInv:
            errorText:-  'Offset outside logical page';
        EMSErrRegionGT1MB:
            errorText:-  'Region size > 1 megabyte';
        EMSErrOverlapFatal:
            errorText:-  'Source/dest overlap prevented move';
        EMSErrMemTypeInv:
            errorText:-  'Memory source/dest types invalid';
        EMSErrDMARegUnsupp:
            errorText:-  'Specified alternate register set unsupported';
        EMSErrNoDMARegs:
            errorText:-  'No available alternate register sets';
        EMSErrAltRegsUnsupp:
            errorText:-  'Alternate registers unsupported';
        EMSErrDMARegUndef:
            errorText:-  'Specified alternate register set undefined';
        EMSErrDMAChanUnsupp:
            errorText:-  'Dedicated DMA channels unsupported';
        EMSErrChanUnsupp:
            errorText:-  'Specified DMA channel unsupported';
        EMSErrNameNotFound:
            errorText:-  'No handle found for name';
        EMSErrNameExists:
            errorText:-  'Handle with same name already exists';
        EMSErrPointerInv:
            errorText:-  'Invalid pointer or source array bogus';
        EMSErrAccess:
            errorText:-  'Access denied by operating system';
    else
            errorText:- 'Unknown error 0x' + hex(err, 2);
        end;

end;
```

```
procedure ems_demoError(func: String);

begin

    (*
     *  Report the error:
     *)
    writeln('Error on ',
                func, '(): "', ems.errorText(errno), '"');
    Halt;
end;

end.
```

Figure 3-7 presents the source code listing to EMSDEFS.ASM. This definition file will be included in all the EMS-based assembly bindings. It defines error codes and EMS function and subfunction values for assembly language programming.

3-7 The source code listing to EMSDEFS.ASM.

```
;*************************************************
;***                                          ***
;***        EmsDefs.ASM                       ***
;***                                          ***
;***        Contains definitions for EMS routines ***
;***                                          ***
;*************************************************
;
;   Define the EMS interrupt:
;
Ems             equ     67h


;
;   Now define the 3.0 EMS function codes.
;   These are 8 bit values which are loaded into
;   AH before calling the EMS interrupt.
;
GetStatus               equ     40h
GetPFA                  equ     41h
GetPSEG                 equ     41h
GetFreeEM               equ     42h
AllocateEM              equ     43h
MapEMPage               equ     44h
FreeEM                  equ     45h
GetVersion              equ     46h
SavePageMap             equ     47h
RestorePageMap          equ     48h
Reserved1               equ     49h
Reserved2               equ     4ah
GetNumActHandles        equ     4bh
GetPagesForHandle       equ     4ch
GetPagesAllHandles      equ     4dh
```

3-7 Continued.

```
;
;   Define the 3.2 and 4.0 EMS function codes:
;
;   Note that these are 16 bit values that
;   are loaded into AX prior to calling
;   the EMS interrupt. (These can be regarded
;   as an 8-bit function plus an 8 bit sub-
;   function.
;
;   The 3.2 codes:
;

SavePageMap32          equ     4e00h
RestPageMap32          equ     4e01h
SwapPageMap32          equ     4e02h
GetMapInfoSize32       equ     4e03h


;
;   The 4.0 codes:
;
SavePartialMap40       equ     4f00h
RestPartialMap40       equ     4f01h
GetPMapInfoSize40      equ     4f02h

MapPagesByNum40        equ     5000h
MapPagesByAddr40       equ     5001h

ReallocHandPages40     equ     5100h

GetHandleAttr40        equ     5200h
SetHandleAttr40        equ     5201h
GetAttrCapability40    equ     5202h

GetHandleName40        equ     5300h
SetHandleName40        equ     5301h

GetAllHandleNames40    equ     5400h
SearchHandleName40     equ     5401h
GetTotalHandles40      equ     5402h

MapPagesJumpNum40      equ     5500h
MapPagesJumpSeg40      equ     5501h

MapPagesCallNum40      equ     5600h
MapPagesCallSeg40      equ     5601h
GetStackNeeded40       equ     5602h

MoveMemRegion40        equ     5700h
SwapMemRegions40       equ     5701h

GetAddrsMappable40     equ     5800h
GetNumMappable40       equ     5801h

GetHWConfig40          equ     5900h
GetNumRawPages40       equ     5901h

AllocHandleStd40       equ     5a00h
AllocHandleRaw40       equ     5a01h
GetAltMapRegs40        equ     5b00h
SetAltMapRegs40        equ     5b01h
```

```
GetAltMapRegSize40    equ    5b02h
AllocAltMapRegs40     equ    5b03h
ReleaseAltMapRegs40   equ    5b04h
AllocDMARegs40        equ    5b05h
EnableDMA40           equ    5b06h
DisableDMA40          equ    5b07h
ReleaseDMARegs40      equ    5b08h

PrepEmmWarmBoot40     equ    5c00h

EnableEmmOSFuncs40    equ    5d00h
DisableEmmOSFuncs40   equ    5d01h
ReleaseAccessKey40    equ    5d02h
```

EMS 3.0 functions

Initialize EMS

Function EMS__Ems.init checks for the presence of EMS. If there is no Expanded Memory Manager present in the system, it will return an error.

Function EMS__Ems.init

```
function EMS__Ems.init
        : Boolean;
```

This function is defined in Pascal in __EMS.PAS.

Get the EMM status

Figure 3-8 presents the source code list to EMS40.ASM.

3-8 The source code listing to EMS40.ASM.

```
;*************************************************************
;***                                                      ***
;***    EMS40.ASM                                         ***
;***                                                      ***
;***    function          EMS_Ems.getStatus               ***
;***                        : Boolean;                     ***
;***                                                      ***
;***    Returns 0 for OK status or an error               ***
;***    code.                                             ***
;***                                                      ***
;***    (Ems Version 3.0)*********************************  ***
;*************************************************************


;— — — — — — — — —
;
; Declare memory model and language
;
        .model  large,pascal
;— — — — — — — — —
```

3-8 Continued.

```
;— — — — — — — — — —
;
; Include ems definition file
;

        include emsdefs.asm
;— — — — — — — — — —
;
; Declare errno as extrn to this
; module
;

        extrn    errno:WORD
;— — — — — — — — — —
;
; Declare function as PUBLIC
;

        public   EMS_Ems@getStatus
;— — — — — — — — — —
;
; Begin code segment
;

        .code
EMS_Ems@getStatus    proc     self: DWord

        mov      ah,GetStatus      ; Move function code
        int      Ems               ; Do the ems call

;
;   Return AH to caller
;
        mov      al,ah
        xor      ah,ah             ; Zero high byte
        mov      errno,ax          ; Save in errno too
        ret                        ; Return to caller

EMS_Ems@getStatus    endp          ; End of procedure

        end                        ; End of source file
```

Function EMS__Ems.getStatus is used to get the status of the Expanded Memory Manager. It should be called only after function EMS__Ems.init has been called successfully. If the status indicates an error, EMS__Ems.getStatus returns True and errno is set to the error code.

Function EMS__Ems.getStatus

function EMS__Ems.getStatus
        : Boolean;

Get the Page Frame Address

Figure 3-9 presents the source code listing to EMS41.ASM.

3-9 The source code listing to EMS41.ASM.

```
;*****************************************************************
;***                                                        ***
;***      EMS41.ASM                                         ***
;***                                                        ***
;***      function         EMS_Ems.getPFA(                 ***
;***                          var page_frame: EMS_PageFrame) ***
;***                          : Boolean;                    ***
;***                                                        ***
;***      Returns PFA through pfa_ptr parameter.           ***
;***      Gives 0 if no error, or an error code.           ***
;***                                                        ***
;***                                                        ***
;***      (Ems Version 3.0)                                 ***
;*****************************************************************
;
          .model   large,pascal

          include  emsdefs.asm

          extrn    errno:WORD

;
;    Define entry point
;
          public   EMS_Ems@getPFA

          .code
EMS_Ems@getPFA  proc     pfa:Far Ptr DWord, self:DWord
          mov      ah,GetPFA           ; Move function code
          int      Ems                 ; Do the ems call

;
;    Check AH to see if an error occurred:
;
          or       ah,ah               ; Set flags
          jnz      error

;
;    BX has a segment address, put it in the high Word
;    of the caller's location, and put zero in the low
;    word giving BX:0000 for an address.
;
          mov      ax,bx               ; Save bx
          les      bx,pfa              ; Get address for return
          mov      es:[bx+2],ax        ; Put segment down
          xor      ax,ax               ; AX gets a zero
          mov      es:[bx],ax          ; Put offset down

          ret                          ; Return to caller (AX -- 0)

error:
          mov      al,ah               ; Zero high byte
          xor      ah,ah               ; Save in errno too
          mov      errno,ax            ; Return to caller
          ret
EMS_Ems@getPFA          endp           ; End of procedure

          end                          ; End of source file
```

Function ems.getPFA(...) is used to obtain a pointer to the EMS page frame. This pointer will be used by the caller to write data to and read data from the EMS pages which have been mapped into the page frame area.

Function ems.getPFA(...)

```
function EMS__Ems.getPFA(
              var page__frame:EMS__PageFrame)
      : Boolean;
```

where

page__frame   Receives pointer to the EMS page frame

Get the number of free EMS pages

Figure 3-10 presents the source code listing to EMS42.ASM.

3-10 The source code listing to EMS42.ASM.

```
;***************************************************************
;***      EMS42.ASM                                        ***
;***                                                        ***
;***      function        EMS_Ems.getFreeEM(               ***
;***                         var total:     Word;          ***
;***                         var free:      Word)          ***
;***                         : Boolean;                    ***
;***                                                        ***
;***      Returns the total number of EMS pages and the    ***
;***      number of pages available. Returns 0 if no error ***
;***      or an error code.                                 ***
;***                                                        ***
;***                                                        ***
;***      (Ems Version 3.0)                                ***
;***************************************************************
          .model   large,pascal
          include emsdefs.asm
          extrn    errno:WORD
;
;    Define entry point
;
          public  EMS_Ems@getFreeEM

          .code
EMS_Ems@getFreeEM    proc    total:Far Ptr word, free:Far Ptr Word,
self:Dword
          mov     ah,GetFreeEM          ; Move function code
          int     Ems                   ; Do the ems call

          or      ah,ah                 ; Set flags
          jnz     error
;
;    BX now has the number of free EMS pages, DX has the total
;    number of EMS pages. Return the values:
```

```
;
        mov     ax,bx               ; Save free pages
        les     bx,free             ; Get address of free
        mov     es:[bx],ax          ; Put free pages down
        les     bx,total            ; Get address of total
        mov     es:[bx],dx          ; Put total pages down

        xor     ax,ax
        ret                         ; AX has zero
error:
        mov     al,ah
        xor     ah,ah               ; Zero high byte
        mov     errno,ax            ; Save in errno too
        ret

EMS_Ems@getFreeEM    endp           ; End of procedure

        end                         ; End of source file
```

Function EMS__Ems.getFreeEM(...) gets the total number of EMS pages installed and the number of EMS pages available.

Function EMS__Ems.getFreeEM(...)

```
function EMS__Ems.getFreeEM(
            var total:  Word;
            var free:   Word)
    : Boolean;
```

where

total Receives number of EMS pages installed
free Receives number of free EMS pages available

Allocate EMS handle and pages

Figure 3-11 presents the source code listing to EMS43.ASM.

3-11 The source code listing to EMS43.ASM.

```
;************************************************************
;***                                                    ***
;***     EMS43.ASM                                      ***
;***                                                    ***
;***     function       EMS_EmBlk.allocEM(              ***
;***                         pages:          Word)      ***
;***                     : Boolean;                     ***
;***                                                    ***
;***     Takes the number of pages to allocate and returns  ***
;***     a handle with that number of pages. On error,  ***
;***     returns a non-zero error code.                 ***
;***                                                    ***
;***                                                    ***
;***     (Ems Version 3.0)                              ***
;************************************************************
;
```

3-11 Continued.

```
        .model  large,pascal

        include emsdefs.asm

        extrn   errno:WORD
;
;   Define entry point
;
        public  EMS_EmBLk@allocEM

        .code

EMS_EmBlk@allocEM    proc     pages:Word, handle:Far Ptr Word
;
;   BX takes the number of pages to allocate:
;
        mov     bx,pages

        mov     ah,AllocateEM       ; Move function code
        int     Ems                 ; Do the ems call

        or      ah,ah               ; Set flags
        jnz     error
;
;   DX now has the EMM handle. Return it:
;
        les     bx,handle           ; Get address of handle
        mov     es:[bx],dx          ; Put handle down

        xor     ax,ax               ; AX gets 0
        ret                         ; Return to caller

error:
        mov     al,ah               ; Transfer return code to al
        xor     ah,ah               ; Zero high byte
        mov     errno,ax            ; Save in errno too
        ret                         ; Return to caller

EMS_EmBlk@allocEM    endp            ; End of procedure

        end                         ; End of source code
```

Function EMS__EmBlk.allocEM(...) is used to allocate a specified number of EMS pages required for use by your program. This function initializes an object of type EMS__EmBlk by allocating EMS memory for it. Subsequent operations work on the EMS__EmBlk object. This is essentially the constructor for EMS__EmBlk, although it is not defined as a constructor. This is because we want to keep the error reporting consistent, and constructors report errors by returning False rather than True.

Function EMS__EmBlk.allocEM(...)

```
function EMS__EmBlk.allocEM(
              pages:  Word)
        : Boolean;
```

where

pages   The number of 16K pages you want to allocate

Map an Expanded Memory Page

Figure 3-12 presents the source code listing to EMS44.ASM.

3-12   The source code listing to EMS44.ASM

```
;*********************************************************    ***
;***     EMS44.ASM                                            ***
;***                                                          ***
;***     function        EMS_EmBlk.mapPage(                   ***
;***                        physical_page:  Word;             ***
;***                        logical_page:   Word)             ***
;***                        : Boolean;                        ***
;***                                                          ***
;***     Maps a physical page into a specified logical page.  ***
;***                                                          ***
;***                                                          ***
;***     (Ems Version 3.0)                                    ***
;*********************************************************
;

        .model   large,pascal

        include emsdefs.asm

        extrn    errno:WORD


;
;   Define entry point
;
        public   EMS_EmBlk@mapPage

        .code

EMS_EmBlk@mapPage    proc    physical_page:Word, logical_page:Word,
                             handle:Far Ptr Word


;
;   AL takes the physical page number, BX, the logical page number,
;   and DX, the handle.
;
        les      bx,handle
        mov      dx,es:[bx]             ; Get the handle
        mov      ax,physical_page
        mov      bx,logical_page

        mov      ah,MapEMPage           ; Move function code
        int      Ems                    ; Do the ems call

        or       ah,ah                  ; Set flags
        jnz      error

        xor      ax,ax                  ; AX gets 0
        ret                             ; Return to caller
```

```
error:
        mov     al,ah               ; Transfer return code to al
        xor     ah,ah               ; Zero high byte
        mov     errno,ax            ; Save in errno too
        ret                         ; Return to caller

EMS_EmBlk@mapPage   endp            ; End of procedure

        end                         ; End of source file
```

Function EMS__EmBlk.mapPage(...) is used to map EMS logical pages to one of the four physical pages located in the 64K page frame segment.

Function Ems__EmBlk.mapPage(...)

```
function EMS__EmBlk.mapPage(
                physical__page:  Word;
                logical__page:   Word)
        : Boolean;
```

where

physical__page   The physical page number (0-3)
logical__page   The EMS logical page to be mapped

Free a handle and the associated EMS pages

Figure 3-13 presents the source code listing to EMS45.ASM.

3-13 The source code listing to EMS45.ASM.

```
;****************************************************************
;***    EMS45.ASM                                           ***
;***                                                        ***
;***    function         EMS_EmBlk.freeEM                   ***
;***                      : Boolean;                        ***
;***                                                        ***
;***    Releases an EMM handle along with the associated    ***
;***    pages.                                              ***
;***                                                        ***
;***                                                        ***
;***    (Ems Version 3.0)                                   ***
;****************************************************************

        .model  large,pascal

        include emsdefs.asm

        extrn   errno:WORD

;
;   Define entry point
;
```

```
        public  EMS_EmBlk@freeEM

        .code

EMS_EmBlk@freeEM    proc    handle:Far Ptr Word

;
;   DX takes the number of pages to allocate:
;
        les     bx,handle
        mov     dx,es:[bx]              ; Get handle

        mov     ah,FreeEM               ; Move function code
        int     Ems                     ; Do the ems call

        or      ah,ah                   ; Set flags
        jnz     error

        xor     ax,ax                   ; AX gets 0
        ret                             ; Return to caller

error:
        mov     al,ah                   ; Transfer return code to al
        xor     ah,ah                   ; Zero high byte
        mov     errno,ax                ; Save in errno too
        ret                             ; Return to caller

EMS_EmBlk@freeEM    endp                ; End of procedure

        end                             ; End of source file
```

Function EMS_EmBlk.freeEM frees all the EMS memory that had been previously allocated and associated with a specified handle. This is essentially the destructor for EMS_EmBlk, although it is not defined as a destructor.

Function EMS_EmBlk.freeEM

function EMS_EmBlk.freeEM
    : Boolean;

Get the EMS version number

Figure 3-14 presents the source code listing to EMS46.ASM.

3-14 The source code listing to EMS46.ASM.

```
;****************************************************************
;***      EMS46.ASM                                        ***
;***                                                       ***
;***      function          EMS_Ems.getVersion(           ***
;***                          var version:    Word)        ***
;***                          : Boolean;                   ***
;***                                                       ***
;***      Gives the EMS version.                           ***
;***                                                       ***
;***                                                       ***
;***      (Ems Version 3.0)                                ***
;****************************************************************

        .model  large,pascal

        include emsdefs.asm

        extrn   errno:WORD

;
;   Define entry point
;
        public  EMS_Ems@getVersion

        .code

EMS_Ems@getVersion proc     version:Far Ptr Word, self:DWord

        mov     ah,GetVersion       ; Move function code
        int     Ems                 ; Do the ems call

        or      ah,ah               ; Set flags
        jnz     error

;
;   AL now has the EMS version.
;
        xor     ah,ah               ; Zero extend
        les     bx,version          ; Get address of version
        mov     es:[bx],ax          ; Return it

        xor     ax,ax               ; AX gets 0
        ret                         ; Return to caller
error:
        mov     al,ah               ; Transfer return code to al
        xor     ah,ah               ; Zero high byte
        mov     errno,ax            ; Save in errno too
        ret                         ; Return to caller

EMS_Ems@getVersion endp             ; End of procedure

        end                         ; End of source file
```

Function EMS_Ems.getVersion(...) returns the current version number in Binary Coded Decimal (BCD) format. So, for example, v4.13 would be represented by $0413.

Function EMS_Ems.getVersion(...)

function EMS_Ems.getVersion(
                    var version: Word)
                    : Boolean;

where

version   Receives the EMS version number in BCD format

Save the contents of page map registers

Figure 3-15 presents the source code listing to EMS47.ASM.

3-15 The source code listing to EMS47.ASM.

```
;*******************************************************************
;***      EMS47.ASM                                          ***
;***                                                          ***
;***      function          EMS_EmBlk.savePageMap            ***
;***                        : Boolean;                        ***
;***                                                          ***
;***      Saves the page map state for the                   ***
;***      specified handle.                                  ***
;***                                                          ***
;***                                                          ***
;***      (Ems Version 3.0)                                  ***
;*******************************************************************

        .model  large,pascal

        include emsdefs.asm

        extrn   errno:WORD

;
;   Define entry point
;
        public  EMS_EmBlk@savePageMap

        .code

EMS_EmBlk@savePageMap    proc     handle:Far Ptr Word

;
;   DX takes the handle
;
        les     bx,handle
        mov     dx,es:[bx]

        mov     ah,SavePageMap        ; Move function code
        int     Ems                   ; Do the ems call

        or      ah,ah                 ; Set flags
        jnz     error
```

```
        xor     ax,ax                   ; AX gets 0
        ret                             ; Return to caller
error:
        mov     al,ah                   ; Transfer return code to al
        xor     ah,ah                   ; Zero high byte
        mov     errno,ax                ; Save in errno too
        ret                             ; Return to caller

EMS_EmBlk@savePageMap    endp           ; End of procedure

        end                             ; End of source file
```

Function Ems__EmBlk.savePageMap saves the page map (the mapping of physical pages to logical pages) to a save area associated with the specified EMS__EmBlk.

Function EMS__EmBlk.savePageMap

```
function EMS__EmBlk.savePageMap
                : Boolean;
```

Restore the contents of page map registers

Figure 3-16 presents the source code listing to EMS48.ASM.

3-16 The source code listing to EMS48.ASM.

```
;***************************************************************
;***     EMS48.ASM                                          ***
;***                                                        ***
;***     function        EMS_EmBlk.restorePageMap           ***
;***                      : Boolean;                        ***
;***                                                        ***
;***     Restores the page map state for the                ***
;***     specified handle.                                  ***
;***                                                        ***
;***                                                        ***
;***     (Ems Version 3.0)                                  ***
;***************************************************************

        .model  large,pascal

        include emsdefs.asm

        extrn   errno:WORD

;
;   Define entry point
;
        public  EMS_EmBlk@restorePageMap

        .code

EMS_EmBlk@restorePageMap        proc    handle:Far Ptr Word
```

```
;
;   DX takes the handle
;
        les     bx,handle
        mov     dx,es:[bx]

        mov     ah,RestorePageMap       ; Move function code
        int     Ems                     ; Do the ems call

        or      ah,ah                   ; Set flags
        jnz     error

        xor     ax,ax                   ; AX gets 0
        ret                             ; Return to caller

error:
        mov     al,ah                   ; Transfer return code to al
        xor     ah,ah                   ; Zero high byte
        mov     errno,ax                ; Save in errno too
        ret                             ; Return to caller

EMS_EmBlk@restorePageMap    endp        ; End of procedure

        end                             ; End of source file
```

Function EMS__EmBlk.restorePageMap restores the map registers that had previously been saved using the EMS__EmBlk.savePageMap function.

Function EMS__EmBlk.restorePageMap

function EMS__EmBlk.restorePageMap
            : Boolean;

Get the active EMM handles

Figure 3-17 presents the source code listing to EMS4B.ASM.

3-17 The source code listing to EMS4B.ASM.

```
;******************************************************
;***                                               ***
;***     EMS4B.ASM                                  ***
;***                                               ***
;***     function       EMS_Ems.getNumActiveHandles(  ***
;***                     var num_handles: Word)     ***
;***                         : Boolean;             ***
;***                                               ***
;***     Gives the number of active EMM handles     ***
;***                                               ***
;***                                               ***
;***     (Ems Version 3.0)                          ***
;******************************************************
;
        .model  large,pascal

        include emsdefs.asm

        extrn   errno:WORD
```

3-17 Continued.

```
;
;   Define entry point
;
        public  EMS_Ems@getNumActiveHandles
        .code

EMS_Ems@getNumActiveHandles proc     num_handles:Far Ptr Word, self:DWord

        mov     ah,GetNumActHandles      ; Move function code
        int     Ems                      ; Do the ems call

        or      ah,ah                    ; Set flags
        jnz     error

;
;   Return the result:
;
        mov     ax,bx                    ; Number of handles
        les     bx,num_handles
        mov     es:[bx],ax               ; Give it back

        xor     ax,ax                    ; AX gets 0
        ret                              ; Return to caller

error:
        mov     al,ah
        xor     ah,ah                    ; Zero high byte
        mov     errno,ax                 ; Save in errno too
        ret                              ; Return to caller

EMS_Ems@getNumActiveHandles endp        ; End of procedure

        end                              ; End of source file
```

Function EMS__Ems.getNumActiveHandles(...) gives the number of active EMM handles.

Function EMS__Ems.getNumActiveHandles(...)

```
function EMS__Ems.getNumActiveHandles(
              var num__handles:  Word)
         : Boolean;
```

where

num__handles   Receives number of active handles

Get number of pages for handle

Figure 3-18 presents the source code listing to EMS4C.ASM.

3-18 The source code listing to EMS4C.ASM.

```
;****************************************************************
;***                                                        ***
;***      EMS4C.ASM                                         ***
;***                                                        ***
;***      function        EMS_EmBlk.getPagesForHandle(      ***
;***                          var num_pages:  Word)         ***
;***                          : Boolean;                    ***
;***                                                        ***
;***      Gives the number of pages associated with a       ***
;***      given EMM handle.                                 ***
;***                                                        ***
;***                                                        ***
;***      (Ems Version 3.0)                                 ***
;****************************************************************

        .model  large,pascal

        include emsdefs.asm

        extrn   errno:WORD


;
;    Define entry point
;
        public  EMS_EmBlk@getPagesForHandle

        .code

EMS_EmBlk@getPagesForHandle proc    num_pages:Far Ptr Word, handle:Far Ptr
                                    Word


;
;    DX takes the handle
;
        les     bx,handle
        mov     dx,es:[bx]

        mov     ah,GetPagesForHandle    ; Move function code
        int     Ems                     ; Do the ems call

        or      ah,ah                   ; Set flags
        jnz     error


;
;    Return the result:
;
        mov     ax,bx                   ; Number of pages
        les     bx,num_pages
        mov     es:[bx],ax              ; Give it back

        xor     ax,ax                   ; AX gets 0
        ret                             ; Return to caller

error:
        mov     al,ah                   ; Transfer return code to al
        xor     ah,ah                   ; Zero high byte
        mov     errno,ax                ; Save in errno too
        ret                             ; Return to caller

EMS_EmBlk@getPagesForHandle endp        ; End of procedure

        end                             ; End of source file
```

Function EMS_EmBlk.getPagesForHandle(...) gets the number of Extended Memory pages associated with a given handle.

Function EMS_EmBlk.getPagesForHandle(...)

function EMS_EmBlk.getPagesForHandle(
            var num_pages: Word)
        : Boolean;

where

num_pages   Receives number of pages associated with handle.

Get number of pages for all handles

Figure 3-19 presents the source code listing to EMS4D.ASM.

3-19 The source code listing to EMS4D.ASM.

```
;********************************************************
;***      EMS4D.ASM                                  ***
;***                                                 ***
;***      function     EMS_Ems.getPagesAllHandles(   ***
;***                   var info:       EMS_HandleInfoArr ***
;***                   var num_handles: Word)        ***
;***                   : Boolean;                    ***
;***                                                 ***
;***      Gives the number of pages associated with each ***
;***      active EMM handle, and the number of active ***
;***      EMM handles.                               ***
;***                                                 ***
;***                                                 ***
;***      (Ems Version 3.0)                          ***
;********************************************************

        .model  large,pascal

        include emsdefs.asm

        extrn   errno:WORD

;
;   Define entry point
;
        public  EMS_Ems@getPagesAllHandles

        .code

EMS_Ems@getPagesAllHandles proc     info:Far Ptr DWord, num_handles:Far Ptr
                                    Word, self:DWord

        push    di                  ; Save DI, we need it

;
;   ES:[DI] gets the buffer address
;
        les     di,info
```

3-19 Continued.

```
        mov     ah,GetPagesAllHandles   ; Move function code
        int     Ems                     ; Do the ems call

        or      ah,ah                   ; Set flags
        jnz     error

;
;   Return the number of handles:
;
        mov     ax,bx                   ; Number of handles
        les     bx,num_handles
        mov     es:[bx],ax              ; Give it back

        xor     ax,ax                   ; AX gets 0
        pop     di                      ; Restore di
        ret                             ; Return to caller

error:
        pop     di                      ; Restore di

        mov     al,ah                   ; Transfer return code to al
        xor     ah,ah                   ; Zero high byte
        mov     errno,ax                ; Save in errno too
        ret                             ; Return to caller

EMS_Ems@getPagesAllHandles endp        ; End of procedure

        end                             ; End of source file
```

Function EMS_Ems.getPagesAllHandles(...) gives the number of active handles and the number of pages associated with each of those handles.

Function EMS_Ems.getPagesAllHandles(...)

function EMS_Ems.getPagesAllHandles(
        var info: EMS_HandleInfoArr;
        var num_handles: Word)
    : Boolean;

where

info   An array big enough to accommodate each handle/page count pair

num_handles Receives the number of active handles

EMS 3.2 functions

Four more functions are added with EMS 3.2; these functions provide greater flexibility in saving and restoring the map state.

Save page map to a buffer

Figure 3-20 presents the source code listing to EMS4E0.ASM.

3-20 The source code listing to EMS4E0.ASM.

```
;****************************************************************
;***      EMS4E0.ASM                                        ***
;***                                                        ***
;***      function          EMS_Ems.savePageMap32(         ***
;***                          save_buffer:    Pointer)      ***
;***                          : Boolean;                    ***
;***                                                        ***
;***      Returns 0 for OK status or an error              ***
;***      code.                                             ***
;***                                                        ***
;***      (Ems Version 3.2)                                 ***
;****************************************************************

        .model  large,pascal

        include emsdefs.asm

        extrn   errno:WORD

;
;   Define entry point
;
        public  EMS_Ems@savePageMap32

        .code

EMS_Ems@savePageMap32   proc save_buff:Far Ptr DWord, self:DWord

        push    di                      ; Save di

        les     di,save_buff            ; Get address of buffer into ES:DI

        mov     ax,SavePageMap32        ; Make the EMS call to save the map
        int     Ems

        or      ah,ah                   ; Check for error
        jnz     error

        xor     ax,ax                   ; AX gets 0
        pop     di                      ; Restore di
        ret                             ; Return to caller
error:
        pop     di                      ; Restore di

        mov     al,ah
        xor     ah,ah                   ; Zero high byte
        mov     errno,ax                ; Save in errno too
        ret                             ; Return to caller

EMS_Ems@savePageMap32   endp            ; End of procedure

        end                             ; End of source file
```

Function EMS__Ems.savePageMap32 allows the programmer to save the map registers into a specified buffer. The 3.0 function only allowed them to be saved in a special area associated with a handle.

Function EMS__Ems.savePageMap32(...)

```
function EMS__Ems.savePageMap32(
              save__buffer:   Pointer)
        : Boolean;
```

where

save__buffer   A pointer to an area of sufficient size (the size can be determined via a call to EMS__Ems.getMapInfoSize)

Restore page map from a buffer

Figure 3-21 presents the source code listing to EMS4E1.ASM.

3-21 The source code listing to EMS4E1.ASM.

```
;***************************************************************
;***       EMS4E1.ASM                                   ***
;***                                                    ***
;***       function       EMS_Ems.restPageMap32(        ***
;***                       restore_buffer: Pointer)     ***
;***                        : Boolean;                  ***
;***                                                    ***
;***       Returns 0 for OK status or an error          ***
;***       code.                                        ***
;***                                                    ***
;***       (Ems Version 3.2)                            ***
;***************************************************************
;
        .model   large,pascal

        include emsdefs.asm

        extrn    errno:WORD


;
;   Define entry point
;
        public  EMS_Ems@restPageMap32

        .code

EMS_Ems@restPageMap32    proc restore_buff:Far Ptr DWord, self:DWord

        push    ds                  ; Save ds
        push    si                  ; Save si

        lds     si,restore_buff     ; Get buffer address into DS:SI

        mov     ax,RestPageMap32
        int     Ems

        or      ah,ah               ; Check for error
```

3-21 Continued.

```
        jnz     error

        xor     ax,ax                   ; Return a zero meaning no error

        pop     si                      ; Restore si
        pop     ds                      ; Restore ds
        ret                             ; Return to caller
error:
        pop     si                      ; Restore si
        pop     ds                      ; Restore ds

        mov     al,ah
        xor     ah,ah                   ; Zero high byte
        mov     errno,ax                ; Save in errno too
        ret                             ; Return to caller

EMS_Ems@restPageMap32    endp           ; End of procedure

        end                             ; End of source file
```

Function EMS__Ems.restPageMap32(...) allows the programmer to restore the map registers from a buffer previously filled by a call to EMS__Ems.save-PageMap32.

Function EMS__Ems.restPageMap32(...)

```
function EMS__Ems.restPageMap32(
             restore__buffer: Pointer)
       : Boolean;
```

where

restore__buffer   A pointer to an area initialized by a call to EMS__Ems.savePageMap32.

Swap page maps

Figure 3-22 presents the source code listing to EMS4E2.ASM.

3-22 The source code listing to EMS4E2.ASM.

```
;*****************************************************************
;***     EMS4E2.ASM                                        ***
;***                                                       ***
;***     function          EMS_Ems.swapPageMap32(          ***
;***                        rest_buffer:    Pointer;        ***
;***                        save_buffer:    Pointer)        ***
;***                         : Boolean;                     ***
;***                                                       ***
;***     Returns 0 for OK status or an error               ***
;***     code.                                             ***
;***                                                       ***
;***     (Ems Version 3.2)                                 ***
;*****************************************************************
```

3-22 Continued.

```
        .model  large,pascal

        include emsdefs.asm

        extrn   errno:WORD

;
;   Define entry point
;
        public  EMS_Ems@swapPageMap32

        .code
EMS_Ems@swapPageMap32   proc restore_buff:Far Ptr DWord, save_buff:Far Ptr
                        DWord, self:DWord

        push    ds                      ; Save ds
        push    si                      ; Save si
        push    di                      ; Save di

        lds     si,restore_buff         ; Get map to restore into DS:SI
        les     di,save_buff            ; Get save area address into ES:DI

        mov     ax,SwapPageMap32        ; Call EMS to swap
        int     Ems

        or      ah,ah                   ; Check for error
        jnz     error

        xor     ax,ax                   ; Return a zero meaning no error

        pop     di                      ; Restore di
        pop     si                      ; Restore si
        pop     ds                      ; Restore ds
        ret                             ; Return to caller

error:
        pop     di                      ; Restore di
        pop     si                      ; Restore si
        pop     ds                      ; Restore ds

        mov     al,ah
        xor     ah,ah                   ; Zero high byte
        mov     errno,ax                ; Save in errno too
        ret                             ; Return to caller

EMS_Ems@swapPageMap32   endp            ; End of procedure

        end                             ; End of source file
```

Function EMS__Ems.swapPageMap32(...) allows the programmer to save the current page map in a buffer and restore the page map from another buffer in one call.

Function EMS__Ems.swapPageMap32(...)

```
function EMS__Ems.swapPageMap32(
                rest__buffer:  Pointer;
                save__buffer:  Pointer;
        : Boolean;
```

where

rest__buffer   The map register buffer to be restored

save__buffer   The buffer in which to save the current map state

Get the size of a map register save area

Figure 3-23 presents the source code listing to EMS4E3.ASM.

3-23 The source code listing to EMS4E3.ASM.

```
;*******************************************************************
;***      EMS4E3.ASM                                          ***
;***                                                          ***
;***      function         EMS_Ems.getMapInfoSize32(         ***
;***                          var size:      Word)           ***
;***                          : Boolean;                     ***
;***                                                          ***
;***      Returns 0 for OK status or an error                ***
;***      code.                                               ***
;***                                                          ***
;***      (Ems Version 3.2)                                   ***
;*******************************************************************

        .model  large,pascal

        include emsdefs.asm

        extrn   errno:WORD

;
;   Define entry point
;
        public  EMS_Ems@getMapInfoSize32

        .code

EMS_Ems@getMapInfoSize32  proc map_size:Far Ptr Word, self:DWord

        mov     ax,GetMapInfoSize32     ; Make the call to get the size
        int     Ems

        or      ah,ah                   ; Check for an error
        jnz     error

;
;   Return the info. Size is in AL. We zero extend it to
;   16 bits and return it.
;
        les     bx,map_size             ; Get address of return spot
        xor     ah,ah                   ; Zero extend to 16 bits
        mov     es:[bx],ax              ; Return the size

        xor     ax,ax                   ; Return a zero meaning no error
        ret                             ; Return to caller
```

```
error:
        pop     di                          ; Restore di
        pop     es                          ; Restore es

        mov     al,ah
        xor     ah,ah                       ; Zero high byte
        mov     errno,ax                    ; Save in errno too
        ret                                 ; Return to caller

EMS_Ems@getMapInfoSize32    endp            ; End of procedure

        end                                 ; End of source file
```

Function EMS__Ems.getMapInfoSize32(...) returns the number of bytes required to save a page map. This function should be called before calling EMS__Ems.savePageMap32 in order to ensure that sufficient buffer space is being provided.

Function EMS__Ems.getMapInfoSize32(...)

function EMS__Ems.getMapInfoSize32(
                var size: Word)
        : Boolean;

where

size   Gets the size in bytes of the space required to save the page map

Summary

This chapter presented a Turbo Pascal interface to the EMS 3.0 and 3.2 functions. Some of the routines presented allow you to determine if an EMM is installed, if the EMM's status is OK, to allocate a specified number of EMS pages, to map logical pages to the EMS page frame, to get a far pointer to the page frame, and to release the previously allocated memory.

These routines will form the foundation for the EMS portion of the Virtual Memory Management system presented in Chapter 6.

4
EMS 4.0

In a similar fashion to that of Chapter 3, this chapter will present the functional capabilities of EMS 4.0. Although EMS 4.0 adds wide ranging capabilities to your memory management bag of tricks, you must be thoughtful about using EMS 4.0 functions in commercial application programs.

The reason, of course, is that there might still be some computers in the market with EMM's supporting only EMS 3.0 or 3.2. If your program will be reaching the commercial marketplace, then you'll have to think hard about whether you must support pre-revision 4.0 EMM.

On the other hand, if you're writing a program to work in a known environment that does indeed support EMS 4.0, then it makes great sense to use as many features of EMS 4.0 as you want.

EMS 4.0 enhancements

EMS 4.0 has two important enhancements that merit some discussion. In EMS 3.0 and 3.2, the only place in addressable memory where an EMS page can be mapped is the Page Frame Area. This means that only four EMS pages can be mapped at any given time. In EMS 4.0, many or most of the pages in low memory (below 640K) can be remapped. Thus, a programmer can, for example, replace the normal memory at segment $4000 with a page from an EMS block. Several calls are required to support this functionality. First, calls are required to determine which pages are mappable. Second, calls are required for saving the map status of a specified set of physical pages. In EMS 3.0 and 3.2, the save page map routines only save the page map for the Page Frame Area.

The second major enhancement for applications programmers is the existence of handle names. The programmer can associate a name with an EMS handle. This proves useful in two ways: memory display utilities can provide more meaningful information if names are associated with EMS blocks, and—more important—a program can avoid having to pass handle numbers to every part of the program that requires access to an EMS block. Instead, a meaningful name for the EMS block can be agreed upon by all parts of a program.

We now turn to the demonstration programs that illustrate the use of the enhancements.

EMS 4.0 demonstration programs

The programs presented in this section of Chapter 4 demonstrate the use of many EMS 4.0 functions. The source code has been heavily documented to facilitate your understanding of these functions.

Figure 4-1 presents the source code listing to PROG4-1.PAS, which demonstrates the following:

- getting the number of mappable pages
- getting the addresses of mappable pages

4-1 The source code listing to PROG4-1.PAS.

```
(* * * * * * * * * * * * * * * * * *
 *
 * prog4-1.pas
 *
 *      Demonstrates
 *          - Get number of mappable pages
 *          - Get addresses of mappable pages
 *
 * * * * * * * * * * * * * * * * * * *)

program prog4_1;

uses    _globals,
        _ems;


var
    ems:                    EMS_Ems;

    numMappablePages:       Word;
    numMappablePages2:      Word;

    i:                      Word;


    pageAddress:            ^EMS_MappablePagesInfoArr;
```

4-1 Continued.

```
begin

    (*
     *  First check for presence of EMS
     *)
    if ems.init then begin
        writeln('EMS is not present');
        Halt;
        end;

    (*
     *  Find out how many mappable pages we have all together. In
     *  4.0, we do not have a fixed size page frame, we may have
     *  many more than 4 mappable pages.
     *)
    if ems.getNumMappable40(numMappablePages) then begin
        ems_demoError('EMS_Ems.getNumMappable40');
        end;

    (*
     *  Now allocate a buffer big enough to hold the addresses
     *  of these pages.
     *)
    GetMem(pageAddress, sizeof(EMS_MappablePagesInfo) * numMappablePages);

    (*
     *  Get the info
     *)
    if ems.getAddrsMappable40(pageAddress^, numMappablePages2) then begin
        ems_demoError('EMS_Ems.getAddrsMappable40');
        end;

    (*
     *  Sanity check that the page counts match.
     *)
    if numMappablePages <> numMappablePages2 then begin
        writeln('There is something really wrong here!');
        Halt;
        end;

    (*
     *  Now print the info out:
     *)
    writeln('╔══════Segment═Address═════════╦══Physical═Page═#═════╗');

    for i:= 0 to numMappablePages-1 do begin
        writeln('║          0x',
                hex(pageAddress^[i].pageSegment, 4),
                '           │',
                pageAddress^[i].physNumber:4,
                '          ║');

        if i < numMappablePages-1 then begin
            writeln('║──────────────────────────────┼─────────────────────║');
            end;
        end;
    writeln('╚══════════════════════════════╧═════════════════════╝');
end.
```

Figure 4-2 presents the source code listing to PROG4-2.PAS, which demonstrates the following:

- getting the hardware configuration
- getting the number of raw pages

4-2 The source code listing to PROG4-2.PAS.

```
(* * * * * * * * * * * * * * * * * *
 *
 * prog4-2.pas
 *
 *      Demonstrates
 *              - Get hardware configuration
 *              - Get number of raw pages
 *
 * * * * * * * * * * * * * * * * * *)

program        prog4_2;

uses           _globals,
               _ems;

var
    ems:                    EMS_Ems;

    hwConfig:               EMS_HardwareConfigInfo;

    freeRawPages:           Word;
    totalRawPages:          Word;

    totalHandles:           Word;


begin
    (*
     *  First check for presence of EMS
     *)
    if ems.init then begin
        writeln('EMS is not present');
        Halt;
        end;

    (*
     *  Start by getting the hardware configuration
     *)
    if ems.getHWConfig40(hwConfig) then begin
        ems_demoError('EMS_Ems.getHWConfig40');
        end;

    (*
     *  Now get the raw page counts
     *)
    if ems.getNumRawPages40(totalRawPages, freeRawPages) then begin
        ems_demoError('EMS_Ems.getNumRawPages40');
        end;
```

4-2 Continued.

```
(*
 *  Get the total handles that can be used.
 *)
if ems.getTotalHandles40(totalHandles) then begin
    ems_demoError('EMS_Ems.getTotalHandles40');
    end;

(*
 *  Print the info out:
 *)
writeln('Total # of raw pages:        ', totalRawPages);
writeln('# of free raw pages:         ', freeRawPages);
writeln;
writeln('Total # of handles:          ', totalHandles);
writeln;
writeln('Raw page size (bytes):       ', 16*hwConfig.rawPgSize);
writeln('Alternate reg sets:          ', hwConfig.altRegSets);
writeln('Context Save area size:      ', hwConfig.saveAreaSz);
writeln('# Regs assignable to DMA:    ', hwConfig.regsDma);
writeln;
write('DMA ');
if hwConfig.dmaType - 0 then begin
    write('can');
    end
else begin
    write('cannot');
    end;
writeln(' be used with alternate registers');
end.
```

Figure 4-3 presents the source code listing to PROG4-3.PAS, which demonstrates the following:

- getting and setting the handle name
- searching for the handle name

4-3 The source code listing to PROG4-3.PAS.

```
(* * * * * * * * * * * * * * * * * * *
 *
 *  prog4-3.pas
 *
 *      Demonstrates
 *          - Get/Set handle name
 *          - Search for handle name
 *
 * * * * * * * * * * * * * * * * * * * *)

program prog4_3;

uses    crt,
        _globals,
        _ems;
```

4-3 Continued.

```
var
    ems:                    EMS_Ems;


procedure displayActiveHandles;

var

    handleInfoArray:    ^EMS_HandleInfoArr;

    numActiveHandles:   Word;
    numActiveHandles2:  Word;

    i:                  Word;

    tmpHandle:          EMS_EmBlk;

    nameBuff:           EMS_HandleName;

begin
    (*
     *  First find out how many active handles there are:
     *)
    if ems.getNumActiveHandles(numActiveHandles) then begin
        ems_demoError('EMS_Ems.getNumActiveHandles');
        end;

    (*
     *  Now allocate a block of handleInfo packets big enough to
     *  hold them.
     *)
    GetMem(handleInfoArray, numActiveHandles * sizeof(EMS_HandleInfo));

    (*
     *  Now get the info.
     *)
    if ems.getPagesAllHandles(handleInfoArray^, numActiveHandles2) then begin
        ems_demoError('EMS_Ems.getNumActiveHandles');
        end;

    (*
     *  The following is a brief sanity clause (Everybody knows
     *  there ain't no sanity clause).
     *)
    if numActiveHandles2 <> numActiveHandles then begin
        writeln('A most unusual situation has occured...');
        Halt;
        end;

    (*
     *  Finally, display it.
     *)
    writeln('                    |_____|_____|_____|_____|');

    for i:= 0 to numActiveHandles-1 do begin
        tmpHandle.handle:= handleInfoArray^[i].handle;
        if tmpHandle.getHandleName40(nameBuff) then begin
            ems_demoError('EMS_EmBlk.getHandleName40');
            end;
```

4-3 Continued.

```
    writeln(
        ,                                          3  ',
        handleInfoArray^[i].handle:3,
        '   3  ',
        handleInfoArray^[i].numPages:3,
        '  3 ',
        nameBuff,
        ' 3');

    if i+1 < numActiveHandles then begin
        writeln(
        ,
        end;                                    |——+——+——|');
    end;

writeln('═══════════════════════════|——|——|——|');

(*
 *  Now free up the arrays.
 *)
FreeMem(handleInfoArray, numActiveHandles * sizeof(EMS_HandleInfo));
end;

procedure pause;

var
    c:                  Char;

begin

    (*
     *  Display a little message:
     *)
    writeln('Hit <CR> to continue...');

    (*
     *  Wait for a <CR>
     *)
    c:= ReadKey;
    while c <> #13 do begin
        c:= ReadKey;
        end;

end;

var

    totalPages:         Word;
    freePages:          Word;

    handle1:            EMS_EmBlk;
    handle2:            EMS_EmBlk;
    handle3:            EMS_EmBlk;
    tmpHandle:          EMS_EmBlk;

    nameBuff:           EMS_HandleName;
```

```
begin
    (*
     * First check for presence of EMS
     *)
    if ems.init then begin
        writeln('EMS is not present');
        Halt;
        end;

    (*
     * Get the number of free pages
     *)
    if ems.getFreeEM(totalPages, freePages) then begin
        ems_demoError('EMS_Ems.getFreeEM');
        end;

    (*
     * Print header:
     *)
    writeln('          Operation          Avail Pages        Active Handles');
    writeln('═══════════════════════════════════════╤═══════════╤═══════════════════════');
    writeln('After initialization      |      ',
                freePages:3,
              '      | Handle   Pages       Name   |');

    displayActiveHandles;
    pause;

    (*
     * Now allocate 5 pages.
     *)
    if handle1.allocEM(5) then begin
        ems_demoError('EMS_Ems.allocEM');
        end;

    (*
     * Set the name for the handle
     *)
    nameBuff:= 'Aramis    ';
    if handle1.setHandleName40(nameBuff) then begin
        ems_demoError('EMS_EmBlk.setHandleName40');
        end;

    (*
     * Get the number of free pages
     *)
    if ems.getFreeEM(totalPages, freePages) then begin
        ems_demoError('EMS_Ems.getFreeEM');
        end;

    (*
     * Print header:
     *)
    writeln('          Operation          Avail Pages        Active Handles');
    writeln('═══════════════════════════════════════╤═══════════╤═══════════════════════');
    writeln('After 5 page allocate     |      ',
                freePages:3,
              '      | Handle   Pages       Name   |');
```

```
displayActiveHandles;
pause;

(*
 *  Now allocate 7 pages.
 *)
if handle2.allocEM(7) then begin
    ems_demoError('EMS_Ems.allocEM');
    end;

(*
 *  Set the name for the handle
 *)
nameBuff:= 'Athos    ';
if handle2.setHandleName40(nameBuff) then begin
    ems_demoError('EMS_EmBlk.setHandleName40');
    end;

(*
 *  Get the number of free pages
 *)
if ems.getFreeEM(totalPages, freePages) then begin
    ems_demoError('EMS_Ems.getFreeEM');
    end;

(*
 *  Print header:
 *)
writeln('          Operation        Avail Pages      Active Handles');
writeln('============================================================');
writeln('After 7 page allocate  |      ',
         freePages:3,
         '        | Handle   Pages    Name   |');

displayActiveHandles;
pause;

(*
 *  Now allocate 6 pages.
 *)
if handle3.allocEM(6) then begin
    ems_demoError('EMS_Ems.allocEM');
    end;

(*
 *  Set the name for the handle
 *)
nameBuff:= 'Porthos ';
if handle3.setHandleName40(nameBuff) then begin
    ems_demoError('EMS_EmBlk.setHandleName40');
    end;

(*
 *  Get the number of free pages
 *)
if ems.getFreeEM(totalPages, freePages) then begin
    ems_demoError('EMS_Ems.getFreeEM');
    end;
```

4-3 Continued.

```
(*
 *  Print header:
 *)
writeln('          Operation          Avail Pages        Active Handles');
writeln('════════════════════════════════╤══════════╤═══════════════════');
writeln('After 6 page allocate    |      ',
          freePages:3,
          '         | Handle   Pages      Name   |');

displayActiveHandles;
pause;

(*
 *  Now find and free the 'Aramis' block.
 *)
nameBuff:= 'Aramis   ';
if tmpHandle.searchHandleName40(nameBuff) then begin
    ems_demoError('EMS_EmBlk.searchHandleName40');
    end;
if tmpHandle.freeEM then begin
    ems_demoError('EMS_EmBlk.freeEM');
    end;

(*
 *  Get the number of free pages
 *)
if ems.getFreeEM(totalPages, freePages) then begin
    ems_demoError('EMS_Ems.getFreeEM');
    end;

(*
 *  Print header:
 *)
writeln('          Operation          Avail Pages        Active Handles');
writeln('════════════════════════════════╤══════════╤═══════════════════');
writeln('After "Aramis" free      |      ',
          freePages:3,
          '         | Handle   Pages      Name   |');

displayActiveHandles;
pause;

(*
 *  Now free the 'Athos' block.
 *)
nameBuff:= 'Athos    ';
if tmpHandle.searchHandleName40(nameBuff) then begin
    ems_demoError('EMS_EmBlk.searchHandleName40');
    end;
if tmpHandle.freeEM then begin
    ems_demoError('EMS_EmBlk.freeEM');
    end;

(*
 *  Get the number of free pages
 *)
if ems.getFreeEM(totalPages, freePages) then begin
    ems_demoError('EMS_Ems.getFreeEM');
    end;
```

4-3 Continued.

```
(*
 *   Print header:
 *)
writeln('        Operation            Avail Pages        Active Handles');
writeln('══════════════════════════════════════════════════════════╗ ');
writeln('After "Athos" free        |        ',
           freePages:3,
        '        | Handle    Pages       Name    |');

displayActiveHandles;
pause;

(*
 *   Now free the 'Porthos' block
 *)
nameBuff:= 'Porthos ';
if tmpHandle.searchHandleName40(nameBuff) then begin
    ems_demoError('EMS_EmBlk.searchHandleName40');
    end;
if tmpHandle.freeEM then begin
    ems_demoError('EMS_EmBlk.freeEM');
    end;

(*
 *   Get the number of free pages
 *)
if ems.getFreeEM(totalPages, freePages) then begin
    ems_demoError('EMS_Ems.getFreeEM');
    end;

(*
 *   Print header:
 *)
writeln('        Operation            Avail Pages        Active Handles');
writeln('══════════════════════════════════════════════════════════╗ ');
writeln('After "Porthos" free      |        ',
           freePages:3,
        '        | Handle    Pages       Name    |');

displayActiveHandles;
end.
```

Figure 4-4 presents the source code listing to PROG4-4.PAS, which demonstrates the following:

- getting all the handle names

4-4 The source code listing to PROG4-4.PAS.

```
(* * * * * * * * * * * * * * * * *
 *
 * prog4-4.pas
 *
 *      Demonstrates
 *          - Get all handle names
 *
 * * * * * * * * * * * * * * * * * *)

program prog4_4;

uses    _globals,
        _ems;

var
    ems:                EMS_Ems;

    handle1:            EMS_EmBlk;
    handle2:            EMS_EmBlk;
    handle3:            EMS_EmBlk;

    numHandles:         Word;

    handleNameArray:    ^EMS_HandleNameInfoArr;

    nameBuff:           EMS_HandleName;

    i:                  Word;

begin

    (*
     *  First check for presence of EMS
     *)
    if ems.init then begin
        writeln('EMS is not present');
        Halt;
        end;

    (*
     *  Allocate some handles and name them:
     *)
    if handle1.allocEM(1) then begin
        ems_demoError('EMS_EmBlk.allocEM');
        end;
    if handle2.allocEM(1) then begin
        ems_demoError('EMS_EmBlk.allocEM');
        end;
    if handle3.allocEM(1) then begin
        ems_demoError('EMS_EmBlk.allocEM');
        end;
    nameBuff:= 'Larry    ';
    if handle1.setHandleName40(nameBuff) then begin
        ems_demoError('EMS_EmBlk.setHandleName40');
        end;
    nameBuff:= 'Moe      ';
    if handle2.setHandleName40(nameBuff) then begin
        ems_demoError('EMS_EmBlk.setHandleName40');
        end;
```

```
    nameBuff:- 'Curly    ';
    if handle3.setHandleName40(nameBuff) then begin
        ems_demoError('EMS_EmBlk.setHandleName40');
        end;

    (*
     *  Allocate space for the names.
     *)
    if ems.getNumActiveHandles(numHandles) then begin
        ems_demoError('EMS_Ems.getNumActiveHandles');
        end;

    GetMem(handleNameArray, sizeof(EMS_HandleNameInfo) * numHandles);

    (*
     *  Get the names for the handles.
     *)
    if ems.getAllHandleNames40(handleNameArray^) then begin
        ems_demoError('EMS_Ems.getAllHandleNames40');
        end;

    (*
     *  Now print the info out:
     *)
    writeln('┌═Handle══════╤══Name═══┐');

    for i:- 0 to numHandles-1 do begin
        writeln('║        ',
                handleNameArray^[i].handle:4,
                '   │   ',
                handleNameArray^[i].name,
                '   ║');

        if i < numHandles-1 then begin
            writeln('╟───────────────┼──────────────╢');
            end;
        end;
    writeln('╚═══════════════╧══════════════╝');

    if handle1.freeEM then begin
        ems_demoError('EMS_EmBlk.freeEM');
        end;
    if handle2.freeEM then begin
        ems_demoError('EMS_EmBlk.freeEM');
        end;
    if handle3.freeEM then begin
        ems_demoError('EMS_EmBlk.freeEM');
        end;

end.
```

Figure 4-5 presents the source code listing to PROG4-5.PAS, which demonstrates the following:

- resizing an expanded memory block

4-5 The source code listing to PROG4-5.PAS.

```
(* * * * * * * * * * * * * * * * * *
 *
 * prog4-5.pas
 *
 *      Demonstrates
 *           - Resize handle
 *
 * * * * * * * * * * * * * * * * * *)

program prog4_5;

uses    crt,
        _globals,
        _ems;

var
    ems:                    EMS_Ems;


procedure displayActiveHandles;

var

    handleInfoArray:    ^EMS_HandleInfoArr;

    numActiveHandles:   Word;
    numActiveHandles2:  Word;

    i:                  Word;

    tmpHandle:          EMS_EmBlk;

    nameBuff:           EMS_HandleName;

begin

    (*
     *  First find out how many active handles there are:
     *)
    if ems.getNumActiveHandles(numActiveHandles) then begin
        ems_demoError('EMS_Ems.getNumActiveHandles');
        end;

    (*
     *  Now allocate a block of handleInfo packets big enough to
     *  hold them.
     *)
    GetMem(handleInfoArray, numActiveHandles * sizeof(EMS_HandleInfo));

    (*
     *  Now get the info.
     *)
    if ems.getPagesAllHandles(handleInfoArray^, numActiveHandles2) then begin
        ems_demoError('EMS_Ems.getNumActiveHandles');
        end;
```

```
    (*
     *   The following is a brief sanity clause (Everybody knows
     *   there ain't no sanity clause).
     *)
    if numActiveHandles2 <> numActiveHandles then begin
        writeln('A most unusual situation has occured...');
        Halt;
        end;

    (*
     *   Finally, display it.
     *)
    writeln('                              └────────┼──────┴──────┤');

    for i:= 0 to numActiveHandles-1 do begin
        tmpHandle.handle:= handleInfoArray^[i].handle;
        if tmpHandle.getHandleName40(nameBuff) then begin
            ems_demoError('EMS_EmBlk.getHandleName40');
            end;

        writeln(
            ,
            handleInfoArray^[i].handle:3,
            ' | ',
            handleInfoArray^[i].numPages:3,
            ' | ',
            nameBuff,
            ' |');

        if i+1 < numActiveHandles then begin
            writeln(
                ,
            end;                      ├──────┼──────┼──────┤');
        end;

    writeln('═══════════════════════════┴──────┴──────┘');
    (*
     *   Now free up the arrays.
     *)
    FreeMem(handleInfoArray, numActiveHandles * sizeof(EMS_HandleInfo));
end;

procedure pause;

var
    c:                  Char;

begin

    (*
     *   Display a little message:
     *)
    writeln('Hit <CR> to continue...');

    (*
     *   Wait for a <CR>
     *)
    c:= ReadKey;
```

```
    while c <> #13 do begin
        c:- ReadKey;
        end;

end;


var
    totalPages:          Word;
    freePages:           Word;
    handle1:             EMS_EmBlk;

    nameBuff:            EMS_HandleName;

begin
    (*
     *  First check for presence of EMS
     *)
    if ems.init then begin
        writeln('EMS is not present');
        Halt;
        end;

    (*
     *  Now allocate 5 pages.
     *)
    if handle1.allocEM(5) then begin
        ems_demoError('EMS_EmBlk.allocEM');
        end;

    (*
     *  Set the name for the handle
     *)
    nameBuff:- 'OurBlock';
    if handle1.setHandleName40(nameBuff) then begin
        ems_demoError('EMS_EmBlk.setHandleName40');
        end;

    (*
     *  Get the number of free pages
     *)
    if ems.getFreeEM(totalPages, freePages) then begin
        ems_demoError('EMS_Ems.getFreeEM');
        end;

    (*
     *  Print header:
     *)
    writeln('      Operation          Avail Pages      Active Handles');
    writeln('=                                                       ');
    writeln('After 5 page allocate    |       .
                 freePages:3,
                 '      | Handle   Pages    Name    |');

    displayActiveHandles;
    pause;
```

4-5 Continued.

```
(*
 *  Now resize the block:
 *)
if handle1.reallocHandPages40(8) then begin
    ems_demoError('EMS_EmBlk.reallocHandPages40');
    end;

(*
 *  Get the number of free pages
 *)
if ems.getFreeEM(totalPages, freePages) then begin
    ems_demoError('EMS_Ems.getFreeEM');
    end;

(*
 *  Print header:
 *)
writeln('        Operation          Avail Pages        Active Handles');
writeln('=                                                          ');
writeln('After Resize of handle  |        ',
          freePages,
          '       | Handle   Pages    Name   |');

displayActiveHandles;

if handle1.freeEM then begin
    ems_demoError('EMS_EmBlk.freeEM');
    end;
end.
```

Figure 4-6 presents the source code listing to PROG4-6.PAS, which demonstrates the following:

- mapping multiple pages by segment number
- saving and restoring the partial map
- mapping pages in low memory (below 640K)

4-6 The source code listing to PROG4-6.PAS.

```
(* * * * * * * * * * * * * * * * * *
 *
 *  prog4-6.pas
 *
 *      Demonstrates
 *          - Map multiple pages by #/segment
 *          - Save/restore partial map
 *          - Mapping pages in lower 640K
 *
 * * * * * * * * * * * * * * * * * * *)

program prog4_6;

uses    _globals,
        _ems;
```

4-6 Continued.

```
var
    ems:                    EMS_Ems;

    i:                      Word;

    numMappablePages:       Word;
    numMappablePages2:      Word;
    numAvailableFrames:     Word;

    pfa:                    EMS_PageFrame;

    pageAddress:            ^EMS_MappablePagesInfoArr;
    availableFrame:         ^EMS_MappablePagesInfoArr;

    mapByNumber:            array[0..5] of EMS_MapByNumber;
    mapByAddress:           array[0..5] of EMS_MapByAddress;

    restOfMem:              Pointer;
    memLeft:                DWord;

    mapPageList:            array[0..6] of Word;
    mapSize:                Word;
    mapSave1:               Pointer;
    mapSave2:               Pointer;

    handle:                 EMS_EmBlk;

    frame:                  array[0..5] of ^EMS_Page;

begin
    (*
     *  First check for presence of EMS
     *)
    if ems.init then begin
        writeln('EMS is not present');
        Halt;
        end;

    (*
     *  Now get the Page Frame Address:
     *)
    if ems.getPFA(pfa) then begin
        ems_demoError('EMS_Ems.getPFA');
        end;

    (*
     *  We'll want a dozen pages of EMS, so allocate them now.
     *)
    if handle.allocEM(12) then begin
        ems_demoError('EMS_EmBlk.allocEM');
        end;

    (*
     *  Find out how many mappable pages we have all together. In
     *  4.0, we do not have a fixed size page frame; we might have
     *  many more than 4 mappable pages.
     *)
    if ems.getNumMappable40(numMappablePages) then begin
        ems_demoError('EMS_Ems.getNumMappable40');
        end;
```

```
    (*
     *  Now allocate a buffer big enough to hold the addresses
     *  of these pages.
     *)
    GetMem(pageAddress, sizeof(EMS_MappablePagesInfo) * numMappablePages);
    GetMem(availableFrame, sizeof(EMS_MappablePagesInfo) *
numMappablePages);

    (*
     *  Get the info
     *)
    if ems.getAddrsMappable40(pageAddress^, numMappablePages2) then begin
        ems_demoError('EMS_Ems.getAddrsMappable40');
        end;

    (*
     *  We now allocate half of memory in order to control
     *  some of the remappable pages.
     *)
    memLeft:- 327680;
    GetMem(restOfMem, memLeft);
    if restOfMem - Nil then begin
        writeln('Unable to allocate conventional memory');
        Halt;
        end;

    (*
     *  Record the mappable pages which fall inside the bounds of
     *  our memory block OR are part of the standard (3.0) page
     *  frame area. Keep count of how many mappable pages
     *  we have in total.
     *)
    numAvailableFrames:- 0;
    for i:- 0 to numMappablePages-1 do begin
        if (segToPhys(pageAddress^[i].pageSegment) >-
segOffToPhys(restOfMem)) and
                (SegToPhys(pageAddress^[i].pageSegment) +
EMS_STD_PAGE_SIZE <-
                    segOffToPhys(restOfMem) + memLeft)
            or (SegToPhys(pageAddress^[i].pageSegment) >-
segOffToPhys(pfa)) and
                (SegToPhys(pageAddress^[i].pageSegment) +
EMS_STD_PAGE_SIZE <-
                    segOffToPhys(pfa) + EMS_STD_PAGE_SIZE*4) then begin
            availableFrame^[numAvailableFrames].physNumber:-
                pageAddress^[i].physNumber;
            availableFrame^[numAvailableFrames].pageSegment:-
                pageAddress^[i].pageSegment;
            numAvailableFrames:- numAvailableFrames + 1;
            end;
        end;

    (*
     *  We will be using 6 page frames. Make sure we have enough.
     *)
    if numAvailableFrames < 6 then begin
        writeln('Insufficient number of available remappable pages');
        Halt;
        end;
```

```
(*
 *  We'll be working with the first six available page frames.
 *  Let's create an array that will allow us to easily
 *  access them.
 *
 *  At the same time, set up the map list for saving the state.
 *)
for i:= 0 to 5 do begin
    frame[i]:= Ptr(availableFrame^[i].pageSegment, 0);
    mapPageList[i+1]:= availableFrame^[i].pageSegment;
    end;
mapPageList[0]:= 6;

(*
 *  Let's put some text into the area.
 *)
StrPtr(@frame[0]^[123])^:=
    'CM:      In perpetrating a revolution there are two';
StrPtr(@frame[1]^[456])^:=
    'CM:      requirements: someone or something to revolt';
StrPtr(@frame[2]^[789])^:=
    'CM:      against and someone to actually show up and';
StrPtr(@frame[3]^[12])^:=
    'CM:      do the revolting. Dress is usually casual';
StrPtr(@frame[4]^[345])^:=
    'CM:';
StrPtr(@frame[5]^[678])^:=
    'CM:                         -- Woody Allen'#13#10;

(*
 *  Let's examine the current state of these pages. Note that because
 *  they (with the exception of those in the standard PFA), are
 *  in the conventional memory area, they already have pages mapped
 *  to them.
 *)
if ems.getPMapInfoSize40(6, mapSize) then begin
    ems_demoError('EMS_Ems.getPMapInfoSize');
    end;

GetMem(mapSave1, mapSize);
GetMem(mapSave2, mapSize);

if ems.savePartialMap40(@mapPageList, mapSave1) then begin
    ems_demoError('EMS_Ems.savePartialMap40');
    end;

(*
 *  Now that we've saved the current state, let's map some
 *  new pages in. We'll do it by number here.
 *)
for i:= 0 to 5 do begin
    mapByNumber[i].logicalPage:= i;
    mapByNumber[i].physicalPage:= availableFrame^[i].physNumber;
    end;

if handle.mapPagesByNum40(6, @mapByNumber) then begin
    ems_demoError('EMS_EmBlk.mapPagesByNum40');
    end;
```

4-6 Continued.

```
(*
 *  Now let's put some new text in:
 *)
StrPtr(@frame[0]^[123])^:-
    'EMA:     Someone did a study of the three most-often-heard phrases';
StrPtr(@frame[1]^[456])^:-
    'EMA:     in New York City. One is "Hey taxi." Two is "What train';
StrPtr(@frame[2]^[789])^:-
    'EMA:     do I take to get to Bloomingdales?" And three is "Don''t';
StrPtr(@frame[3]^[12])^:-
    'EMA:     worry, it''s only a flesh wound."';
StrPtr(@frame[4]^[345])^:-
    'EMA:';
StrPtr(@frame[5]^[678])^:-
    'EMA:                          -- David Letterman'#13#10;

(*
 *  Let's save this map.
 *)
if ems.savePartialMap40(@mapPageList, mapSave2) then begin
    ems_demoError('EMS_Ems.savePartialMap40');
    end;

(*
 *  Now let's map a third set of pages, this time by segment
 *)
for i:- 0 to 5 do begin
    mapByAddress[i].logicalPage:- 6 + i;
    mapByAddress[i].physicalSeg:- availableFrame^[i].pageSegment;
    end;

if handle.mapPagesByAddr40(6, @mapByAddress) then begin
    ems_demoError('EMS_EmBlk.mapPagesByAddr40');
    end;

(*
 *  Put some text in
 *)
StrPtr(@frame[0]^[123])^:-
    'EMB:     I grew up to have my father''s looks, my father''s';
StrPtr(@frame[1]^[456])^:-
    'EMB:     speech patterns, my father''s posture, my father''s';
StrPtr(@frame[2]^[789])^:-
    'EMB:     walk, my father''s opinions and my mother''s contempt';
StrPtr(@frame[3]^[12])^:-
    'EMB:     for my father.';
StrPtr(@frame[4]^[345])^:-
    'EMB:';
StrPtr(@frame[5]^[678])^:-
    'EMB:                          -- Jules Feiffer'#13#10;

(*
 *  Now let's print out the stuff in the newest map.
 *)
writeln(StrPtr(@frame[0]^[123])^);
writeln(StrPtr(@frame[1]^[456])^);
writeln(StrPtr(@frame[2]^[789])^);
writeln(StrPtr(@frame[3]^[12])^);
writeln(StrPtr(@frame[4]^[345])^);
writeln(StrPtr(@frame[5]^[678])^);
```

```
(*
 *  Let's restore the second map and print the contents.
 *)
if ems.restPartialMap40(mapSave2) then begin
    ems_demoError('EMS_Ems.restPartialMap40');
    end;

writeln(StrPtr(@frame[0]^[123])^);
writeln(StrPtr(@frame[1]^[456])^);
writeln(StrPtr(@frame[2]^[789])^);
writeln(StrPtr(@frame[3]^[12])^);
writeln(StrPtr(@frame[4]^[345])^);
writeln(StrPtr(@frame[5]^[678])^);

(*
 *  And finally, let's restore the original map (the conventional
 *  memory pages), and print the contents.
 *)
if ems.restPartialMap40(mapSave1) then begin
    ems_demoError('EMS_Ems.restPartialMap40');
    end;

writeln(StrPtr(@frame[0]^[123])^);
writeln(StrPtr(@frame[1]^[456])^);
writeln(StrPtr(@frame[2]^[789])^);
writeln(StrPtr(@frame[3]^[12])^);
writeln(StrPtr(@frame[4]^[345])^);
writeln(StrPtr(@frame[5]^[678])^);

(*
 *  Now we free that which must be freed.
 *)
FreeMem(restOfMem, memLeft);

if handle.freeEM then begin
    ems_demoError('EMS_EmBlk.freeEM');
    end;

end.
```

Figure 4-7 presents the source code listing to PROG4-7.PAS, which demonstrates the following:

- Moving memory between low memory and EMS

4-7 The source code listing to PROG4-7.PAS.

```
(* * * * * * * * * * * * * * * * * *
 *
 * prog4-7.pas
 *
 *      Demonstrates
 *          - Xfer to/from EMS and Conventional memory
 *
 * * * * * * * * * * * * * * * * * * *)
```

4-7 Continued.

```pascal
program prog4_7;

uses    _globals,
        _ems;

var

    ems:                EMS_Ems;

    handle1:            EMS_EmBlk;
    handle2:            EMS_EmBlk;
    handle3:            EMS_EmBlk;
    handle4:            EMS_EmBlk;

    movePacket:         EMS_MoveMemoryInfo;

    text:               String;
    buff:               String;

begin
    (*
     *  First check for presence of EMS
     *)
    if ems.init then begin
        writeln('EMS is not present');
        Halt;
        end;

    (*
     *  Allocate some EMS pages
     *)
    if handle1.allocEM(1) then begin
        ems_demoError('EMS_EmBlk.allocEM');
        end;
    if handle2.allocEM(1) then begin
        ems_demoError('EMS_EmBlk.allocEM');
        end;
    if handle3.allocEM(1) then begin
        ems_demoError('EMS_EmBlk.allocEM');
        end;
    if handle4.allocEM(1) then begin
        ems_demoError('EMS_EmBlk.allocEM');
        end;

    (*
     *  Now let's copy some text into various places in the
     *  EM blocks, and then copy it back and print it out.
     *)

    (*
     *  Set up a pointer to a string:
     *)
    text:= '    Every year when it''s Chinese New Year here in New York,';

    (*
     *  Set up the move packet. Note that we round the length
     *  up to an even number. The call requires an even length
     *  transfer.
     *)
    movePacket.length:= Ord(text[0])+1;          { +1 for terminator }
```

```
movePacket.srcType:- EMS_MOVE_CONV;     { Conventional }
movePacket.srcHandle:- 0;               { indicates real memory }
movePacket.srcOffset:- Ofs(text);       { actual offset }
movePacket.srcPage:- Seg(text);         { actual segment }
movePacket.destType:- EMS_MOVE_EMS;     { EMS }
movePacket.destHandle:- handle1.handle; { 1st 1K block }
movePacket.destOffset:- 42;             { A random offset into block }
movePacket.destPage:- 0;                { page zero }

(*
 *   Do the actual EMS call:
 *)
if ems.moveMemRegion40(movePacket) then begin
    ems_demoError('EMS_Ems.moveMemRegion40');
    end;

(*
 *   Now put the next string into the next EM block:
 *)
text:- '        there are fireworks going off at all hours. New York mothers';

movePacket.length:- Ord(text[0])+1;     { +1 for terminator }
movePacket.srcType:- EMS_MOVE_CONV;     { Conventional }
movePacket.srcHandle:- 0;               { indicates real memory }
movePacket.srcOffset:- Ofs(text);       { actual offset }
movePacket.srcPage:- Seg(text);         { actual segment }
movePacket.destType:- EMS_MOVE_EMS;     { EMS }
movePacket.destHandle:- handle2.handle; { 2nd 1K block }
movePacket.destOffset:- 911;            { A random offset into block }
movePacket.destPage:- 0;                { page zero }

if ems.moveMemRegion40(movePacket) then begin
    ems_demoError('EMS_Ems.moveMemRegion40');
    end;

(*
 *   And something for the third block:
 *)
text:- '      calm their frightened children by telling them it''s just
            gunfire'#13#10;


movePacket.length:- Ord(text[0])+1;     { +1 for terminator }
movePacket.srcType:- EMS_MOVE_CONV;     { Conventional }
movePacket.srcHandle:- 0;               { indicates real memory }
movePacket.srcOffset:- Ofs(text);       { actual offset }
movePacket.srcPage:- Seg(text);         { actual segment }
movePacket.destType:- EMS_MOVE_EMS;     { EMS }
movePacket.destHandle:- handle3.handle; { 3rd 1K block }
movePacket.destOffset:- 800;            { A random offset into block }
movePacket.destPage:- 0;                { page zero }

if ems.moveMemRegion40(movePacket) then begin
    ems_demoError('EMS_Ems.moveMemRegion40');
    end;

(*
 *   Now the fourth and last block:
 *)
text:- '                            -- David Letterman';
```

4-7 Continued.

```
movePacket.length:- Ord(text[0])+1;   { +1 for terminator }
movePacket.srcType:- EMS_MOVE_CONV;   { Conventional }
movePacket.srcHandle:- 0;             { indicates real memory }
movePacket.srcOffset:- Ofs(text);     { actual offset }
movePacket.srcPage:- Seg(text);       { actual segment }
movePacket.destType:- EMS_MOVE_EMS;   { EMS }
movePacket.destHandle:- handle4.handle; { 4th 1K block }
movePacket.destOffset:- 212;          { A random offset into block }
movePacket.destPage:- 0;              { page zero }

if ems.moveMemRegion40(movePacket) then begin
    ems_demoError('EMS_Ems.moveMemRegion40');
    end;

(*
 *  Now we've copies four strings into EMS blocks.
 *        Block 1 at offset 42,
 *        Block 2 at offset 911,
 *        Block 3 at offset 800,
 *        Block 4 at offset 212.
 *
 *  Now let's retrieve them and print them out.
 *)
movePacket.length:- 128;              { +1 for terminator }
movePacket.srcType:- EMS_MOVE_EMS;    { EMS }
movePacket.srcHandle:- handle1.handle; { First handle }
movePacket.srcOffset:- 42;            { A random offset into block }
movePacket.srcPage:- 0;               { page zero }
movePacket.destType:- EMS_MOVE_CONV;  { Conventional memory }
movePacket.destHandle:- 0;            { Conventional memory }
movePacket.destOffset:- Ofs(buff);    { actual offset }
movePacket.destPage:- Seg(buff);      { actual segment }

if ems.moveMemRegion40(movePacket) then begin
    ems_demoError('EMS_Ems.moveMemRegion40');
    end;

writeln(buff);

(*
 *  Now pick up the second piece:
 *)
movePacket.length:- 128;              { +1 for terminator }
movePacket.srcType:- EMS_MOVE_EMS;    { EMS }
movePacket.srcHandle:- handle2.handle; { Second handle }
movePacket.srcOffset:- 911;           { A random offset into block }
movePacket.srcPage:- 0;               { page zero }
movePacket.destType:- EMS_MOVE_CONV;  { Conventional memory }
movePacket.destHandle:- 0;            { Conventional memory }
movePacket.destOffset:- Ofs(buff);    { actual offset }
movePacket.destPage:- Seg(buff);      { actual segment }

if ems.moveMemRegion40(movePacket) then begin
    ems_demoError('EMS_Ems.moveMemRegion40');
    end;

writeln(buff);

(*
 *  Now pick up the third piece:
 *)
```

```
    movePacket.length:- 128;                { +1 for terminator }
    movePacket.srcType:- EMS_MOVE_EMS;      { EMS }
    movePacket.srcHandle:- handle3.handle;  { Third handle }
    movePacket.srcOffset:- 800;             { A random offset into block }
    movePacket.srcPage:- 0;                 { page zero }
    movePacket.destType:- EMS_MOVE_CONV;    { Conventional memory }
    movePacket.destHandle:- 0;              { Conventional memory }
    movePacket.destOffset:- Ofs(buff);      { actual offset }
    movePacket.destPage:- Seg(buff);        { actual segment }

    if ems.moveMemRegion40(movePacket) then begin
        ems_demoError('EMS_Ems.moveMemRegion40');
        end;

    writeln(buff);

    (*
     *  Now pick up the fourth piece:
     *)
    movePacket.length:- 128;                { +1 for terminator }
    movePacket.srcType:- EMS_MOVE_EMS;      { EMS }
    movePacket.srcHandle:- handle4.handle;  { Fourth handle }
    movePacket.srcOffset:- 212;             { A random offset into block }
    movePacket.srcPage:- 0;                 { page zero }
    movePacket.destType:- EMS_MOVE_CONV;    { Conventional memory }
    movePacket.destHandle:- 0;              { Conventional memory }
    movePacket.destOffset:- Ofs(buff);      { actual offset }
    movePacket.destPage:- Seg(buff);        { actual segment }

    if ems.moveMemRegion40(movePacket) then begin
        ems_demoError('EMS_Ems.moveMemRegion40');
        end;

    writeln(buff);

    (*
     *  Free up the blocks of memory.
     *)
    if handle1.freeEM then begin
        ems_demoError('EMS_EmBlk.freeEM');
        end;
    if handle2.freeEM then begin
        ems_demoError('EMS_EmBlk.freeEM');
        end;
    if handle3.freeEM then begin
        ems_demoError('EMS_EmBlk.freeEM');
        end;
    if handle4.freeEM then begin
        ems_demoError('EMS_EmBlk.freeEM');
        end;

end.
```

Now that we have presented the source code for the EMS 4.0 demonstration programs, it's time to present the interface functions.

EMS 4.0 interface functions

Save a partial page map

Figure 4-8 presents the source code listing to EMS4F0.ASM.

4-8 The source code listing to EMS4F0.ASM.

```
;*********************************************************************
;***    EMS4F0.ASM                                                ***
;***                                                              ***
;***    function        EMS_Ems.savePartialMap40(                ***
;***                         map:              Pointer;           ***
;***                         buffer:           Pointer)           ***
;***                         : Boolean;                           ***
;***                                                              ***
;***    Saves the state of a subset of expanded mem page         ***
;***    mapping in buffer                                         ***
;***                                                              ***
;***    Returns 0 if no error or an error code.                  ***
;***                                                              ***
;***                                                              ***
;***                                                              ***
;***    (Ems Version 4.0)                                         ***
;*********************************************************************

        .model  large,pascal

        include emsdefs.asm

        extrn   errno:WORD

;
;   Define entry point
;
        public  EMS_Ems@savePartialMap40

        .code

EMS_Ems@savePartialMap40 proc       map:Far Ptr Word, buffer:Far Ptr Word,
                                    self:DWord

        push    ds                          ; Save some registers
        push    si
        push    di

;
;   DS:SI needs a list of segment addresses of pages for which
;   to save the mapping state.
;
        lds     si,map

;
;   ES:DI gets the address of the buffer to save the info into
;
        les     di,buffer

        mov     ax,SavePartialMap40     ; Do the call
        int     Ems
```

4-8 Continued.

```
        or      ah,ah                       ; Set flags
        jnz     error

        xor     ax,ax                       ; Return OK

        pop     di                          ; Restore regs
        pop     si
        pop     ds
        ret

error:
        pop     di                          ; Restore regs
        pop     si
        pop     ds

        mov     al,ah                       ; Transfer return code
        xor     ah,ah                       ; Zero extend
        mov     errno,ax                    ; Save in errno too
        ret

EMS_Ems@savePartialMap40 endp              ; End of procedure

        end                                 ; End of source file
```

The EMS__Ems.savePartialMap40(...) function saves the state of the specified expanded page mapping registers into a designated buffer.

Function EMS__Ems.savePartialMap40(...)

function EMS__Ems.savePartialMap40(
                map: Pointer;
                buffer: Pointer)
        : Boolean;

where

map   Points to a list of segment addresses
buffer Receives the register state information for the specified pages

Restore a partial page map

Figure 4-9 presents the source code listing to EMS4F1.ASM.

4-9 The source code listing to EMS4F1.ASM.

```
;***************************************************************
;***      EMS4F1.ASM                                       ***
;***                                                       ***
;***      function          EMS_Ems.restPartialMap40(      ***
;***                            buffer:        Pointer)    ***
;***                            : Boolean;                 ***
;***                                                       ***
;***      Restores the state of a subset of expanded mem page ***
;***      mapping from buffer                              ***
;***                                                       ***
;***      Returns 0 if no error or an error code.         ***
;***                                                       ***
;***                                                       ***
;***      (Ems Version 4.0)                                ***
;***************************************************************
         .model   large,pascal

         include emsdefs.asm

         extrn    errno:WORD

;
;    Define entry point
;
         public  EMS_Ems@restPartialMap40

         .code

EMS_Ems@restPartialMap40 proc      buffer:Far Ptr Word, self:DWord

         push    ds                      ; Save registers
         push    si

         lds     si,buffer               ; DS:SI gets buffer address

         mov     ax,RestPartialMap40     ; Make EMS call
         int     Ems

         or      ah,ah                   ; Set flags
         jnz     error

         xor     ax,ax                   ; return OK

         pop     si                      ; Restore regs
         pop     ds
         ret

error:
         pop     si                      ; Restore regs
         pop     ds

         mov     al,ah                   ; AL gets error code
         xor     ah,ah                   ; Zero extend
         mov     errno,ax                ; Save in errno too

         ret

EMS_Ems@restPartialMap40 endp           ; End of procedure

         end                            ; End of source file
```

The EMS__Ems.restPartialMap40(...) function restores the state of the previously saved page mapping registers.

Function EMS__Ems.restPartialMap40(...)

function EMS__Ems.restPartialMap40(
              buffer: Pointer)
      : Boolean;

where

  buffer   Holds the register state information

Get the size of partial page map information

Figure 4-10 presents the source code listing to EMS4F2.ASM.

4-10 The source code listing to EMS4F2.ASM.

```
;***********************************************************
;***      EMS4F2.ASM                                    ***
;***                                                    ***
;***      function        EMS_Ems.getPMapInfoSize40(    ***
;***                         pages: Word;               ***
;***                         var buffSize:    Word)     ***
;***                         : Boolean;                 ***
;***                                                    ***
;***      Pointer gets size of partial page map buffer in ***
;***      bytes.                                        ***
;***                                                    ***
;***      Returns 0 if no error or an error code.       ***
;***                                                    ***
;***                                                    ***
;***      (Ems Version 4.0)                             ***
;***********************************************************
;

        .model   large,pascal

        include emsdefs.asm

        extrn    errno:WORD


;
;    Define entry point
;
        public   EMS_Ems@getPMapInfoSize40

        .code

EMS_Ems@getPMapInfoSize40 proc pages:Word, buffSize:Far Ptr Word,
self:DWord

        mov      bx,pages              ; BX gets number of pages

        mov      ax,GetPMapInfoSize40  ; Make the EMS call
        int      Ems

        or       ah,ah                 ; Set flags
        jnz      error
```

```
        xor     ah,ah               ; Zero extend size in AL
        les     bx,buffSize         ; Return it
        mov     es:[bx],ax

        xor     ax,ax               ; Return OK
        ret

error:
        mov     al,ah               ; AL gets error code
        xor     ah,ah               ; Zero extend
        mov     errno,ax            ; Save in errno too
        ret

EMS_Ems@getPMapInfoSize40 endp      ; End of procedure

        end                         ; End of source file
```

The EMS__Ems.getPMapInfoSize40(...) function returns the amount of space required to save the specified number of map registers using the EMS__Ems.savePartialMap40 function.

Function EMS__Ems.getPMapInfoSize40(...)

```
function EMS__Ems.getPMapInfoSize40(
            pages:      Word;
            var buffSize:  Word)
        : Boolean;
```

where

pages The number of physical pages for which state is to be saved
size   Receives the amount of space required in bytes

Map multiple pages by number

Figure 4-11 presents the source code listing to EMS500.ASM.

4-11 The source code listing to EMS500.ASM.

```
;****************************************************************
;***    EMS500.ASM                                        ***
;***                                                      ***
;***    function        EMS_EmBlk.mapPagesByNum40(        ***
;***                     pages:          Word;            ***
;***                     buffer:         Pointer)         ***
;***                     : Boolean;                       ***
;***                                                      ***
;***    Fill buffer with 32 bit entries that control pages ***
;***    to be mapped by page number                       ***
;***                                                      ***
;***    Returns 0 if no error or an error code.           ***
;***                                                      ***
;***                                                      ***
```

4-11 Continued.

```
;***                                                                      ***
;***      (Ems Version 4.0)                                               ***
;***********************************************************************

        .model  large,pascal

        include emsdefs.asm

        extrn   errno:WORD

;
;    Define entry point
;
        public  EMS_EmBlk@mapPagesByNum40

        .code

EMS_EmBlk@mapPagesByNum40    proc num:Word, buffer:Far Ptr Word, handle:Far
                             Ptr DWord

        push    ds                      ; Save regs
        push    si

        les     bx,handle
        mov     dx,es:[bx]              ; EMS handle
        mov     cx,num                  ; Number of pages to map

        lds     si,buffer               ; Map info buffer

        mov     ax,MapPagesByNum40      ; Make the EMS call
        int     Ems

        or      ah,ah                   ; Set flags
        jnz     error

        xor     ax,ax                   ; return OK

        pop     si                      ; Restore regs
        pop     ds
        ret

error:
        pop     si                      ; Restore regs
        pop     ds

        mov     al,ah                   ; AL get error code
        xor     ah,ah                   ; Zero extend
        mov     errno,ax                ; Save in errno too

        ret

EMS_EmBlk@mapPagesByNum40    endp       ; End of procedure

        end                             ; End of source file
```

The EMS_EmBlk.mapPagesByNum40(...) function maps several logical pages at one time. A mapping buffer gives pairs of a logical EMS page and a physical page number.

Function EMS_EmBlk.mapPagesByNum40(...)

```
function EMS_EmBlk.mapPagesByNum40(
            pages: Word;
            buffer:  Pointer)
        : Boolean;
```

where

pages   The number of pages to map

buffer Points to a table of 32-bit entries giving the logical and physical pages to be mapped (see _EMS.PAS, FIG. 3-6 for EMS_MapByNumber structure)

Map multiple pages by address

Figure 4-12 presents the source code listing to EMS501.ASM.

4-12 The source code listing to EMS501.ASM.

```
;*****************************************************************
;***        EMS501.ASM                                       ***
;***                                                         ***
;***        function        EMS_EmBlk.mapPagesByAddr40(      ***
;***                        pages:        Word;              ***
;***                        buffer:       Pointer)           ***
;***                        : Boolean;                       ***
;***                                                         ***
;***        Fill buffer with 32 bit entries that control pages ***
;***        to be mapped by segment address                  ***
;***                                                         ***
;***        Returns 0 if no error or an error code.          ***
;***                                                         ***
;***                                                         ***
;***                                                         ***
;***        (Ems Version 4.0)                                ***
;*****************************************************************

        .model  large,pascal

        include emsdefs.asm

        extrn   errno:WORD

;
;   Define entry point
;
        public  EMS_EmBlk@mapPagesByAddr40

        .code

EMS_EmBlk@mapPagesByAddr40  proc num:Word, buffer:Far Ptr Word, handle:Far
                            Ptr Word
```

4-12 Continued.

```
        push    ds                              ; Save regs
        push    si

        les     bx,handle
        mov     dx,es:[bx]                      ; EMS handle
        mov     cx,num                          ; Number of pages to map
        lds     si,buffer                       ; Mapping info

        mov     ax,MapPagesByAddr40             ; Make the EMS call
        int     Ems

        or      ah,ah                           ; Set flags
        jnz     error

        xor     ax,ax                           ; Return OK

        pop     si                              ; Restore regs
        pop     ds
        ret

error:
        pop     si
        pop     ds

        mov     al,ah                           ; AL get error code
        xor     ah,ah                           ; Zero extend
        mov     errno,ax                        ; Save in errno too

        ret

EMS_EmBlk@mapPagesByAddr40    endp              ; End of procedure

        end                                     ; End of source file
```

The EMS__EmBlk.mapPagesByAddr40(...) function maps several logical pages at one time. A mapping buffer gives pairs of a logical EMS page and a physical segment number.

Function EMS__Ems.mapPagesByAddr40(...)

```
function EMS__EmBlk.mapPagesByNum40(
                pages: Word;
                buffer: Pointer)
        : Boolean;
```

where

pages   The number of pages to map
buffer Points to a table of 32-bit entries giving logical and physical segment addresses (see __EMS.PAS, FIG. 3-6 for EMS__MapByAddress structure).

Reallocate pages for handle

Figure 4-13 presents the source code listing to EMS51.ASM.

4-13 The source code listing to EMS51.ASM.

```
;********************************************************************
;***      EMS51.ASM                                              ***
;***                                                             ***
;***      function          EMS_EmBlk.reallocHandPages40(        ***
;***                          pages:         Word)               ***
;***                          : Boolean;                         ***
;***                                                             ***
;***      Reallocates number of pages to EMM handle              ***
;***                                                             ***
;***      Returns 0 if no error or an error code.                ***
;***                                                             ***
;***                                                             ***
;***                                                             ***
;***      (Ems Version 4.0)                                      ***
;********************************************************************

        .model  large,pascal

        include emsdefs.asm

        extrn   errno:WORD

;
;   Define entry point
;
        public  EMS_EmBlk@reallocHandPages40

        .code

EMS_EmBlk@reallocHandPages40        proc num:Word, handle:Far Ptr Word

        les     bx,handle
        mov     dx,es:[bx]              ; EMS handle
        mov     bx,num                  ; New page count

        mov     ax,ReallocHandPages40   ; Make the call
        int     Ems

        or      ah,ah                   ; Set flags
        jnz     error

        xor     ax,ax                   ; Return OK
        ret

error:
        mov     al,ah                   ; AL get error code
        xor     ah,ah                   ; Zero extend
        mov     errno,ax                ; Save in errno too
        ret

EMS_EmBlk@reallocHandPages40        endp    ; End of procedure

        end                             ; End of source file
```

The function EMS__EmBlk.reallocHandlePages40(...) alters the number
of pages allocated to a specified handle.

Function EMS__EmBlk.reallocHandlePages40(...)

function EMS__EmBlk.reallocHandPages40(
                     pages: Word)
        : Boolean;

where

pages   The new handle page count.

Get handle attribute

Figure 4-14 presents the source code listing to EMS520.ASM.

4-14 The source code listing to EMS520.ASM.

```
;***********************************************************  ***
;***      EMS520.ASM                                         ***
;***                                                         ***
;***      function        EMS_EmBlk.getHandleAttr40(         ***
;***                          var attribute:  Word)          ***
;***                          : Boolean;                     ***
;***                          external;                      ***
;***                                                         ***
;***      Get volatile (0) or non-volatile (1) attribute     ***
;***      associated with the handle.                        ***
;***                                                         ***
;***      Returns 0 if no error or an error code.            ***
;***                                                         ***
;***                                                         ***
;***                                                         ***
;***      (Ems Version 4.0)                                  ***
;***********************************************************

        .model   large,pascal

        include emsdefs.asm

        extrn    errno:WORD


;
;   Define entry point
;
        public   EMS_EmBlk@getHandleAttr40

        .code

EMS_EmBlk@getHandleAttr40    proc attr:Far Ptr Word, handle:Far Ptr Word

        les      bx,handle
        mov      dx,es:[bx]          ; DX gets EMS handle

        mov      ax,GetHandleAttr40  ; Do call
        int      Ems

        or       ah,ah               ; Set flags
        jnz      error
```

```
        xor     ah,ah                   ; Zero extend attr to 16 bits
        les     bx,attr                 ; Return attribute
        mov     es:[bx],ax

        xor     ax,ax                   ; return OK
        ret

error:
        mov     al,ah                   ; AL get error code
        xor     ah,ah                   ; Zero extend
        mov     errno,ax                ; Save in errno too
        ret


EMS_EmBlk@getHandleAttr40       endp    ; End of procedure

        end                             ; End of source file
```

The function EMS__Ems.getHandleAttr40(...) retrieves the attribute associated with a specified handle.

Function EMS__EmBlk.getHandleAttr40(...)

```
function EMS__EmBlk.getHandleAttr40(
            var attribute:  Word)
        : Boolean;
```

where

attr Receives 1=nonvolatile (ems data held on warm boot) or 0= volatile
      (ems data destroyed on warm boot)

Set handle attribute

Figure 4-15 presents the source code listing to EMS521.ASM.

4-15 The source code listing to EMS521.ASM.

```
;*****************************************************************
;***    EMS521.ASM                                            ***
;***                                                          ***
;***                                                          ***
;***    function        EMS_EmBlk.setHandleAttr40(            ***
;***                        attribute:      Word)             ***
;***                        : Boolean;                        ***
;***                                                          ***
;***    Set volatile (0) or non-volatile (1) attribute        ***
;***    associated with the handle.                           ***
;***                                                          ***
;***    Returns 0 if no error or an error code.               ***
;***                                                          ***
;***                                                          ***
;***                                                          ***
;***                                                          ***
;***    (Ems Version 4.0)                                     ***
;*****************************************************************
```

```
        .model  large,pascal

        include emsdefs.asm

        extrn   errno:WORD

;
;   Define entry point
;
        public  EMS_EmBlk@setHandleAttr40

        .code

EMS_EmBlk@setHandleAttr40    proc attr:Word, handle:Far Ptr Word

        les     bx,handle
        mov     dx,es:[bx]              ; DX gets EMS handle
        mov     bx,attr                 ; BL gets attribute

        mov     ax,SetHandleAttr40      ; Make EMS call
        int     Ems

        or      ah,ah                   ; Set flags
        jnz     error

        xor     ax,ax                   ; Return OK
        ret

error:
        mov     al,ah                   ; AL gets error code
        xor     ah,ah                   ; Zero extend
        mov     errno,ax                ; Save in errno too
        ret

EMS_EmBlk@setHandleAttr40    endp       ; End of procedure
        end                             ; End of source file
```

The function EMS__EmBlk.setHandleAttr40(...) sets the attribute associated with a specified handle.

Function EMS__EmBlk.setHandleAttr40(...)

function EMS__EmBlk.setHandleAttr40(
                attribute: Word)
        : Boolean;

where

   attr Set 1= nonvolatile (ems data held on warm boot) or 0= volatile
         (ems data destroyed on warm boot)

Get attribute capabilities

Figure 4-16 presents the source code listing to EMS522.ASM.

4-16 The source code listing to EMS522.ASM.

```
;**********************************************************
;***      EMS522.ASM                                  ***
;***                                                  ***
;***      function        EMS_Ems.getAttrCapability40( ***
;***                         var capability: Word)    ***
;***                         : Boolean;               ***
;***                                                  ***
;***      Gets EMM support status for handle volatility. ***
;***         volatile (0) or non-volatile (1) attribute ***
;***                                                  ***
;***      Returns 0 if no error or an error code.     ***
;***                                                  ***
;***                                                  ***
;***                                                  ***
;***      (Ems Version 4.0)                           ***
;**********************************************************

        .model  large,pascal

        include emsdefs.asm

        extrn   errno:WORD

;
;   Define entry point
;
        public  EMS_Ems@getAttrCapability40

        .code

EMS_Ems@getAttrCapability40 proc attr:Far Ptr Word, self:DWord

        mov     ax,GetAttrCapability40  ; Make EMS call
        int     Ems

        or      ah,ah           ; Set flags
        jnz     error

        xor     ah,ah           ; Zero extend attr to 16 bits
        les     bx,attr         ; Return it
        mov     es:[bx],ax

        xor     ax,ax           ; Return OK
        ret

error:
        mov     al,ah           ; AL gets error code
        xor     ah,ah           ; Zero extend
        mov     errno,ax        ; Save in errno too
        ret

EMS_Ems@getAttrCapability40 endp    ; End of procedure

        end                         ; End of source file
```

EMS 4.0 interface functions   **121**

The function EMS__Ems.getAttrCapability40(...) retrieves a code that indicates the EMM's capability of supporting nonvolatile EMS data.

Function EMS__Ems.getAttrCapability40(...)

```
function EMS__Ems.getAttrCapability40(
              var capability:  Word)
    : Boolean;
```

where

capability   Receives 1=nonvolatile (ems data held on warm boot) or 0= volatile (ems data destroyed on warm boot)

Get handle name

Figure 4-17 presents the source code listing to EMS530.ASM.

4-17 The source code listing to EMS530.ASM.

```
;***********************************************************
;***       EMS530.ASM                                   ***
;***                                                    ***
;***       function      EMS_EmBlk.getHandleName40(     ***
;***                      var handle_name: EMS_HandleName)***
;***                        : Boolean;                  ***
;***                                                    ***
;***       Fill 8 byte handle name buffer with handle name. ***
;***                                                    ***
;***       Returns 0 if no error or an error code.      ***
;***                                                    ***
;***                                                    ***
;***                                                    ***
;***       (Ems Version 4.0)                            ***
;***********************************************************
;
        .model  large,pascal

        include emsdefs.asm

        extrn   errno:WORD

;
;   Define entry point
;
        public  EMS_EmBlk@getHandleName40

        .code
EMS_EmBlk@getHandleName40  proc handle_name:Far Ptr Word, handle:Far Ptr WOrd

        push    di                      ; Save di

        les     bx,handle
        mov     dx,es:[bx]              ; DX gets EMS handle
        les     di,handle_name          ; ES:DI gets name

        mov     ax,GetHandleName40      ; Make EMS call
        int     Ems
```

4-17 Continued.

```
        or      ah,ah                   ; Set flags
        jnz     error

        xor     ax,ax                   ; Return OK
        pop     di
        ret

error:
        pop     di                      ; Restore DI

        mov     al,ah                   ; AL gets error code
        xor     ah,ah                   ; Zero extend
        mov     errno,ax                ; Save in errno too
        ret

EMS_EmBlk@getHandleName40    endp       ; End of procedure

        end                             ; End of source file
```

The EMS__EmBlk.getHandleName40(...) function returns the designated name of a specified handle.

Function EMS__EmBlk.getHandleName40(...)

```
function EMS__EmBlk.getHandleName40(
            var handle__name:  EMS__HandleName)
        : Boolean;
```

where

name   An 8-byte buffer into which the name is copied

Set handle name

Figure 4-18 presents the source code listing to EMS531.ASM.

4-18 The source code listing to EMS531.ASM.

```
;****************************************************************
;***       EMS531.ASM                                       ***
;***                                                        ***
;***       function       EMS_EmBlk.setHandleName40(        ***
;***                      var handle_name: EMS_HandleName)  ***
;***                      : Boolean;                        ***
;***                                                        ***
;***       Set handle name buffer (bytes)                   ***
;***                                                        ***
;***       Returns 0 if no error or an error code.          ***
;***                                                        ***
;***                                                        ***
;***                                                        ***
;***       (Ems Version 4.0)                                ***
;****************************************************************
```

4-18 Continued.

```
        .model  large,pascal

        include emsdefs.asm

        extrn   errno:WORD

;
;   Define entry point
;
        public  EMS_EmBlk@setHandleName40

        .code

EMS_EmBlk@setHandleName40    proc handle_name:Far Ptr Word, handle:Far Ptr Word

        push    ds                      ; Save regs
        push    si

        les     bx,handle
        mov     dx,es:[bx]              ; DX gets the EMS handle
        lds     si,handle_name          ; DS:SI get handle name

        mov     ax,SetHandleName40      ; Make the EMS call
        int     Ems

        or      ah,ah                   ; Set flags
        jnz     error

        xor     ax,ax                   ; Return OK
        pop     si                      ; Restore regs
        pop     ds
        ret

error:
        pop     si                      ; Restore regs
        pop     ds

        mov     al,ah                   ; AL gets error code
        xor     ah,ah                   ; Zero extend
        mov     errno,ax                ; Save in errno too
        ret

EMS_EmBlk@setHandleName40    endp       ; End of procedure

        end                             ; End of source file
```

The EMS__EmBlk.setHandleName40(...) function sets the name of a specified handle.

Function EMS__EmBlk.setHandleName40(...)

```
function EMS__EmBlk.setHandleName40(
            var handle__name:  EMS__HandleName)
        : Boolean;
```

where

name   An 8-byte buffer where the name taken from

Get all handle names

Figure 4-19 presents the source code listing to EMS540.ASM.

4-19 The source code listing to EMS540.ASM.

```
;******************************************************************
;***      EMS540.ASM                                         ***
;***                                                         ***
;***      function    EMS_Ems.getAllHandleNames40(           ***
;***                   var info_list:  EMS_HandleNameInfoArr;***
;***                   : Boolean;                            ***
;***                                                         ***
;***                                                         ***
;***      Fill 8 byte handle names to 2550 MAX entries       ***
;***                                                         ***
;***      Returns 0 if no error or an error code.            ***
;***                                                         ***
;***                                                         ***
;***                                                         ***
;***      (Ems Version 4.0)                                  ***
;******************************************************************

          .model   large,pascal

          include emsdefs.asm

          extrn    errno:WORD

;
;   Define entry point
;
          public   EMS_Ems@getAllHandleNames40

          extrn    errno:WORD

          .code

EMS_Ems@getAllHandleNames40 proc info_list:Far Ptr Byte, self:DWord

          push     di                      ; Save DI

          les      di,info_list            ; ES:DI gets address of buffer

          mov      ax,GetAllHandleNames40  ; Make the EMS call
          int      Ems

          or       ah,ah                   ; Set flags
          jnz      error

          xor      ax,ax                   ; Return OK
          pop      di                      ; Restore DI
          ret
```

```
error:
        pop     di                      ; Restore DI

        mov     al,ah                   ; AL gets error code
        xor     ah,ah                   ; Zero extend
        mov     errno,ax                ; Save in errno too
        ret

EMS_Ems@getAllHandleNames40 endp        ; End of procedure

        end                             ; End of source file
```

Function EMS__Ems.getAllHandleNames40(...) returns a list of names for all the active handles.

Function EMS__Ems.getAllHandleNames40(...)

function EMS__Ems.getAllHandleNames40(
                var info__list: EMS__HandleNameInfoArr)
        : Boolean;

where

info__list An array of EMS__HandleNameInfo records (see __EMS.PAS, FIG. 3-6, for EMS__HandleNameInfo structure)

Search for handle name

Figure 4-20 presents the source code listing to EMS541.ASM.

4-20 The source code listing to EMS541.ASM.

```
;*********************************************************
;***                                                 ***
;***    EMS541.ASM                                   ***
;***                                                 ***
;***    function       EMS_EmBlk.searchHandleName40( ***
;***                   var name:     EMS_HandleName) ***
;***                     : Boolean;                  ***
;***                                                 ***
;***    Returns handle number of specified handle name. ***
;***                                                 ***
;***    Returns 0 if no error or an error code.      ***
;***                                                 ***
;***                                                 ***
;***                                                 ***
;***                                                 ***
;***    (Ems Version 4.0)*****************************
;*********************************************************

        .model  large,pascal

        include emsdefs.asm

        extrn   errno:WORD
```

4-20 Continued.

```
;
;   Define entry point
;
        public  EMS_EmBlk@searchHandleName40

        .code

EMS_EmBlk@searchHandleName40        proc handle_name:Far Ptr Byte, handle:Far
                                    Ptr Word

        push    ds                      ; Save regs
        push    si

        lds     si,handle_name          ; DS:SI gets handle name

        mov     ax,SearchHandleName40   ; Do EMS call
        int     Ems

        or      ah,ah                   ; Set flags
        jnz     error

        les     bx,handle               ; Return handle we found
        mov     es:[bx],dx

        xor     ax,ax                   ; Return OK
        pop     si                      ; Restore regs
        pop     ds
        ret

error:
        pop     si                      ; Restore regs
        pop     ds

        mov     al,ah                   ; AL gets error code
        xor     ah,ah                   ; Zero extend
        mov     errno,ax                ; Save in errno too
        ret

EMS_EmBlk@searchHandleName40        endp        ; End of procedure

        end                             ; End of source file
```

Function EMS_EmBlk.searchHandleName40(...) initializes the target EMS__EmBlk with the handle associated with the specified name.

Function EMS__EmBlk.searchHandleName40(...)
```
function EMS__EmBlk.searchHandleName40(
                var name:  EMS__HandleName)
        : Boolean;
```

where

name   Points to an 8-byte handle name

Get total number of handles

Figure 4-21 presents the source code listing to EMS542.ASM.

4-21 The source code listing to EMS542.ASM.

```
;********************************************************
;***                                                 ***
;***     EMS542.ASM                                  ***
;***                                                 ***
;***     function         EMS_Ems.getTotalHandles40( ***
;***                        var handles:    Word)    ***
;***                        : Boolean;               ***
;***                                                 ***
;***     Returns total number of allocated handles to ***
;***     pointer.                                    ***
;***                                                 ***
;***     Returns 0 if no error or an error code.     ***
;***                                                 ***
;***                                                 ***
;***                                                 ***
;***     (Ems Version 4.0)                           ***
;********************************************************
;

        .model  large,pascal

        include emsdefs.asm

        extrn   errno:WORD


;
;   Define entry point
;
        public  EMS_Ems@getTotalHandles40

        .code

EMS_Ems@getTotalHandles40 proc handles:Far Ptr Word, self:DWord

        mov     ax,GetTotalHandles40    ; Do EMS call
        int     Ems

        or      ah,ah                   ; Set flags
        jnz     error

        mov     ax,bx                   ; Number of handles
        les     bx,handles              ; Return it
        mov     es:[bx],ax

        xor     ax,ax                   ; Return OK
        ret

error:
        mov     al,ah                   ; AL gets error code
        xor     ah,ah                   ; Zero extend
        mov     errno,ax                ; Save in errno too
        ret

EMS_Ems@getTotalHandles40 endp         ; End of procedure

        end                             ; End of source file
```

Function EMS__Ems.getTotalHandles40(...) returns the total number of active EMS handles.

Function EMS__Ems.getTotalHandles40(...)

```
function EMS__Ems.getTotalHandles40(
            var handles:  Word)
      : Boolean;
```

where

handles Receives total number of active EMS handles

Map pages by number and jump

Figure 4-22 presents the source code listing to EMS550.ASM.

4-22 The source code listing to EMS550.ASM.

```
;*******************************************************************
;***    EMS550.ASM                                          ***
;***                                                        ***
;***    function       EMS_EmBlk.mapPagesJumpNum40(         ***
;***                       var buffer:     DWord)           ***
;***                       : Boolean;                       ***
;***                                                        ***
;***    Transfers control to EMS location mapped by phys.   ***
;***    page by JUMP                                        ***
;***                                                        ***
;***    Returns 0 if no error or an error code.             ***
;***                                                        ***
;***                                                        ***
;***                                                        ***
;***    (Ems Version 4.0)                                   ***
;*******************************************************************

        .model  large,pascal

        include emsdefs.asm

        extrn   errno:WORD

;
;   Define entry point
;
        public  EMS_EmBlk@mapPagesJumpNum40

        .code

EMS_EmBlk@mapPagesJumpNum40 proc buffer:Far Ptr DWord, handle:Far Ptr DWord

        push    ds                      ; Save regs
        push    si
```

```
        les     bx,handle
        mov     dx,es:[bx]              ; DX gets the EMS handle
        lds     si,buffer               ; DS:SI gets the buffer address

        mov     ax,MapPagesJumpNum40    ; Make EMS call
        int     Ems

        or      ah,ah                   ; Set flags
        jnz     error

        xor     ax,ax                   ; Return OK
        pop     si
        pop     ds
        ret

error:
        pop     si                      ; Restore regs
        pop     ds

        mov     al,ah                   ; AL gets error code
        xor     ah,ah                   ; Zero extend
        mov     errno,ax                ; Save in errno too
        ret

EMS_EmBlk@mapPagesJumpNum40 endp        ; End of procedure

        end                             ; End of source file
```

Function EMS_EmBlk.mapPagesJumpNum40(...) changes the context of the EMS pages and transfers to a specified address via a JMP (jump).

Function EMS_EmBlk.mapPagesJumpNum40(...)

function EMS_EmBlk.mapPagesJumpNum40(
            buffer: pointer)
        : Boolean;

where

buffer   Points to a buffer of the following form:
          jump_target: DWord;
          num_pages_to_map; Byte;
          page_map_list: Pointer; (* to logical page #, physical page # pairs *)

Map pages by segment and jump

Figure 4-23 presents the source code listing to EMS551.ASM.

4-23 The source code listing to EMS551.ASM.

```
;*************************************************************
;***      EMS551.ASM                                      ***
;***                                                      ***
;***      function      EMS_EmBlk.mapPagesJumpSeg40(      ***
;***                       var buffer:    DWord)          ***
;***                       : Boolean;                     ***
;***                                                      ***
;***      Transfers control to EMS location mapped by segment ***
;***      location by JUMP                                ***
;***                                                      ***
;***      Returns 0 if no error or an error code.         ***
;***                                                      ***
;***                                                      ***
;***                                                      ***
;***      (Ems Version 4.0)                               ***
;*************************************************************

        .model  large,pascal

        include emsdefs.asm

        extrn   errno:WORD

;
;   Define entry point
;
        public  EMS_EmBlk@mapPagesJumpSeg40

        .code

EMS_EmBlk@mapPagesJumpSeg40 proc buffer:Far Ptr DWord, handle:Far Ptr Word

        push    ds                       ; Save regs
        push    si

        les     bx,handle
        mov     dx,es:[bx]               ; DX gets the EMS handle
        lds     si,buffer                ; DS:SI gets the buffer address

        mov     ax,MapPagesJumpSeg40     ; Make the EMS call
        int     Ems

        or      ah,ah                    ; Set flags
        jnz     error

        xor     ax,ax                    ; Return OK
        pop     si                       ; Restore regs
        pop     ds
        ret

error:
        pop     si                       ; Restore regs
        pop     ds

        mov     al,ah                    ; AL gets error code
        xor     ah,ah                    ; Zero extend
        mov     errno,ax                 ; Save in errno too
        ret

EMS_EmBlk@mapPagesJumpSeg40 endp         ; End of procedure

        end                              ; End of source file
```

Function EMS__EmBlk.mapPagesJumpSeg40(...) changes the context of the EMS pages and transfers to a specified address via a JMP (jump).

Function EMS__EmBlk.mapPagesJumpSeg40(...)

```
function EMS__EmBlk.mapPagesJumpSeg40(
              buffer:  pointer)
    : Boolean;
```

where

buffer   Points to a buffer of the following form:
   jump__target: DWord;
   num__pages__to__map: Byte;
   page__map__list: Pointer (* to logical page #, physical page
                             segment pairs *)

Map pages by number and call

Figure 4-24 presents the source code listing to EMS560.ASM.

4-24 The source code listing to EMS560.ASM.

```
;*******************************************************      ***
;***      EMS560.ASM                                          ***
;***                                                          ***
;***      function        EMS_EmBlk.mapPagesCallNum40(        ***
;***                      var buffer:      Word)              ***
;***                      : Boolean;                          ***
;***                                                          ***
;***      Transfers control to EMS location mapped by phys.   ***
;***      page by CALL                                        ***
;***                                                          ***
;***      Returns 0 if no error or an error code.             ***
;***                                                          ***
;***                                                          ***
;***                                                          ***
;***                                                          ***
;***      (Ems Version 4.0)                                   ***
;*******************************************************************

        .model  large,pascal

        include emsdefs.asm

        extrn   errno:WORD


;
;   Define entry point
;
        public  EMS_EmBlk@mapPagesCallNum40

        .code

EMS_EmBlk@mapPagesCallNum40 proc buffer:Far Ptr DWord, handle:Far Ptr Word
```

4-24 Continued.

```
        push    ds                          ; Save regs
        push    si

        les     bx,handle
        mov     dx,es:[bx]                  ; DX gets EMS handle
        lds     si,buffer                   ; DS:SI gets buffer address

        mov     ax,MapPagesCallNum40        ; Make EMS call
        int     Ems

        or      ah,ah                       ; Set flags
        jnz     error

        xor     ax,ax                       ; Return OK
        pop     si                          ; Restore regs
        pop     ds
        ret

error:
        pop     si                          ; Restore regs
        pop     ds

        mov     al,ah                       ; AL gets error code
        xor     ah,ah                       ; Zero extend
        mov     errno,ax                    ; Save in errno too
        ret

EMS_EmBlk@mapPagesCallNum40 endp            ; End of procedure

        end                                 ; End of source file
```

Function EMS__EmBlk.mapPagesCallNum40(...) changes the context of the EMS pages and transfers to a specified address via a CALL (call).

Function EMS__EmBlk.mapPagesCallNum40(...)

function EMS__EmBlk.mapPagesCallNum40(
        buffer: Pointer)
   : Boolean;

where

buffer Points to a buffer of the following form:
     call__target: DWord;
     precall__num__pages: Byte;
     precall__map__list: Pointer (* to logical page #, physical page #
                              pairs);

Map pages by segment and call

Figure 4-25 presents the source code listing to EMS561.ASM.

4-25 The source code listing to EMS561.ASM.

```
;****************************************************************
;***      EMS561.ASM                                        ***
;***                                                        ***
;***      function          EMS_EmBlk.mapPagesCallSeg40(    ***
;***                          var buffer:     Word)         ***
;***                             : Boolean;                 ***
;***                                                        ***
;***      Transfers control to EMS location mapped by segment ***
;***      location by CALL                                  ***
;***                                                        ***
;***      Returns 0 if no error or an error code.           ***
;***                                                        ***
;***                                                        ***
;***                                                        ***
;***      (Ems Version 4.0)                                 ***
;****************************************************************

        .model  large,pascal

        include emsdefs.asm

        extrn   errno:WORD

;
;   Define entry point
;
        public  EMS_EmBlk@mapPagesCallSeg40

        .code

EMS_EmBlk@mapPagesCallSeg40 proc buffer:Far Ptr DWord, handle:Far Ptr Word

        push    ds                      ; Save regs
        push    si

        les     bx,handle
        mov     dx,es:[bx]              ; DX gets EMS handle
        lds     si,buffer               ; DS:SI gets buffer address

        mov     ax,MapPagesCallSeg40    ; Make EMS call
        int     Ems

        or      ah,ah                   ; Set flags
        jnz     error

        xor     ax,ax                   ; Return OK
        pop     si                      ; Restore regs
        pop     ds
        ret

error:
        pop     si                      ; Restore regs
        pop     ds

        mov     al,ah                   ; AL gets error code
        xor     ah,ah                   ; Zero extend
        mov     errno,ax                ; Save in errno too
        ret

EMS_EmBlk@mapPagesCallSeg40 endp        ; End of procedure

        end                             ; End of source file
```

Function EMS__Ems.mapPagesCallSeg40(...) changes the context of the EMS pages and transfers to a specified address via a CALL (call).

Function EMS__EmBlk.mapPagesCallSeg40(...)

```
function EMS__EmBlk.mapPagesCallSeg40(
              buffer:  Pointer)
        : Boolean;
```

where

buffer   Points to a buffer of the following form:
call__target: DWord;
precall__num__pages: Byte;
precall__map__list: Pointer (* to logical page #, physical page #
                                            pairs);
postcall__num__pages: Byte;
postcall__map__list: Pointer (* to logical page #, physical page
                                            segment pairs *);

Get map page stack space for call

Figure 4-26 presents the source code listing to EMS562.ASM.

4-26   The source code listing to EMS562.ASM.

```
;****************************************************************
;***      EMS562.ASM                                        ***
;***                                                        ***
;***      function           EMS_Ems.getStackNeeded40(      ***
;***                          var stack_space: Word)        ***
;***                          : Boolean;                    ***
;***                                                        ***
;***      Returns stack space for map page and call to      ***
;***      pointer.                                          ***
;***                                                        ***
;***      Returns 0 if no error or an error code.           ***
;***                                                        ***
;***                                                        ***
;***                                                        ***
;***      (Ems Version 4.0)                                 ***
;****************************************************************

        .model   large,pascal

        include emsdefs.asm

        extrn    errno:WORD

;
;   Define entry point
;
        public   EMS_Ems@getStackNeeded40

        .code

EMS_Ems@getStackNeeded40     proc stack_space:Far Ptr Word, self:DWord
```

```
        mov     ax,GetStackNeeded40    ; Make EMS call
        int     Ems

        or      ah,ah                  ; Set flags
        jnz     error

        les     bx,stack_space         ; Return stack size to caller
        mov     es:[bx],dx

        xor     ax,ax                  ; Return OK
        ret
error:
        mov     al,ah                  ; AL gets error code
        xor     ah,ah                  ; Zero extend
        mov     errno,ax               ; Save in errno too
        ret

EMS_Ems@getStackNeeded40    endp       ; End of procedure

        end                            ; End of source file
```

Function EMS__Ems.getStackNeeded40(...) retrieves the extra stack space required by the EMS__EmBlk.mapPagesCallNum40(...) and EMS__Em Blk.map PagesCallSeg40(...) functions.

Function EMS__Ems.getStackNeeded40(...)

function EMS__Ems.getStackNeeded40(
            var stack__space: Word)
        : Boolean;

where

stack__size Receives the extra stack size required by the
            EMS__Ems.mapPagesCallNum40(...)
            and EMS__Ems.mapPagesCallSeg40(...) functions

Move a memory region

Figure 4-27 presents the source code listing to EMS570.ASM.

4-27 The source code listing to EMS570.ASM.

```
;*****************************************************************
;***      EMS570.ASM                                        ***
;***                                                        ***
;***      function    EMS_Ems.moveMemRegion40(             ***
;***                  var buffer:      EMS_MoveMemoryInfo)  ***
;***                  : Boolean;                            ***
;***                                                        ***
;***      Moves memory region from source to destination    ***
;***      described in MoveMemoryInfo_type structure        ***
;***                                                        ***
;***      Buffer Structure                                  ***
```

4-27 Continued.

```
;***     ----------------                                        ***
;***     DWORD    length;        ; memory length               ***
;***     BYTE     srce_type;     ; 0-conventional,1-expanded   ***
;***     WORD     srce_handle;   ; source memory handle        ***
;***     WORD     srce_offset;   ; source memory offset        ***
;***     WORD     srce_id;       ; source seg or phys page     ***
;***     BYTE     dest_type;     ; 0-conventional,1-expanded   ***
;***     WORD     dest_handle;   ; source memory handle        ***
;***     WORD     dest_offset;   ; source memory offset        ***
;***     WORD     dest_id;       ; source seg or phys page     ***
;***                                                            ***
;***     Returns 0 if no error or an error code.                ***
;***                                                            ***
;***                                                            ***
;***                                                            ***
;***     (Ems Version 4.0)                                      ***
;*******************************************************************

         .model   large,pascal

         include emsdefs.asm

         extrn    errno:WORD

;
;    Define entry point
;
         public   EMS_Ems@moveMemRegion40

         .code

EMS_Ems@moveMemRegion40 proc buffer:Far Ptr Byte, self:DWord

         push     ds                    ; Save regs
         push     si

         lds      si,buffer             ; DS:SI gets move buffer address

         mov      ax,MoveMemRegion40    ; Do the EMS call
         int      Ems

         or       ah,ah                 ; Set flags
         jnz      error

         xor      ax,ax                 ; Return OK
         pop      si                    ; Restore regs
         pop      ds
         ret

error:
         pop      si                    ; Restore regs
         pop      ds

         mov      al,ah                 ; AL gets error code
         xor      ah,ah                 ; Zero extend
         mov      errno,ax              ; Save in errno too
         ret

EMS_Ems@moveMemRegion40 endp            ; End of procedure
         end                            ; End of source file
```

The EMS__Ems.moveMemRegion40(...) function moves a portion of expanded or conventional memory to any other location without disturbing the expanded memory page mapping context.

Function EMS__Ems.moveMemRegion40(...)

function EMS__Ems.moveMemRegion40(
                var buffer: EMS__MoveMemoryInfo)
        : Boolean;

where

buffer A EMS__MoveMemoryInfo structure (see __EMS.PAS, FIG. 3-6, for
        EMS__MoveMemoryInfo structure)

Swap memory regions

Figure 4-28 presents the source code listing to EMS571.ASM.

4-28 The source code listing to EMS571.ASM.

```
;**************************************************************  ***
;***    EMS571.ASM                                              ***
;***                                                            ***
;***    function     EMS_Ems.swapMemRegions40(                  ***
;***                    var buffer:      EMS_MoveMemoryInfo)     ***
;***                       : Boolean;                           ***
;***                                                            ***
;***    Swaps memory region from source to destination          ***
;***    described in MoveMemoryInfo_type structure              ***
;***                                                            ***
;***    Buffer Structure                                        ***
;***    ----------------                                        ***
;***    DWORD    length;      ; memory length                   ***
;***    BYTE     srce_type;   ; 0-conventional,1-expanded       ***
;***    WORD     srce_handle; ; source memory handle            ***
;***    WORD     srce_offset; ; source memory offset            ***
;***    WORD     srce_id;     ; source seg or phys page         ***
;***    BYTE     dest_type;   ; 0-conventional,1-expanded       ***
;***    WORD     dest_handle; ; source memory handle            ***
;***    WORD     dest_offset; ; source memory offset            ***
;***    WORD     dest_id;     ; source seg or phys page         ***
;***                                                            ***
;***    Returns 0 if no error or an error code.                 ***
;***                                                            ***
;***                                                            ***
;***                                                            ***
;***    (Ems Version 4.0)                                       ***
;**************************************************************
;
        .model  large,pascal

        include emsdefs.asm

        extrn   errno:WORD
```

```
;
;   Define entry point
;
        public  EMS_Ems@swapMemRegions40

        .code

EMS_Ems@swapMemRegions40 proc buffer:Far Ptr Byte, self:DWord

        push    ds                      ; Save regs
        push    si

        lds     si,buffer               ; DS:SI gets swap buffer address

        mov     ax,SwapMemRegions40     ; Do the EMS call
        int     Ems

        or      ah,ah                   ; Set flags
        jnz     error

        xor     ax,ax                   ; Return OK
        pop     si                      ; Restore regs
        pop     ds
        ret

error:
        pop     si                      ; Restore regs
        pop     ds

        mov     al,ah                   ; AL gets error code
        xor     ah,ah                   ; Zero extend
        mov     errno,ax                ; Save in errno too
        ret

EMS_Ems@swapMemRegions40 endp          ; End of procedure

        end                             ; End of source file
```

The EMS__Ems.swapMemRegion40(...) function swaps a portion of expanded or conventional memory with any other memory without disturbing the expanded memory page mapping context.

Function EMS__Ems.swapMemRegion40(...)

```
function EMS__Ems.swapMemRegions40(
            var buffer:  EMS__MoveMemoryInfo)
        : Boolean;
```

where

buffer   Points to EMS__MoveMemoryInfo structure (see __EMS.PAS, FIG. 3-6, for EMS__MoveMemoryInfo structure).

Get addresses of mappable pages

Figure 4-29 presents the source code listing to EMS580.ASM.

4-29 The source code listing to EMS580.ASM.

```
;*************************************************************
;***                                                      ***
;***    EMS580.ASM                                        ***
;***                                                      ***
;***    function  EMS_Ems.getAddrsMappable40(             ***
;***              var buffer:     EMS_MappablePagesInfoArr; ***
;***              var num_entries: Word)                  ***
;***              : Boolean;                              ***
;***                                                      ***
;***    Returns, in the buffer specified a list of the    ***
;***    pages in memory which can be mapped. These include ***
;***    pages in the middle of the 640K area so caution   ***
;***    must be exercised in mapping them.                ***
;***                                                      ***
;***    Returns 0 if no error or an error code.           ***
;***                                                      ***
;***    (Ems Version 4.0)                                 ***
;*************************************************************

        .model  large,pascal

        include emsdefs.asm

        extrn   errno:WORD

;
;   Define entry point
;
        public  EMS_Ems@getAddrsMappable40

        .code

EMS_Ems@getAddrsMappable40 proc buffer:Far Ptr Byte, num_entries:Far Ptr
                           Word, self:DWord

        push    di                      ; Save di

        les     di,buffer               ; Get the buffer address into ES:DI

        mov     ax,GetAddrsMappable40   ; Make the EMS call
        int     Ems

        or      ah,ah                   ; Set flags
        jnz     error

        les     bx,num_entries          ; Return number of pages
        mov     word ptr es:[bx],cx

        xor     ax,ax                   ; return OK
        pop     di                      ; restore di
        ret

error:
        pop     di                      ; restore di

        mov     al,ah                   ; AL gets error code
```

4-29 Continued.

```
        xor     ah,ah                   ; Zero extend
        mov     errno,ax                ; Save in errno too
        ret

EMS_Ems@getAddrsMappable40 endp        ; End of procedure

        end                             ; End of source file
```

The EMS_Ems.getAddrsMappable40(...) function retrieves the segment base address and physical page number for each mappable page in the EMS system.

Function EMS_Ems.getAddrsMappable40(...)

```
function EMS_Ems.getAddrsMappable40(
            var buffer:        EMS_MappablePagesInfoArr;
            var num_entries: Word)
        : Boolean;
```

where

buffer   Array of EMS_MappablePagesInfo records (see _EMS.PAS, FIG. 3-6, for EMS_MappablePagesInfo structure)

num_entries   Receives the number of entries in mappable physical page array

Get number of mappable pages

Figure 4-30 presents the source code listing to EMS581.ASM.

4-30 The source code listing to EMS581.ASM.

```
;******************************************************************
;***     EMS581.ASM                                          ***
;***                                                         ***
;***     function        EMS_Ems.getNumMappable40(          ***
;***                        var mappablePages: Word)         ***
;***                        : Boolean;                       ***
;***                                                         ***
;***     Returns total number of mappable pages to pointer.  ***
;***                                                         ***
;***     Returns 0 if no error or an error code.             ***
;***                                                         ***
;***     (Ems Version 4.0)                                   ***
;******************************************************************

        .model  large,pascal

        include emsdefs.asm

        extrn   errno:WORD
```

4-30 Continued.

```
;
;   Define entry point
;
        public  EMS_Ems@getNumMappable40

        .code

EMS_Ems@getNumMappable40 proc mappable_pages:Far Ptr Word, self:DWord

        mov     ax,GetNumMappable40      ; Make the call
        int     Ems

        or      ah,ah                    ; Check for error
        jnz     error

        les     bx,mappable_pages        ; Return the number of...
        mov     es:[bx],cx               ; ... mappable pages

        xor     ax,ax                    ; return OK
        ret

error:
        mov     al,ah                    ; AL gets error code
        xor     ah,ah                    ; Zero extend
        mov     errno,ax                 ; Save in errno too
        ret

EMS_Ems@getNumMappable40     endp        ; End of procedure

        end                              ; End of source file
```

The EMS__Ems.getNumMappable40(...) function retrieves the number of mappable physical pages. This information may be used to calculate the size of the buffer required by the EMS__Ems.getAddrsMappable40(...) function. A DWORD (4 bytes) of buffer space is required for each mappable page.

Function EMS__Ems.getNumMappable40(...)

```
function EMS__Ems.getNumMappable40(
            var mappablePages:  Word)
        : Boolean;
```

where

num__entries Receives the number of mappable physical pages

Get hardware configuration

Figure 4-31 presents the source code listing to EMS590.ASM.

4-31 The source code listing to EMS590.ASM.

```
;****************************************************************
;***     EMS590.ASM                                          ***
;***                                                         ***
;***     function  EMS_Ems.getHWConfig40(                    ***
;***                 var buffer:      EMS_HardwareConfigInfo) ***
;***                 : Boolean;                              ***
;***                                                         ***
;***     HardwareConfigInfo_type structure                  ***
;***     --------------------------------                    ***
;***     WORD    raw_p_size;  ; size of raw pages in paras   ***
;***     WORD    alt_regs;    ; number of alt reg sets       ***
;***     WORD    save_area;   ; size of map sav area (bytes) ***
;***     WORD    regs_to_dma; ; max num regs assigned to dma ***
;***     WORD    dma_type;    ; 0-alt dma regs OK,           ***
;***                          ; 1-one dma reg only           ***
;***                                                         ***
;***     Returns hardware config info to structure pointer.  ***
;***                                                         ***
;***     Returns 0 if no error or an error code.             ***
;***                                                         ***
;***                                                         ***
;***                                                         ***
;***     (Ems Version 4.0)                                   ***
;****************************************************************

        .model  large,pascal

        include emsdefs.asm

        extrn   errno:WORD

;
;   Define entry point
;
        public  EMS_Ems@getHWConfig40

        .code

EMS_Ems@getHWConfig40 proc buffer:Far Ptr Word, self:DWord

        push    di                  ; Save DI

        les     di,buffer           ; ES:DI gets buffer address

        mov     ax,GetHWConfig40    ; Do the EMS call
        int     Ems

        or      ah,ah               ; Set flags
        jnz     error

        xor     ax,ax               ; Return OK
        pop     di                  ; Restore DI
        ret
```

4-31 Continued.

```
error:
        pop     di                      ; Restore DI

        mov     al,ah                   ; AL gets error code
        xor     ah,ah                   ; Zero extend
        mov     errno,ax                ; Save in errno too
        ret

EMS_Ems@getHWConfig40 endp              ; End of procedure

        end                             ; End of source file
```

The EMS__Ems.getHWConfig40(...) function returns information about the EMM configuration.

Function EMS__Ems.getHWConfig40(...)

function EMS__Ems.getHWConfig40(
           var buffer: EMS__HardwareConfigInfo)
   : Boolean;

where

buff Points to EMS__HardwareConfigInfo structure (see __EMS.PAS, FIG. 3-6, for EMS__HardwareConfigInfo structure)

Get number of raw pages

Figure 4-32 presents the source code listing to EMS591.ASM.

4-32 The source code listing to EMS591.ASM.

```
;**********************************************************
;***                                                   ***
;***     EMS591.ASM                                    ***
;***                                                   ***
;***     function        EMS_Ems.getNumRawPages40(     ***
;***                        var total_pages: Word;     ***
;***                        var free_pages: Word)       ***
;***                        : Boolean;                 ***
;***                                                   ***
;***     Returns the total number of free raw pages and the  ***
;***     number of raw pages available.                ***
;***                                                   ***
;***     Returns 0 if no error or an error code.       ***
;***                                                   ***
;***                                                   ***
;***     (Ems Version 4.0)                             ***
;**********************************************************

        .model  large,pascal

        include emsdefs.asm

        extrn   errno:WORD
```

4-32 Continued.

```
;
;   Define entry point
;
        public   EMS_Ems@getNumRawPages40

        .code

EMS_Ems@getNumRawPages40 proc     total:Far Ptr Word, free:Far Ptr Word,
                                  self:DWord

        mov     ax,GetNumRawPages40     ;  Do the EMS call
        int     Ems

        or      ah,ah                   ; Set flags
        jnz     error

        mov     ax,bx                   ; Save free pages
        les     bx,free                 ; Return it to caller
        mov     es:[bx],ax
        les     bx,total                ; Return total pages to caller
        mov     es:[bx],dx

        xor     ax,ax                   ; Return OK
        ret

error:
        mov     al,ah                   ; AL gets error code
        xor     ah,ah                   ; Zero extend
        mov     errno,ax                ; Save in errno too
        ret

EMS_Ems@getNumRawPages40 endp         ; End of procedure

        end                           ; End of source file
```

The EMS_Ems.getNumRawPages40(...) function retrieves the number of raw pages that have been allocated and the total number of raw pages. A raw page's size may vary from the 16K page size standard.

Function EMS__Ems.getNumRawPages40(...)

```
function EMS__Ems.getNumRawPages40(
            var total__pages:  Word;
            var free__pages:  Word)
     : Boolean;
```

where

free__pages   Receives the number of free raw pages

total__pages   Receives the total number of raw pages

Allocate handle and standard pages

Figure 4-33 presents the source code listing to EMS5A0.ASM.

4-33 The source code listing to EMS5A0.ASM.

```
;*************************************************************
;***                                                    ***
;***       EMS5A0.ASM                                   ***
;***                                                    ***
;***       function       EMS_EmBlk.allocHandleStd40(   ***
;***                        pages:          Word)       ***
;***                        : Boolean;                  ***
;***                                                    ***
;***       Allocates standards pages and returns handle to   ***
;***       pointer.                                     ***
;***                                                    ***
;***       Returns 0 if no error or an error code.      ***
;***                                                    ***
;***                                                    ***
;***                                                    ***
;***       (Ems Version 4.0)                            ***
;*************************************************************

          .model   large,pascal

          include emsdcfs.asm

          extrn    errno:WORD


;
;   Define entry point
;
          public   EMS_EmBlk@allocHandleStd40

          .code

EMS_EmBlk@allocHandleStd40  proc pages:Word, handle:Far Ptr Word

          mov      bx,pages            ; BX gets # pages to allocate

          mov      ax,AllocHandleStd40 ; Do EMS call
          int      Ems

          or       ah,ah               ; Set flags
          jnz      error


          les      bx,handle           ; Return handle to caller
          mov      es:[bx],dx

          xor      ax,ax               ; Return OK
          ret

   error:
          mov      al,ah               ; AL gets error code
          xor      ah,ah               ; Zero extend
          mov      errno,ax            ; Save in errno too
          ret

EMS_EmBlk@allocHandleStd40  endp        ; End of procedure

          end                          ; End of source file
```

The EMS_EmBlk.allocHandleStd40(...) function allocates a specified number of standard (16K) pages and initializes the target EMS_EmBlk with the handle.

Function EMS_EmBlk.allocHandleStd40(...)

```
function EMS_EmBlk.allocHandleStd40(
              pages:  Word)
        : Boolean;
```

where

> pages Holds the number of standard pages to allocate

Allocate handle and raw pages

Figure 4-34 presents the source code listing to EMS5A1.ASM.

4-34 The source code listing to EMS5A1.ASM.

```
;***************************************************************
;***     EMS5A0.ASM                                         ***
;***                                                        ***
;***     function        EMS_EmBlk.allocHandleRaw40(        ***
;***                      pages:          Word)             ***
;***                      : Boolean;                        ***
;***                                                        ***
;***     Allocates raw pages and returns handle to pointer  ***
;***                                                        ***
;***     Returns 0 if no error or an error code.            ***
;***                                                        ***
;***                                                        ***
;***                                                        ***
;***     (Ems Version 4.0)                                  ***
;***************************************************************

        .model  large,pascal

        include emsdefs.asm

        extrn   errno:WORD

;
;   Define entry point
;
        public  EMS_EmBlk@allocHandleRaw40

        .code

EMS_EmBlk@allocHandleRaw40  proc pages:Word, handle:Far Ptr Word

        mov     bx,pages            ; BX gets # pages to allocate

        mov     ax,AllocHandleRaw40 ; Do EMS call
        int     Ems
```

```
        or      ah,ah                   ; Set flags
        jnz     error


        les     bx,handle               ; Return handle to caller
        mov     es:[bx],dx

        xor     ax,ax                   ; Return OK
        ret

error:
        mov     al,ah                   ; AL gets error code
        xor     ah,ah                   ; Zero extend
        mov     errno,ax                ; Save in errno too
        ret

EMS_EmBlk@allocHandleRaw40  endp        ; End of procedure

        end                             ; End of source file
```

The EMS__EmBlk.allocHandleRaw40(...) function allocates a specified number of raw pages and retrieves the handles associated with those standard pages.

Function EMS__EmBlk.allocHandleRaw40(...)

function EMS__EmBlk.allocHandleRaw40(
            pages: Word)
    : Boolean;

where

pages   Holds the number of raw pages to allocate

Prepare EMM for warm boot

Figure 4-35 presents the source code listing to EMS5C.ASM.

4-35 The source code listing to EMS5C.ASM.

```
;*******************************************************
;***                                                ***
;***    EMS5C.ASM                                   ***
;***                                                ***
;***    function        EMS_Ems.prepEmmWarmBoot40   ***
;***                        : Boolean;              ***
;***                                                ***
;***    Prep EMM for warm boot process             ***
;***                                                ***
;***    Returns 0 if no error or an error code.     ***
;***                                                ***
;***                                                ***
;***                                                ***
;***
```

4-35 Continued.

```
;***     (Ems Version 4.0)                                              ***
;*******************************************************************
        .model  large,pascal

        include emsdefs.asm

        extrn    errno:WORD
;
;   Define entry point
;
        public  EMS_Ems@prepEmmWarmBoot40

        .code
EMS_Ems@prepEmmWarmBoot40 proc  self:DWord

        mov     ax,PrepEmmWarmBoot40    ; Do the EMS call
        int     Ems

        or      ah,ah                   ; Set flags
        jnz     error

        xor     ax,ax                   ; Return OK
        ret

error:
        mov     al,ah                   ; AL gets error code
        xor     ah,ah                   ; Zero extend
        mov     errno,ax                ; Save in errno too
        ret

EMS_Ems@prepEmmWarmBoot40 endp          ; End of procedure

        end                             ; End of source file
```

The EMS__Ems.prepEmmWarmBoot40(...) function prepares the EMM for an impending warm boot process.

Function EMS__Ems.prepEmmWarmBoot40(...)
function EMS__Ems.prepEmmWarmBoot40
    : Boolean;

EMS 4.0 operating-system-only functions

Table 4-1 lists the EMS 4.0 functions intended only for use by the operating system. These functions may be disabled at any time by the operating system. Using them in your programs is not recommended.

Table 4-1   The EMS 4.0 OS-only function list.

Funct.	Sub.	Description
5B	00	Getting alternate map registers
5B	01	Setting alternate map registers
5B	02	Getting size of alternate map save area
5B	03	Allocating alternate map register set
5B	04	Deallocating alternate map register set
5B	05	Allocating DMA register set
5B	06	Enabling DMA on alternate map register set
5B	07	Disabling DMA on alternate map register set
5B	08	Deallocating DMA register set
5D	00	Enabling EMM operating system functions
5D	01	Disabling EMM operating system functions
5D	02	Releasing access key

Summary

Chapter 4 presented the EMS 4.0 functions that can greatly enhance your use of EMS memory in your programs. If your program is intended for commercial use, it might make sense to stick to EMS 3.0 supported functions. Although many computers do support the EMS 4.0 standard, not every computer that supports EMS conforms to the EMS 4.0 standard.

If your program is intended for an in-house application that supports the EMS 4.0 standard, then it certainly makes sense to use the functions presented in this chapter if they will make your programming task easier.

5
Extended Memory
Specification (XMS) v2.0

One of the early failings for programmers attempting to use extended memory (memory addressed above 1M) was the lack of a standard. In the summer of 1988 Microsoft Corporation, Lotus Development Corporation, Intel Corporation, and AST Research Inc. jointly agreed upon the XMS programming standard. This programming standard provided a series of predefined functions which permit orderly usage of extended memory.

Let's take a look at the basic vocabulary that will be used in this chapter:

Extended Memory Memory in 80286 (386, 486, etc...) computers addressed above the 1M boundary.

High Memory Area (HMA)   The first 64K of extended memory. HMA is unique because code can be located in it and may be executed while the computer is running in real mode. HMA really starts at address $FFFF:$0010.

Upper Memory Block (UMB)   Blocks of memory available between the 640K and 1M addresses. The availability of UMBs depends on the hardware adapter cards installed in the computer.

Extended Memory Blocks (EMB)   Blocks of memory located above the HMA that may only be used for data storage.

A20 Line   The 21st address line of the 80x86 family of microprocessors. Enabling the A20 allows access to the HMA memory area in real mode.

Extended Memory Manager (XMM)   A DOS device driver that allows for the management of Extended Memory.

Here are some comments concerning the overall design of the XMS interface code. Note that there is a function named XMS__Xms.init. This function initializes XMS. It should be used to determine if XMS is in fact available for use by your program. If you do not initialize XMS and make a call to an XMS function, the function will return an error.

Errors are flagged by returning True. If a function takes an error, the error code can be determined by examining the global variable errno, defined in __GLOBALS.PAS. Mnemonics for the error codes are defined in __XMS.PAS. If you want to get the message associated with an error code, XMS__Xms.errorText(errno) will return a string with the message.

The first part of this chapter provides a series of heavily commented demonstration programs clearly showing how to use the XMS interface. Feel free to use these demonstration programs as stepping-stones in your programs' use of Extended Memory.

The second part of this chapter provides the source for the XMS management functions. These functions will provide a solid foundation for your using XMS in your programs.

XMS 2.0 demonstration programs

Figure 5-1 presents the source code listing to PROG5-1.PAS, which demonstrates this task:

- initializing the XMS interface

5-1 The source code listing to PROG5-1.PAS.

```
(* * * * * * * * * * * * * * * * * *
 *
 * prog5-1.pas
 *
 * Test to see if XMS is present
 *
 * * * * * * * * * * * * * * * * * * *)

program prog5_1;

uses
    _Globals,
    _Xms;

var
    xms:            XMS_Xms;
    xmsHandlerAddr: SegOff_type absolute xmsHandler;


begin

    (*
     * Print out the address of the XMS handler before it's
     * initialized.
     *)
```

```
writeln('Before initialization: XMS handler- 0x',
        hex(xmsHandlerAddr.Segment, 4),':0x',
        hex(xmsHandlerAddr.Offset, 4));
(*
 * Attempt to initialize XMS. If there is an error, report it.
 *)
if not xms.init then begin
    writeln('XMS is present');
    end
else begin
    writeln('XMS is not present');
    end;
(*
 * Now print out the address of the XMS handler after it's been
 * initialized.
 *)
writeln('After initialization: XMS handler- 0x',
        hex(xmsHandlerAddr.Segment, 4),':0x',
        hex(xmsHandlerAddr.Offset, 4));
end.
```

Figure 5-2 presents the source code listing to PROG5-2.PAS, which demonstrates the following task:

- reporting the version of the XMS driver

5-2 The source code listing to PROG5-2.PAS.

```
(* * * * * * * * * * * * * * * * * *
 *
 * prog5-2.pas
 *
 * Get XMS Version Number
 *
 * * * * * * * * * * * * * * * * * *)

program prog5_2;

uses
    _Globals,
    _Xms;

type
    SegOff_type - record
        Offset:     Word;
        Segment:    Word;
        end;

var
    xms:                XMS_Xms;
    xmsHandlerAddr: SegOff_type absolute xmsHandler;
    xmsVersion:         Word;
    xmmVersion:         Word;
    hmaFlag:            Word;
```

```
begin
    (*
     *  Print out the address of the XMS handler before it's
     *  initialized.
     *)
    writeln('Before initialization: XMS handler= 0x',
                hex(xmsHandlerAddr.Segment, 4),':0x',
                hex(xmsHandlerAddr.Offset, 4));

    (*
     *  Attempt to initialize XMS. If there is an error, report it.
     *)
    if not xms.init then begin
        writeln('XMS is present');
        end
    else begin
        writeln('XMS is not present');
        end;

    (*
     *  Now print out the address of the XMS handler after it's been
     *  initialized.
     *)
    writeln('After initialization: XMS handler= 0x',
                hex(xmsHandlerAddr.Segment, 4),':0x',
                hex(xmsHandlerAddr.Offset, 4));

    if xms.getVersion(xmsVersion, xmmVersion, hmaFlag) then begin
        xms_demoError('xms.getVersion')
        end;
    write('XMS Version= ', ((xmsVersion div 4096) mod 16):1,
                            ((xmsVersion div 256) mod 16):1, '.',
                            ((xmsVersion div 16) mod 16):1,
                            ((xmsVersion) mod 16):1);
    write(', XMM Version= ', ((xmmVersion div 4096) mod 16):1,
                            ((xmmVersion div 256) mod 16):1, '.',
                            ((xmmVersion div 16) mod 16):1,
                            ((xmmVersion) mod 16):1);
    write(', HMA is ');
    if hmaFlag <> 0 then begin
        writeln('present')
        end
    else begin
        writeln('not present')
        end;

end.
```

Figure 5-3 presents the source code listing to PROG5-3.PAS, which demonstrates the following tasks:

- getting the amount of free XMS
- allocating XMS for program use
- freeing previously allocated XMS memory for other purposes

The source code listing to PROG5-3.PAS.

```
(* * * * * * * * * * * * * * * * * * *
 *
 * prog5-3.pas
 *
 * Get amount of free XMS
 *
 * * * * * * * * * * * * * * * * * * * *)


program prog5_3;


uses
    _Globals,
    _Xms;


var
    xms:            XMS_Xms;
    totalFree:      Word;
    largestFree:    Word;
    handle1:        XMS_XmBlk;
    handle2:        XMS_XmBlk;


begin
    (*
     *  Attempt to initialize XMS. If there is an error, report it.
     *)
    if xms.init then begin
        writeln('XMS is not present');
        end;

    (*
     *  Print header:
     *)
    writeln('                                              Total        Largest Block');
    writeln('══════════════════════════════════════════════╤════════════╤═══════════╗');
    (*
     *  Report the free memory available:
     *)
    if xms.getFreeXM(totalFree, largestFree) then begin
        xms_demoError('XMS_Xms.getFreeXM');
        end;

    writeln('After initialization             |        ',
            totalFree:4,
            ' KB      |        ',
            largestFree:4,
            ' KB      |');
    writeln('─────────────────────────────────┼────────────┼───────────┤');
    (*
     *  Now allocate 16KB and note the change:
     *)
    if handle1.allocXM(16) then begin
        xms_demoError('XMS_XmsBlk.allocXM');
        end;
```

```
if xms.getFreeXM(totalFree, largestFree) then begin
    xms_demoError('XMS_Xms.getFreeXM');
    end;

writeln('After 16 KB allocate        |    ',
        totalFree:4,
        ' KB       |    ',
        largestFree:4,
        ' KB    |');
writeln('-------------------------------+-----------------+----------------|');

(*
 *  Now allocate another 32KB and note the change:
 *)
if handle2.allocXM(32) then begin
    xms_demoError('XMS_XmsBlk.allocXM');
    end;

if xms.getFreeXM(totalFree, largestFree) then begin
    xms_demoError('XMS_Xms.getFreeXM');
    end;

writeln('After 32 KB allocate        |    ',
        totalFree:4,
        ' KB      |    ',
        largestFree:4,
        ' KB    |');
writeln('-------------------------------+-----------------+----------------|');

(*
 *  Now free the FIRST block and see what happens:
 *)
if handle1.freeXM then begin
    xms_demoError('XMS_XmsBlk.freeXM');
    end;

if xms.getFreeXM(totalFree, largestFree) then begin
    xms_demoError('XMS_Xms.getFreeXM');
    end;

writeln('After free of 16 KB block   |    ',
        totalFree:4,
        ' KB       |    ',
        largestFree:4,
        ' KB   |');
writeln('-------------------------------+-----------------+----------------|');

(*
 *  Now free second block of 32KB
 *)
if handle2.freeXM then begin
    xms_demoError('XMS_XmsBlk.freeXM');
    end;
if xms.getFreeXM(totalFree, largestFree) then begin
    xms_demoError('XMS_Xms.getFreeXM');
    end;
writeln('After free of 32 KB block   |    ',
        totalFree:4,
        ' KB      |    ',
        largestFree:4,
        ' KB    |');
```

```
writeln('════════════════════╧════════════════╧════════════════╝');

    (*
    *  Now attempt to free the handles again. We expect errors.
    *)
    if handle1.freeXM then begin
        writeln('XMS_XmsBlk.freeXM() of already freed handle gives "',
                    xms.errorText(errno), '"');
        end;
    if handle2.freeXM then begin
        writeln('XMS_XmsBlk.freeXM() of already freed handle gives "',
                    xms.errorText(errno), '"');
        end;


end.
```

Figure 5-4 presents the source code listing to PROG5-4.PAS, which demonstrates the following task:

- transferring data to and from XMS

5-4 The source code listing to PROG5-4.PAS.

```
(* * * * * * * * * * * * * * * * * *
 *
 *  prog5-4.pas
 *
 *  Demonstrates use of move to/from eXtended Memory
 *
 * * * * * * * * * * * * * * * * * * *)


program prog5_4;

uses
    _Globals,
    _Xms;

var
    xms:            XMS_Xms;

    handle1:        XMS_XmBlk;
    handle2:        XMS_XmBlk;
    handle3:        XMS_XmBlk;
    handle4:        XMS_XmBlk;

    movePacket:     XMS_MovePacket;

    text:           String;
    buff:           String;
```

```
begin
    (*
     *  Attempt to initialize XMS. If there is an error, report it.
     *)
    if xms.init then begin
        writeln('XMS is not present');
        end;

    (*
     *  Now allocate 4 1K blocks:
     *)
    if handle1.allocXM(1) then begin
        xms_demoError('XMS_XmsBlk.allocXM');
        end;
    if handle2.allocXM(1) then begin
        xms_demoError('XMS_XmsBlk.allocXM');
        end;
    if handle3.allocXM(1) then begin
        xms_demoError('XMS_XmsBlk.allocXM');
        end;
    if handle4.allocXM(1) then begin
        xms_demoError('XMS_XmsBlk.allocXM');
        end;

    (*
     *  Now let's copy some text into various places in the
     *  XM blocks, and then copy it back and print it out.
     *)

    (*
     *  Set up a pointer to a string:
     *)
    text:= 'Fourscore and seven years ago our fathers brought forth ';

    (*
     *  Set up the move packet. Note that we round the length
     *  up to an even number. The call requires an even length
     *  transfer.
     *)
    movePacket.length:= even(Ord(text[0])+1);{ +1 for terminator      }
    movePacket.srcHandle:= 0;                { indicates real memory   }
    movePacket.srcOffset:= DWord(@Text);     { actual segment:offset   }
    movePacket.destHandle:= handle1.handle;  { 1st 1K block            }
    movePacket.destOffset:= 42;              { A random offset into block }

    (*
     *  Do the actual XMS call:
     *)
    if xms.moveXM(movePacket) then begin
        xms_demoError('XMS_Xms.moveXM');
        end;

    (*
     *  Now put the next string into the next XM block:
     *)
    text:= 'on this continent a'#13#10'new nation, ';
```

```
movePacket.length:- even(Ord(text[0])+1);{ +1 for terminator        }
movePacket.srcHandle:- 0;                 { indicates real memory     }
movePacket.srcOffset:- DWord(@Text);      { actual segment:offset     }
movePacket.destHandle:- handle2.handle;   { 2nd 1K block              }
movePacket.destOffset:- 911;              { A random offset into block }

if xms.moveXM(movePacket) then begin
    xms_demoError('XMS_Xms.moveXM');
    end;

(*
 *  And something for the third block:
 *)
text:- 'conceived in liberty and dedicated to the proposition ';

movePacket.length:- even(Ord(text[0])+1);{ +1 for terminator        }
movePacket.srcHandle:- 0;                 { indicates real memory     }
movePacket.srcOffset:- DWord(@Text);      { actual segment:offset     }
movePacket.destHandle:- handle3.handle;   { 3rd 1K block              }
movePacket.destOffset:- 800;              { A random offset into block }

if xms.moveXM(movePacket) then begin
    xms_demoError('XMS_Xms.moveXM');
    end;

(*
 *  Now the fourth and last block:
 *)
text:- 'that all'#13#10'men are created equal.'#13#10'';

movePacket.length:- even(Ord(text[0])+1);{ +1 for terminator        }
movePacket.srcHandle:- 0;                 { indicates real memory     }
movePacket.srcOffset:- DWord(@Text);      { actual segment:offset     }
movePacket.destHandle:- handle4.handle;   { 4th 1K block              }
movePacket.destOffset:- 212;              { A random offset into block }

if xms.moveXM(movePacket) then begin
    xms_demoError('XMS_Xms.moveXM');
    end;

(*
 *  Now we've copied four strings into XM blocks.
 *      Block 1 at offset 42,
 *      Block 2 at offset 911,
 *      Block 3 at offset 800,
 *      Block 4 at offset 212.
 *
 *  Now let's retrieve them and print them out.
 *)
movePacket.length:- 96;                   { Length of buffer          }
movePacket.srcHandle:- handle1.handle;    { 1st block                 }
movePacket.srcOffset:- 42;                { offset                    }
movePacket.destHandle:- 0;                { real memory               }
movePacket.destOffset:- DWord(@buff);     { real address              }

if xms.moveXM(movePacket) then begin
    xms_demoError('XMS_Xms.moveXM');
    end;

write(buff);
```

5-4 Continued.

```
(*
 *   Now pick up the second piece:
 *)
movePacket.length:- 96;                      { Length of buffer           }
movePacket.srcHandle:- handle2.handle;       { 2nd block                  }
movePacket.srcOffset:- 911;                  { offset                     }
movePacket.destHandle:- 0;                   { real memory                }
movePacket.destOffset:- DWord(@buff);        { real address               }

if xms.moveXM(movePacket) then begin
    xms_demoError('XMS_Xms.moveXM');
    end;

write(buff);

(*
 *   Now pick up the third piece:
 *)
movePacket.length:- 96;                      { Length of buffer           }
movePacket.srcHandle:- handle3.handle;       { 3rd block                  }
movePacket.srcOffset:- 800;                  { offset                     }
movePacket.destHandle:- 0;                   { real memory                }
movePacket.destOffset:- DWord(@buff);        { real address               }

if xms.moveXM(movePacket) then begin
    xms_demoError('XMS_Xms.moveXM');
    end;

write(buff);

(*
 *   Now pick up the fourth piece:
 *)
movePacket.length:- 96;                      { Length of buffer           }
movePacket.srcHandle:- handle4.handle;       { 4th block                  }
movePacket.srcOffset:- 212;                  { offset                     }
movePacket.destHandle:- 0;                   { real memory                }
movePacket.destOffset:- DWord(@buff);        { real address               }

if xms.moveXM(movePacket) then begin
    xms_demoError('XMS_Xms.moveXM');
    end;

write(buff);

(*
 *   Finally, free up the blocks:
 *)
if handle1.freeXM then begin
    xms_demoError('XMS_XmsBlk.freeXM');
    end;
if handle2.freeXM then begin
    xms_demoError('XMS_XmsBlk.freeXM');
    end;
if handle3.freeXM then begin
    xms_demoError('XMS_XmsBlk.freeXM');
    end;
if handle4.freeXM then begin
    xms_demoError('XMS_XmsBlk.freeXM');
    end;

end.
```

Figure 5-5 presents the source code listing to PROG5-5.PAS, which demonstrates the following tasks:

- securing the HMA
- getting the A20 state
- enabling A20
- disabling A20
- accessing the HMA

5-5 The source code listing to PROG5-5.PAS.

```
(* * * * * * * * * * * * * * * * * *
 *
 * prog5-5.pas
 *
 *   Demonstrates use of the HMA
 *
 * * * * * * * * * * * * * * * * * * *)


program prog5_5;

uses
    _Globals,
    _Xms;

var
    xms:          XMS_Xms;
    text:         ^String;
    a20State:     Word;

    (*
     *   Set up the HMA. It's address is $FFFF:$10.
     *   Note that ($FFFF shl 4) + $10 - 0xFFFF0 + 0x10 - 0x100000.
     *)
    hma:          array[0..$FFEF] of char absolute $FFFF:$10;

begin

    (*
     *   Attempt to initialize XMS. If there is an error, report it.
     *)
    if xms.init then begin
        writeln('XMS is not present');
        end;


    (*
     *   Now try to allocate the HMA
     *)
    if xms.allocHMA($FFFF) then begin
        xms_demoError('XMS_Xms.allocHMA');
        end;
```

```
(*
 *  Now that we've got the HMA, we need to enable the A20
 *  line so that addresses won't wrap.
 *)
if xms.globEnabA20 then begin
    xms_demoError('XMS_Xms.globEnabA20');
    end;

(*
 *  Now let's copy some text into various places in the
 *  HMA, and then copy it back and print it out.
 *)
text:= @hma[0];
text^:= 'Oh say can you see by the dawn''s early light'#13#10;
StrPtr(@hma[100])^:= '  What so proudly we hailed at the twilight''s
last gleaming ?'#13#10;
StrPtr(@hma[200])^:= 'Whose broad stripes and bright stars ';
StrPtr(@hma[300])^:= 'through the perilous fight'#13#10;
StrPtr(@hma[400])^:= '  O''er the ramparts we watched were so gallantly
streaming ?'#13#10;

(*
 *  Query and print out the A20 state (we know it's enabled):
 *)
if xms.getA20State(a20State) then begin
    xms_demoError('XMS_Xms.getA20State');
    end;

write('===============================A20=');
if a20State <> 0 then begin
    writeln('Enabled=================================');
    end
else begin
    writeln('Disabled================================');
    end;

(*
 *  Now print the stuff right out of the HMA
 *)
write(StrPtr(@hma[0])^);
write(StrPtr(@hma[100])^);
write(StrPtr(@hma[200])^);
write(StrPtr(@hma[300])^);
write(StrPtr(@hma[400])^);

(*
 *  Disable the A20 line.
 *)
if xms.globDisabA20 then begin
    xms_demoError('XMS_Xms.globDisabA20');
    end;

(*
 *  Now note the garbage the same code will produce without
 *  the A20 line enabled. This will be looking at addresses
 *  0:0, 0:100, etc. instead of 10000:0, 10000:100, etc.
 *)

if xms.getA20State(a20State) then begin
    xms_demoError('XMS_Xms.getA20State');
    end;
```

```
write('━━━━━━━━━━━━━━━━━━━━━━A20=');
if a20State <> 0 then begin
    writeln('Enabled━━━━━━━━━━━━━━━━━━━━━');
    end
else begin
    writeln('Disabled━━━━━━━━━━━━━━━━━━━━');
    end;

(*
 *  Now print the stuff right out of the HMA
 *)
write(StrPtr(@hma[0])^);
write(StrPtr(@hma[100])^);
write(StrPtr(@hma[200])^);
write(StrPtr(@hma[300])^);
write(StrPtr(@hma[400])^);

(*
 *  Free up the HMA
 *)
if xms.freeHMA then begin
    xms_demoError('XMS_Xms.freeHMA');
    end;

end.
```

Figure 5-6 presents the source code listing to PROG5-6.PAS, which demonstrates the following tasks:

- Locking and unlocking XMS blocks
- Moving data to and from XMS via the Raw move

5-6 The source code listing to PROG5-6.PAS.

```
(* * * * * * * * * * * * * * * * * *
 *
 * prog5-6.pas
 *
 * Demonstrates use of move to/from eXtended Memory using raw move.
 *
 * * * * * * * * * * * * * * * * * * * * * *)

program prog5_6;

uses
    _Globals,
    _Xms;

var
    xms:            XMS_Xms;

    handle1:        XMS_XmBlk;
    handle2:        XMS_XmBlk;
    handle3:        XMS_XmBlk;
    handle4:        XMS_XmBlk;
```

```
    physAddr1:      DWord;
    physAddr2:      DWord;
    physAddr3:      DWord;
    physAddr4:      DWord;

    movePacket:     XMS_MovePacket;

    text:           String;
    buff:           String;


begin
    (*
     *  Attempt to initialize XMS. If there is an error, report it.
     *)
    if xms.init then begin
        writeln('XMS is not present');
        end;

    (*
     *  Now allocate 4 1K blocks:
     *)
    if handle1.allocXM(1) then begin
        xms_demoError('XMS_XmsBlk.allocXM');
        end;
    if handle2.allocXM(1) then begin
        xms_demoError('XMS_XmsBlk.allocXM');
        end;
    if handle3.allocXM(1) then begin
        xms_demoError('XMS_XmsBlk.allocXM');
        end;
    if handle4.allocXM(1) then begin
        xms_demoError('XMS_XmsBlk.allocXM');
        end;


    (*
     *  Now let's lock the blocks, getting their physical addresses
     *  so we can do some raw moves to and from them.
     *)
    if handle1.lockXM(physAddr1) then begin
        xms_demoError('XMS_XmBlk.lockXM');
        end;
    if handle2.lockXM(physAddr2) then begin
        xms_demoError('XMS_XmBlk.lockXM');
        end;
    if handle3.lockXM(physAddr3) then begin
        xms_demoError('XMS_XmBlk.lockXM');
        end;
    if handle4.lockXM(physAddr4) then begin
        xms_demoError('XMS_XmBlk.lockXM');
        end;

    (*
     *  Now let's copy some text into various places in the
     *  XM blocks, and then copy it back and print it out.
     *)
```

5-6 Continued.

```
(*
 *  Set up a pointer to a string:
 *)
text:- 'Fourscore and seven years ago our fathers brought forth ';

(*
 *  Do the raw move. Note that the length must be an
 *  even number of bytes.
 *)
if xms.rawMove(physAddr1+42,
               segOffToPhys(@text),
               even(Ord(text[0])+1)) then begin
    xms_demoError('XMS_Xms.rawMove');
    end;

(*
 *  Now put the next string into the next XM block:
 *)
text:- 'on this continent a'#13#10'new nation, ';
if xms.rawMove(physAddr1+911,
               segOffToPhys(@text),
               even(Ord(text[0])+1)) then begin
    xms_demoError('XMS_Xms.rawMove');
    end;

(*
 *  And something for the third block:
 *)
text:- 'conceived in liberty and dedicated to the proposition ';
if xms.rawMove(physAddr1+800,
               segOffToPhys(@text),
               even(Ord(text[0])+1)) then begin
    xms_demoError('XMS_Xms.rawMove');
    end;

(*
 *  Now the fourth and last block:
 *)
text:- 'that all'#13#10'men are created equal.'#13#10;
if xms.rawMove(physAddr1+212,
               segOffToPhys(@text),
               even(Ord(text[0])+1)) then begin
    xms_demoError('XMS_Xms.rawMove');
    end;

(*
 *  Now we've copied four strings into XM blocks.
 *      Block 1 at offset 42,
 *      Block 2 at offset 911,
 *      Block 3 at offset 800,
 *      Block 4 at offset 212.
 *
 *  Now let's retrieve them and print them out.
 *)
if xms.rawMove(segOffToPhys(@buff),
               physAddr1+42,
               256) then begin
    xms_demoError('XMS_Xms.rawMove');
    end;
```

```
write(buff);


(*
 *   Now pick up the second piece:
 *)
if xms.rawMove(segOffToPhys(@buff),
               physAddr1+911,
               256) then begin
    xms_demoError('XMS_Xms.rawMove');
    end;

write(buff);


(*
 *   Now pick up the third piece:
 *)
if xms.rawMove(segOffToPhys(@buff),
               physAddr1+800,
               256) then begin
    xms_demoError('XMS_Xms.rawMove');
    end;

write(buff);


(*
 *   Now pick up the fourth piece:
 *)
if xms.rawMove(segOffToPhys(@buff),
               physAddr1+212,
               256) then begin
    xms_demoError('XMS_Xms.rawMove');
    end;

write(buff);


(*
 *   Now unlock the blocks.
 *)
if handle1.unlockXM then begin
    xms_demoError('XMS_XmBlk.unlockXM');
    end;
if handle2.unlockXM then begin
    xms_demoError('XMS_XmBlk.unlockXM');
    end;
if handle3.unlockXM then begin
    xms_demoError('XMS_XmBlk.unlockXM');
    end;
if handle4.unlockXM then begin
    xms_demoError('XMS_XmBlk.unlockXM');
    end;

(*
 *   Finally, free up the blocks:
 *)
if handle1.freeXM then begin
    xms_demoError('XMS_XmsBlk.freeXM');
    end;
```

```
    if handle2.freeXM then begin
        xms_demoError('XMS_XmsBlk.freeXM');
        end;
    if handle3.freeXM then begin
        xms_demoError('XMS_XmsBlk.freeXM');
        end;
    if handle4.freeXM then begin
        xms_demoError('XMS_XmsBlk.freeXM');
        end;
end.
```

Figure 5-7 presents the source code listing to PROG5-7.PAS, which demonstrates the following tasks:

- allocating and freeing Upper Memory
- moving data to and from Upper Memory

5-7 The source code listing to PROG5-7.PAS.

```
(* * * * * * * * * * * * * * * * * * *
 *
 * prog5-7.pas
 *
 * Demonstrates use of move to/from Upper Memory
 *
 * * * * * * * * * * * * * * * * * * * * *)

program prog5_7;

uses
    _Globals,
    _Xms;

var
    xms:            XMS_Xms;

    movePacket:     XMS_MovePacket;

    text:           String;
    block1:         ^String;
    block2:         ^String;
    block3:         ^String;
    block4:         ^String;
    block5:         ^String;

    actualSize:     Word;

begin
    (*
     * Attempt to initialize XMS. If there is an error, report it.
     *)
    if xms.init then begin
        writeln('XMS is not present');
        end;
```

```
(*
 *   Now allocate 5 128 byte blocks of Upper Memory
 *)
if xms.allocUM(8, Pointer(block1), actualSize) then begin
    writeln('    Biggest block available was ',
                actualSize * 16, ' bytes');
    xms_demoError('XMS_Xms.allocUM');
    end;
if xms.allocUM(8, Pointer(block2), actualSize) then begin
    writeln('    Biggest block available was ',
                actualSize * 16, ' bytes');
    xms_demoError('XMS_Xms.allocUM');
    end;
if xms.allocUM(8, Pointer(block3), actualSize) then begin
    writeln('    Biggest block available was ',
                actualSize * 16, ' bytes');
    xms_demoError('XMS_Xms.allocUM');
    end;
if xms.allocUM(8, Pointer(block4), actualSize) then begin
    writeln('    Biggest block available was ',
                actualSize * 16, ' bytes');
    xms_demoError('XMS_Xms.allocUM');
    end;
if xms.allocUM(8, Pointer(block5), actualSize) then begin
    writeln('    Biggest block available was ',
                actualSize * 16, ' bytes');
    xms_demoError('XMS_Xms.allocUM');
    end;

(*
 *   Now let's copy some text into various places in the
 *   UM blocks, and then copy it back and print it out.
 *)

(*
 *   Copy the text:
 *)
    block1^:-
'We the people of the United States, in order to form a more perfect
Union,'#13#10;

(*
 *   Now put the next string into the next UM block:
 *)
    block2^:-
'establish justice, ensure domestic tranquility, provide for the com-
mon'#13#10;

(*
 *   And something for the the third block:
 *)
    block3^:-
'defense, promote the general welfare, and secure the blessings of liber-
ty'#13#10;

(*
 *   Now the fourth block:
 *)
    block4^:-
'to ourselves and our posterity do ordain and establish this
Constitution'#13#10;
```

5-7 Continued.

```
      (*
       *  And the fifth and final block:
       *)
      block5^:= 'for the United States of America.'#13#10;

      (*
       *  Now we've copied five strings into UM blocks.
       *
       *  Let's retrieve them and print them out.
       *)
      write(block1^);
      write(block2^);
      write(block3^);
      write(block4^);
      write(block5^);

      (*
       *  Free up the blocks of memory.
       *)
      if xms.freeUM(block1) then begin
         xms_demoError('XMS_Xms.freeUM');
         end;
      if xms.freeUM(block2) then begin
         xms_demoError('XMS_Xms.freeUM');
         end;
      if xms.freeUM(block3) then begin
         xms_demoError('XMS_Xms.freeUM');
         end;
      if xms.freeUM(block4) then begin
         xms_demoError('XMS_Xms.freeUM');
         end;
      if xms.freeUM(block5) then begin
         xms_demoError('XMS_Xms.freeUM');
         end;

end.
```

Figure 5-8 presents the source code listing to PROG5-8.PAS, which demonstrates the following tasks:

- resizing of XMS blocks

5-8 The source code listing to PROG5-8.PAS.

```
(* * * * * * * * * * * * * * * * * *
 *
 *  prog5-8.pas
 *
 *  Demonstrates resizing blocks and getting block info
 *
 * * * * * * * * * * * * * * * * * *)

program prog5_8;
```

5-8 Continued.

```
uses
    _Globals,
    _Xms;

var
    xms:            XMS_Xms;

    lockCount:      Word;
    numFreeHandles: Word;
    blockSize:      Word;

    handle1:        XMS_XmBlk;
    handle2:        XMS_XmBlk;
    handle3:        XMS_XmBlk;

    physAddr1:      DWord;
    physAddr2:      DWord;
    physAddr3:      DWord;


begin
    (*
     *  Attempt to initialize XMS. If there is an error, report it.
     *)
    if xms.init then begin
        writeln('XMS is not present');
        end;


    (*
     *  Print header:
     *)
    writeln(
                              Address     Size (bytes)  Locks');
    writeln(
    ==================================================           ');

    (*
     *  Allocate three blocks:
     *)
    if handle1.allocXM(16) then begin
        xms_demoError('XMS_XmBlk.allocXM');
        end;
    if handle2.allocXM(16) then begin
        xms_demoError('XMS_XmBlk.allocXM');
        end;
    if handle3.allocXM(16) then begin
        xms_demoError('XMS_XmBlk.allocXM');
        end;

    (*
     *  Now lock 'em and get their physical addresses.
     *)
    if handle1.lockXM(physAddr1) then begin
        xms_demoError('xms_lockXM');
        end;
    if handle2.lockXM(physAddr2) then begin
        xms_demoError('xms_lockXM');
        end;
```

```
if handle3.lockXM(physAddr3) then begin
    xms_demoError('xms_lockXM');
    end;

(*
 *  Now one by one get info on them:
 *)
if handle1.getHandInfo(blockSize, numFreeHandles, lockCount) then begin
    xms_demoError('xms_getHandInfo');
    end;
writeln('After allocation:  block 1 |   0x',
        hex(physAddr1, 6),
        '   |      0x',
        hex(blockSize*1024, 6),
        '   |    ',
        lockCount:3,
        ' |');

writeln(
                        ———————————+—————————+————————+|');

if handle2.getHandInfo(blockSize, numFreeHandles, lockCount) then begin
    xms_demoError('xms_getHandInfo');
    end;
writeln('                   block 2 |   0x',
        hex(physAddr2, 6),
        '   |      0x',
        hex(blockSize*1024, 6),
        '   |    ',
        lockCount:3,
        ' |');

writeln(
                        ———————————+—————————+————————+|');

if handle3.getHandInfo(blockSize, numFreeHandles, lockCount) then begin
    xms_demoError('xms_getHandInfo');
    end;
writeln('                   block 3 |   0x',
        hex(physAddr3, 6),
        '   |      0x',
        hex(blockSize*1024, 6),
        '   |    ',
        lockCount:3,
        ' |');

writeln(
=======================+—————————+————————+|');

(*
 *  Now let's resize the middle block and see what happens.
 *  First, however, we want to unlock all of the blocks so
 *  that they can move as necessary.
 *)
if handle1.unlockXM then begin
    xms_demoError('xms_unlockXM');
    end;
if handle2.unlockXM then begin
    xms_demoError('xms_unlockXM');
    end;
```

```
if handle3.unlockXM then begin
    xms_demoError('xms_unlockXM');
    end;

(*
 *  Do the resize:
 *)
if handle2.resizeXM(32) then begin
    xms_demoError('xms_resizeXM');
    end;

(*
 *  Lock them all again.
 *)
if handle1.lockXM(physAddr1) then begin
    xms_demoError('xms_lockXM');
    end;
if handle2.lockXM(physAddr2) then begin
    xms_demoError('xms_lockXM');
    end;
if handle3.lockXM(physAddr3) then begin
    xms_demoError('xms_lockXM');
    end;

(*
 *  Now report on the new situation.
 *)
if handle1.getHandInfo(blockSize, numFreeHandles, lockCount) then begin
    xms_demoError('xms_getHandInfo');
    end;
writeln('After allocation:  block 1 |   0x',
        hex(physAddr1, 6),
        '     |    0x',
        hex(blockSize*1024, 6),
        '    |   ',
        lockCount:3,
        '  |');

writeln('                   -------------+-------------------+-----------|');

if handle2.getHandInfo(blockSize, numFreeHandles, lockCount) then begin
    xms_demoError('xms_getHandInfo');
    end;
writeln('                   block 2 |   0x',
        hex(physAddr2, 6),
        '     |    0x',
        hex(blockSize*1024, 6),
        '    |   ',
        lockCount:3,
        '  |');

writeln('                   -------------+-------------------+-----------|');

if handle3.getHandInfo(blockSize, numFreeHandles, lockCount) then begin
    xms_demoError('xms_getHandInfo');
    end;
writeln('                   block 3 |   0x',
        hex(physAddr3, 6),
        '     |    0x',
```

5-8 Continued.

```
            hex(blockSize*1024, 6),
            '   |   ',
            lockCount:3,
            '  |');
   writeln(
'                                                                    |');
   (*
    *  Unlock the blocks:
    *)
   if handle1.unlockXM then begin
      xms_demoError('xms_unlockXM');
      end;
   if handle2.unlockXM then begin
      xms_demoError('xms_unlockXM');
      end;
   if handle3.unlockXM then begin
      xms_demoError('xms_unlockXM');
      end;

   (*
    *  And free them
    *)
   if handle1.freeXM then begin
      xms_demoError('XMS_XmsBlk.freeXM');
      end;
   if handle2.freeXM then begin
      xms_demoError('XMS_XmsBlk.freeXM');
      end;
   if handle3.freeXM then begin
      xms_demoError('XMS_XmsBlk.freeXM');
      end;

end.
```

XMS-related function prototypes, macros, and error defines

Figure 5-9 presents the source code listing to __XMS.PAS.

This file contains the function prototypes, definitions, and error code definitions for your XMS unit.

5-9 The source code listing to __XMS.PAS.

```
(* * * * * * * * * * * * * * * * *
 *
 *  _xms.pas
 *
 *  XMS related definitions,
 *  structures and function prototypes
 *
 * * * * * * * * * * * * * * * * * * *)
```

5-9 Continued.

```
unit    _Xms;

interface

uses    _Globals;

const
    {*
     *  Define the XMS page size
     *}
    XMS_PAGE_SIZE=      1024;

    {*
     *  Define the XMS error codes.
     *}
    XMSErrOK=           $00;    { No Error }
    XMSErrUnimp=        $80;    { Unimplemented function }
    XMSErrVDISK=        $81;    { VDISK device detected }
    XMSErrA20=          $82;    { A20 error }
    XMSErrNoHMA=        $90;    { HMA does not exist }
    XMSErrHMAInUse=     $91;    { HMA already in use }
    XMSErrHMAMin=       $92;    { HMA space req. < /HMAMIN= parameter }
    XMSErrHMANotAll=    $93;    { HMA not allocated }
    XMSErrA20Enab=      $94;    { A20 still enabled }
    XMSErrNoXMLeft=     $0A0;   { All XM allocated }
    XMSErrNoHandles=    $0A1;   { All handles are allocated }
    XMSErrHandInv=      $0A2;   { Invalid handle }
    XMSErrSHandInv=     $0A3;   { Invalid Source Handle }
    XMSErrSOffInv=      $0A4;   { Invalid Source Offset }
    XMSErrDHandInv=     $0A5;   { Invalid Dest Handle }
    XMSErrDOffInv=      $0A6;   { Invalid Dest Offset }
    XMSErrLenInv=       $0A7;   { Invalid Length }
    XMSErrOverlap=      $0A8;   { Invalid move overlap }
    XMSErrParity=       $0A9;   { Parity error }
    XMSErrNoLock=       $0AA;   { Handle not locked }
    XMSErrLock=         $0AB;   { Handle Locked }
    XMSErrLockOvflo=    $0AC;   { Lock count overflo }
    XMSErrLockFail=     $0AD;   { Lock fail }
    XMSErrSmUMB=        $0B0;   { Smaller UMB available }
    XMSErrNoUMB=        $0B1;   { No UMBs available }
    XMSErrUMBInv=       $0B2;   { Invalid UMB segment }

 type
    {*
     *  Define a type or two:
     *}

    XMS_MovePacket = record
        length:     DWord;     { length of transfer }
        srcHandle:  Word;      { source handle (0 means < 1M
                                 boundary) }
        srcOffset:  DWord;     { source offset }
        destHandle: Word;      { destination handle (0 means < 1MB) }
        destOffset: DWord;     { destination offset }
        end;
```

5-9 Continued.

```
{*
 * Define the Xms object type.
 *}
XMS_xms = object
    function        init
                        : Boolean;
    function        getVersion(
                        var xmsVersion: Word;
                        var xmmVersion: Word;
                        var hmaFlag:    Word)
                        : Boolean;
    function        rawMove(
                        dest:           DWord;
                        source:         DWord;
                        length:         Word)
                        : Boolean;
    function        moveXM(
                        var packet:     XMS_MovePacket)
                        : Boolean;
    function        allocHMA(
                        hmaBytes:       Word)
                        : Boolean;
    function        freeHMA
                        : Boolean;
    function        globEnabA20
                        : Boolean;
    function        globDisabA20
                        : Boolean;
    function        getA20State(
                        var a20State:   Word)
                        : Boolean;
    function        getFreeXM(
                        var totalFree:  Word;
                        var largestFree:Word)
                        : Boolean;
    function        allocUM(
                        size:           Word;
                        var address:    Pointer;
                        var actualSize: Word)
                        : Boolean;
    function        freeUM(
                        address:        Pointer)
                        : Boolean;

    function        errorText(
                        err:            Word)
                        : String;

    end;


XMS_XmBlk = object
    handle:         Word;

    function        allocXM(
                        blockSize:      Word)
                        : Boolean;
    function        freeXM
                        : Boolean;
    function        lockXM(
                        var physAddr:   DWord)
                        : Boolean;
```

```
        function        unlockXM
                            : Boolean;
        function        getHandInfo(
                            var blockSize:   Word;
                            var handlesLeft:Word;
                            var lockCount:   Word)
                            : Boolean;
        function        resizeXM(
                            newSize:         Word)
                            : Boolean;


        end;

    xmsHandlerType= procedure;

    procedure xms_defaultHandler;

var
    xms:            XMS_Xms;

const
    xmshandler: ^xmsHandlerType= @xms_defaultHandler;

procedure   xms_demoError(funcName: String);



{*
 *  Start the implementation
 *}
implementation


{*
 *  Load in all of the assembly modules:
 *}
{$L XMS00}
{$L XMS01}
{$L XMS02}
{$L XMS03}
{$L XMS04}
{$L XMS07}
{$L XMS08}
{$L XMS09}
{$L XMS0A}
{$L XMS0B}
{$L XMS0C}
{$L XMS0D}
{$L XMS0E}
{$L XMS0F}
{$L XMS10}
{$L XMS11}
{$L XMSINIT}
{$L XMSRAW}

{*
 *  Now define all of the XMS externals:
 *}
function        XMS_Xms.init
                    : Boolean;
                    external;
```

```
function          XMS_Xms.getVersion(
                      var xmsVersion: Word;
                      var xmmVersion: Word;
                      var hmaFlag:    Word)
                      : Boolean;
                      external;
function          XMS_Xms.rawMove(
                      dest:           DWord;
                      source:         DWord;
                      length:         Word)
                      : Boolean;
                      external;
function          XMS_Xms.moveXM(
                      var packet:     XMS_MovePacket)
                      : Boolean;
                      external;
function          XMS_Xms.allocHMA(
                      hmaBytes:       Word)
                      : Boolean;
                      external;
function          XMS_Xms.freeHMA
                      : Boolean;
                      external;
function          XMS_Xms.globEnabA20
                      : Boolean;
                      external;
function          XMS_Xms.globDisabA20
                      : Boolean;
                      external;
function          XMS_Xms.getA20State(
                      var a20State:   Word)
                      : Boolean;
                      external;
function          XMS_Xms.getFreeXM(
                      var totalFree:  Word;
                      var largestFree:Word)
                      : Boolean;
                      external;
function          XMS_Xms.allocUM(
                      size:           Word;
                      var address:    Pointer;
                      var actualSize: Word)
                      : Boolean;
                      external;
function          XMS_Xms.freeUM(
                      address:        Pointer)
                      : Boolean;

                      external;

{*
 *  Now define the XMB externals:
 *}
function          XMS_XmBlk.allocXM(
                      blockSize:      Word)
                      : Boolean;
                      external;
function          XMS_XmBlk.freeXM
                      : Boolean;
                      external;
```

5-9 Continued.

```
function         XMS_XmBlk.lockXM(
                     var physAddr:   DWord)
                     : Boolean;
                     external;
function         XMS_XmBlk.unlockXM
                     : Boolean;
                     external;
function         XMS_XmBlk.getHandInfo(
                     var blockSize:   Word;
                     var handlesLeft:Word;
                     var lockCount:   Word)
                     : Boolean;
                     external;
function         XMS_XmBlk.resizeXM(
                     newSize:         Word)
                     : Boolean;
                     external;

{*
 *   And define the sole Pascal function: errorText
 *}
function         XMS_Xms.errorText(
                     err:             Word)
                     : String;
begin
    case err of
        XMSErrOK:
            errorText:- 'No Error';
        XMSErrUnimp:
            errorText:- 'Unimplemented function';
        XMSErrVDISK:
            errorText:- 'VDISK device detected';
        XMSErrA20:
            errorText:- 'A20 error';
        XMSErrNoHMA:
            errorText:- 'HMA does not exist';
        XMSErrHMAInUse:
            errorText:- 'HMA already in use';
        XMSErrHMAMin:
            errorText:- 'HMA space requested < /HMAMIN- parameter';
        XMSErrHMANotAll:
            errorText:- 'HMA not allocated';
        XMSErrA20Enab:
            errorText:- 'A20 still enabled';
        XMSErrNoXMLeft:
            errorText:- 'All eXtended Memory allocated';
        XMSErrNoHandles:
            errorText:- 'All handles are allocated';
        XMSErrHandInv:
            errorText:- 'Invalid handle';
        XMSErrSHandInv:
            errorText:- 'Invalid Source Handle';
        XMSErrSOffInv:
            errorText:- 'Invalid Source Offset';
        XMSErrDHandInv:
            errorText:- 'Invalid Destination Handle';
        XMSErrDOffInv:
            errorText:- 'Invalid Destination Offset';
        XMSErrLenInv:
            errorText:- 'Invalid Length';
        XMSErrOverlap:
            errorText:- 'Invalid move overlap';
```

5-9 Continued.

```
        XMSErrParity:
            errorText:- 'Parity error';
        XMSErrNoLock:
            errorText:- 'Handle not locked';
        XMSErrLock:
            errorText:- 'Handle Locked';
        XMSErrLockOvflo:
            errorText:- 'Lock count overflo';
        XMSErrLockFail:
            errorText:- 'Lock fail';
        XMSErrSmUMB:
            errorText:- 'Smaller UMB available';
        XMSErrNoUMB:
            errorText:- 'No UMB''s available';
        XMSErrUMBInv:
            errorText:- 'Invalid UMB segment';
        else
            errorText:- 'Unknown error';
        end;
end;

(*
 *  Define xms_demoerr, which is used to report errors in the demo
 *  programs.
 *)
procedure    xms_demoError(funcName: String);
begin

    {*
     *  Report the error:
     *}
    writeln('Error on ', funcName, '(): "',
                xms.errorText(errno), '"');
    Halt;
end;


procedure    xms_defaultHandler; external;

end.
```

The XMS assembly language definition file

Figure 5-10 presents the source code listing to XMSDEFS.ASM. This file contains definitions used by the XMSxx.ASM files.

5-10 The source code listing to XMSDEFS.ASM.

```
;**********************************************
;***                                        ***
;***     XmsDefs.ASM                        ***
;***                                        ***
;***     Contains definitions for XMS routines ***
;***                                        ***
;**********************************************
```

```
;
;    Define the extended function interrupt that gives us the
;    XMS handler address:
;
XFunc          equ      2fh


;
;    Define the function code for XMS, and the two sub-codes:
;
XFuncXMS          equ      43h
XFuncXMSPres      equ      0h
XFuncXMSEntry     equ      10h


;
;    Define the XMSPresent response:
;
XMSPresent        equ      80h


;
;    Now define the 2.0 XMS function codes.
;    These are 8 bit values which are loaded into
;    AH before calling the XMS handler (the address of which
;    was determined using XFuncXMSEntry int).
;
XMSGetVersion     equ      00h
XMSAllocHMA       equ      01h
XMSFreeHMA        equ      02h
XMSGlobEnabA20    equ      03h
XMSGlobDisabA20   equ      04h
XMSLocEnabA20     equ      05h
XMSLocDisabA20    equ      06h
XMSGetA20State    equ      07h
XMSGetFreeXM      equ      08h
XMSAllocXM        equ      09h
XMSFreeXM         equ      0ah
XMSMoveXM         equ      0bh
XMSLockXM         equ      0ch
XMSUnlockXM       equ      0dh
XMSGetHandInfo    equ      0eh
XMSResizeXM       equ      0fh
XMSAllocUM        equ      10h
XMSFreeUM         equ      11h


;
;    Now define the XMS error codes:
;
XMSErrOK          equ      00h     ; No error
XMSErrUnimp       equ      80h     ; Unimplemented function
XMSErrVDISK       equ      81h     ; VDISK device detected
XMSErrA20         equ      82h     ; A20 error
XMSErrNoHMA       equ      90h     ; HMA does not exist
XMSErrHMAInUse    equ      91h     ; HMA already in use
XMSErrHMAMin      equ      92h     ; HMA space req. < /HMAMIN- parameter
XMSErrHMANotAll   equ      93h     ; HMA not allocated
XMSErrA20Enab     equ      94h     ; A20 still enabled
XMSErrNoXMLeft    equ      0A0h    ; All XM allocated
XMSErrNoHandles   equ      0A1h    ; All handles are allocated
XMSErrHandInv     equ      0A2h    ; Invalid handle
XMSErrSHandInv    equ      0A3h    ; Invalid Source Handle
```

```
XMSErrSOffInv     equ      0A4h     ; Invalid Source Offset
XMSErrDHandInv    equ      0A5h     ; Invalid Dest Handle
XMSErrDOffInv     equ      0A6h     ; Invalid Dest Offset
XMSErrLenInv      equ      0A7h     ; Invalid Length
XMSErrOverlap     equ      0A8h     ; Invalid move overlap
XMSErrParity      equ      0A9h     ; Parity error
XMSErrNoLock      equ      0AAh     ; Handle not locked
XMSErrLock        equ      0ABh     ; Handle Locked
XMSErrLockOvflo   equ      0ACh     ; Lock count overflo
XMSErrLockFail    equ      0ADh     ; Lock fail
XMSErrSmUMB       equ      0B0h     ; Smaller UMB available
XMSErrNoUMB       equ      0B1h     ; No UMBs available
XMSErrUMBInv      equ      0B2h     ; Invalid UMB segment


;
;   Define the Bios interrupt and function codes
;
XMSBios           equ      15h

;
;   Define the two function codes
;
XMSBiosXMMove     equ      87h      ; Move a block of XMS
XMSBiosXMSize     equ      88h      ; Get size of extended memory

;
;   Define the access byte
;
XMSBiosAccess     equ      93h      ; The "correct" access byte
```

XMS 2.0 functions

Initialize the XMS interface

Figure 5-11 presents the source code listing to XMSINIT.ASM.

5-11 The source code listing to XMSINIT.ASM.

```
;*********************************************************
;***      XMSINIT.ASM                                 ***
;***                                                  ***
;***      function        XMS_Xms.init                ***
;***                        : Boolean;                ***
;***                                                  ***
;***      Initializes the XMS interface. Returns a zero ***
;***      if interface successfully initialized.      ***
;***                                                  ***
;*********************************************************


;----------------------------------------
;
; Declare memory model and language
;
```

5-11 Continued.

```
        .model  large,pascal

;---------------------------------------
;
; Include xms definition file
;
        include xmsdefs.asm

;---------------------------------------
;
; Declare error WORD as extrn to this
; module
;
        extrn   errno:WORD
        extrn   xmsHandler

;---------------------------------------
;
; Declare function as PUBLIC
;
        public  XMS_Xms@init
        public  xms_defaultHandler

;---------------------------------------
;
; Begin code segment
;
        .code

XMS_Xms@init    proc    self: Far Ptr Word

        mov     ah,XFuncXMS      ; XMS functions
        mov     al,XFuncXMSPres  ; Determine is XMS present
        int     XFunc            ; Call extended functions

        cmp     al,XMSPresent    ; See if it's there
        jne     noXMS            ; Nope, return an error

;
;       It's there, so let's get the handler address:
;
        mov     ah,XFuncXMS      ; XMS functions
        mov     al,XFuncXMSEntry; Get handler entry point
        int     XFunc            ; Call extended functions

        mov     word ptr xmsHandler,bx    ; Handler offset
        mov     word ptr xmsHandler+2,es  ; Handler segment

        mov     ax,XMSErrOK      ; no error
        xor     dx,dx
        ret

noXMS:
        mov     ax,XMSErrUnimp   ; No XMS (Unimplemented function)
        mov     errno,ax         ; Copy to errno
        xor     dx,dx
        ret
```

5-11 Continued.

```
XMS_xms@init    endp              ; end of procedure

;
;   The xms_default_handler is used so that a call to
;   xmsHandler before XMS is initialized will return an
;   error. This is replaced by the actual handler when
;   xms_init is called.
;
xms_defaultHandler      proc

        xor     ax,ax            ; ax to zero means error
        mov     bl,XMSErrUnimp   ; Unimplemented function
        ret

xms_defaultHandler      endp

        end                      ; end of source file
```

Function XMS__Xms.init initializes XMS for use by your program. It should be called before any other XMS library functions are called.

Function XMS__Xms.init

function   XMS__Xms.init
                : Boolean;

Get the XMS version numbers

Figure 5-12 presents the source code listing to XMS00.ASM.

5-12 The source code listing to XMS00.ASM.

```
;****************************************************************
;***    XMS00.ASM                                          ***
;***                                                       ***
;***    function        XMS_Xms.getVersion(                ***
;***                         var xmsVersion: Word;         ***
;***                         var xmmVersion: Word;         ***
;***                         var hmaFlag:    Word)         ***
;***                         : Boolean;                    ***
;***                                                       ***
;***    Returns the version number of the XMS, the XMM,    ***
;***    and indicates whether HMA is available.            ***
;***                                                       ***
;****************************************************************

        .model  large,pascal

        include xmsdefs.asm

        extrn   errno:WORD
        extrn   xmsHandler:DWord
```

5-12 Continued.

```
;
;   Define entry point
;
        public  XMS_Xms@getVersion

        .code
XMS_Xms@getVersion  proc    xmsVer:Far Ptr Word, xmmVer: Far Ptr Word,
HMAFlag: Far Ptr Word, self:DWord
        mov     ah,XMSGetVersion        ; Function code
        call    xmsHandler              ; call the guy

        or      ax,ax                   ; AX=0 means error
        jz      errorReturn

;
;   Save BX, which has the XMM version.
;
        mov     cx,bx

;
;   Now return the values.
;
        les     bx,xmsVer
        mov     es:[bx],ax              ; XMS version returned
        les     bx,xmmVer
        mov     es:[bx],cx              ; XMM version returned
        les     bx,HMAFlag
        mov     es:[bx],dx              ; HMA indicator

        mov     ax,XMSErrOK             ; No error
        ret

errorReturn:
        mov     al,bl                   ; Move error code to AL
        xor     ah,ah                   ; Zero extend to 16 bits
        mov     errno,ax                ; Copy to errno
        ret

XMS_Xms@getVersion  endp                ; End of procedure

        end                             ; End of source file
```

This source file contains the code to function XMS__Xms.getVersion(...). This function returns via WORD pointers a 16-bit BCD number representing the revision of the XMS version and indicates the existence of the HMA.

Function XMS__Xms.getVersion(...)

```
function  XMS__Xms.getVersion(
                  var xmsVersion:  Word;
                  var xmmVersion:  Word;
                  var hmaFlag:     Word)
                  : Boolean;
```

where

xmsVersion   Receives the XMS version number
xmmVersion   Receives the XM manager version number
hmaFlag   Receives a value of 1 if the HMA exists and 0 if the HMA
               does not exist

Allocate the HMA (High Memory Area)

Figure 5-13 presents the source code listing to XMS01.ASM.

5-13 The source code listing to XMS01.ASM.

```
;****************************************************************
;***       XMS01.ASM                                         ***
;***                                                         ***
;***       function          XMS_Xms.allocHMA(              ***
;***                             hmaBytes:      Word)        ***
;***                             : Boolean;                  ***
;***                                                         ***
;***       Allocates the High Memory Area to the program.    ***
;***       HmaBytes specifies the amount of HMA which the    ***
;***       the program intends to use. If it asks for a      ***
;***       sufficient amount, the request will be granted.   ***
;***                                                         ***
;****************************************************************
          .model  large,pascal

          include xmsdefs.asm

          extrn   errno:WORD
          extrn   xmsHandler:DWord
;
;    Define entry point
;
          public  XMS_Xms@allocHMA

          .code

XMS_Xms@allocHMA     proc     hmaBytes:Word, self: DWord

          mov     dx,hmaBytes       ; Amount the app expects to use
          mov     ah,XMSAllocHMA    ; Function code
          call    xmsHandler        ; call the guy

          or      ax,ax             ; AX=0 means error
          jz      errorReturn

          mov     ax,XMSErrOK       ; No error
          ret

errorReturn:
          mov     al,bl             ; Move error code to AL
          xor     ah,ah             ; Zero extend to 16 bits
          mov     errno,ax          ; Copy to errno
          ret

XMS_Xms@allocHMA     endp            ; end of procedure
          end
```

This source file holds the code to function XMS__Xms.allocHMA(...).
This function attempts to reserve a maximum of 0xFFF0 bytes in the
HMA for the calling program.

Function XMS__Xms.allocHMA(...)

```
function    XMS__Xms.allocHMA(
                    hmaBytes:   Word)
                : Boolean;
```

where

> hmaBytes Holds 0xFFFF if caller is application program, number of
> bytes required if caller is TSR

Release the HMA (High Memory Area)

Figure 5-14 presents the source code listing to XMS02.ASM.

5-14 The source code listing to XMS02.ASM.

```
;*****************************************************************
;***      XMS02.ASM                                         ***
;***                                                        ***
;***      function        XMS_Xms.freeHMA                   ***
;***                      : Boolean;                        ***
;***                                                        ***
;***      Frees the High Memory Area.                       ***
;***                                                        ***
;*****************************************************************
;
        .model  large,pascal

        include xmsdefs.asm

        extrn   errno:WORD
        extrn   xmsHandler:DWord

;
;   Define entry point
;
        public  XMS_Xms@freeHMA

        .code

XMS_Xms@freeHMA proc     self:DWord

        mov     ah,XMSFreeHMA       ; Function code
        call    xmsHandler          ; call the guy

        or      ax,ax               ; AX=0 means error
        jz      errorReturn

        mov     ax,XMSErrOK         ; No error
        ret
```

```
errorReturn:
        mov     al,bl               ; Move error code to AL
        xor     ah,ah               ; Zero extend to 16 bits
        mov     errno,ax            ; Copy to errno
        ret

XMS_Xms@freeHMA endp                ; end of procedure

        end
```

This source file holds the code to function XMS__Xms.freeHMA(...). This function allows a program to release the HMA area for use by other programs.

Function XMS__Xms.freeHMA(...)

error= XMS__Xms.freeHMA( );

Enable the global A20 line

Figure 5-15 holds the source code listing to XMS03.ASM.

5-15 The source code listing to XMS03.ASM.

```
;****************************************************************
;***        XMS03.ASM                                        ***
;***                                                         ***
;***        function         XMS_Xms.globEnabA20            ***
;***                         : Boolean;                      ***
;***                                                         ***
;***        Enables the A20 address line allowing 21 bit    ***
;***        addressing and access to the HMA                 ***
;***                                                         ***
;****************************************************************

        .model  large,pascal

        include xmsdefs.asm

        extrn   errno:WORD
        extrn   xmsHandler:DWord

;
;   Define entry point
;
        public  XMS_Xms@globEnabA20

        .code

XMS_Xms@globEnabA20 proc    self:DWord

        mov     ah,XMSGlobEnabA20   ; Function code
        call    xmsHandler          ; call the guy
```

```
        or      ax,ax                   ; AX=0 means error
        jz      errorReturn

        mov     ax,XMSErrOK             ; No error
        ret

errorReturn:
        mov     al,bl                   ; Move error code to AL
        xor     ah,ah                   ; Zero extend to 16 bits
        mov     errno,ax                ; Copy to errno
        ret

XMS_Xms@globEnabA20 endp                ; end of procedure

        end
```

This source file holds the code to function XMS__Xms.globEnabA20(...). This function attempts to enable the A20 line. It should only be used by those programs that have control of the HMA.

Function XMS__Xms.globEnabA20

```
function   XMS__Xms.globEnabA20
                 : Boolean;
```

Disable the global A20 line

Figure 5-16 holds the source code listing to XMS04.ASM.

5-16 The source code listing to XMS04.ASM.

```
;****************************************************************
;***    XMS04.ASM                                          ***
;***                                                       ***
;***    function       XMS_Xms.globDisabA20               ***
;***                     : Boolean                         ***
;***                                                       ***
;***    Disables the A20 address line.                     ***
;***                                                       ***
;****************************************************************

        .model  large,pascal

        include xmsdefs.asm

        extrn   errno:WORD
        extrn   xmsHandler:DWord

;
;   Define entry point
;
        public  XMS_Xms@globDisabA20
```

5-16 Continued.

```
        .code

XMS_Xms@globDisabA20      proc      self:DWord

        mov      ah,XMSGlobDisabA20    ; Function code
        call     xmsHandler            ; call the guy

        or       ax,ax                 ; AX=0 means error
        jz       errorReturn

        mov      ax,XMSErrOK           ; No error
        ret

errorReturn:
        mov      al,bl                 ; Move error code to AL
        xor      ah,ah                 ; Zero extend to 16 bits
        mov      errno,ax              ; Copy to errno
        ret

XMS_Xms@globDisabA20      endp          ; end of procedure

        end
```

This source file holds the code to function XMS__Xms.globDisabA20(...). This function attempts to disable the A20 line. It should only be used by those programs that have control of the HMA.

Function XMS__Xms.globDisabA20

```
function   XMS__Xms.globDisabA20
               : Boolean;
```

Get the current A20 line state

Figure 5-17 presents the source code listing to XMS07.ASM.

5-17 The source code listing to XMS07.ASM.

```
;*****************************************************************
;***      XMS07.ASM                                         ***
;***                                                        ***
;***      function          XMS_Xms.getA20State(           ***
;***                            var a20State:   Word)       ***
;***                            : Boolean;                  ***
;***                                                        ***
;***      Returns the enable status of the A20 line.        ***
;***      A20State is TRUE (1) on return if A20 is enabled,  ***
;***      otherwise it is FALSE (0).                         ***
;***                                                        ***
;*****************************************************************

        .model   large,pascal

        include xmsdefs.asm
```

```
        extrn    errno:WORD
        extrn    xmsHandler:DWord

;
;   Define entry point
;
        public   XMS_Xms@getA20State

        .code

XMS_Xms@getA20State proc    a20State:Far Ptr Word, self: DWord

        mov      ah,XMSGetA20State    ; Function code
        call     xmsHandler           ; call the guy

        or       ax,ax                ; AX=0 may mean error
        jnz      goodReturn           ; AX<>0 means A20 enabled
        or       bl,bl                ; BL<>0 means error
        jnz      errorReturn

goodReturn:
        les      bx,a20State          ; Address to return result
        mov      es:[bx],ax           ; Flag gives A20 state
        mov      ax,XMSErrOK          ; No error
        ret

errorReturn:
        mov      al,bl                ; Move error code to AL
        xor      ah,ah                ; Zero extend to 16 bits
        mov      errno,ax             ; Copy to errno
        ret

XMS_Xms@getA20State endp             ; end of procedure

        end
```

This source file holds the code to function XMS_Xms.getA20State(...).
This function checks to see if the A20 line is in fact enabled.

Function XMS__Xms.getA20State(...)

```
function  XMS__Xms.getA20State(
                var a20State:   Word)
            : Boolean;
```

where

a20State   Receives a 1 if A20 is enabled, or a 0 if A20 is disabled

Get amount of free extended memory

Figure 5-18 presents the source code listing to XMS08.ASM.

5-18 The source code listing to XMS08.ASM.

```
;****************************************************************
;***        XMS08.ASM                                        ***
;***                                                         ***
;***        function         XMS_Xms.getFreeXM(             ***
;***                             var totalFree:  Word;       ***
;***                             var largestFree:Word)       ***
;***                             : Boolean;                  ***
;***                                                         ***
;***        Queries the amount of extended memory available. ***
;***                                                         ***
;****************************************************************

        .model  large,pascal

        include xmsdefs.asm

        extrn   errno:WORD
        extrn   xmsHandler:DWord

;
;   Define entry point
;
        public  XMS_Xms@getFreeXM

        .code

XMS_Xms@getFreeXM    proc      total:Far Ptr Word, largest: Far Ptr Word,
                               self:DWord

        mov     ah,XMSGetFreeXM    ; Function code
        call    xmsHandler         ; call the guy

        or      ax,ax              ; AX=0 means error
        jz      errorReturn

;
;   Now return the values.
;
        les     bx,total
        mov     es:[bx],dx         ; total free memory in KB
        les     bx,largest
        mov     es:[bx],ax         ; largest free block

        mov     ax,XMSErrOK        ; No error
        ret

errorReturn:
        mov     al,bl              ; Move error code to AL
        xor     ah,ah              ; Zero extend to 16 bits
        mov     errno,ax           ; Copy to errno
        ret

XMS_Xms@getFreeXM    endp          ; end of procedure

        end
```

This source listing presents the code to function XMS__Xms.get FreeXM(...). This function returns the total amount of free XMS and the largest free XMS block in kilobytes.

Function XMS__Xms.getFreeXM(...)

```
function   XMS__Xms.getFreeXM(
                    var totalFree:      Word;
                    var largestFree:   Word)
```

where

totalFree   Receives the total free XMS in kilobytes
largestFree   Receives the largest free XMS block in kilobytes

Allocating an extended memory block

Figure 5-19 presents the source code listing to XMS09.ASM.

5-19 The source code listing to XMS09.ASM.

```
;***************************************************************
;***        XMS09.ASM                                       ***
;***                                                        ***
;***        function        XMS_XmBlk.allocXM(              ***
;***                          blockSize:        Word)       ***
;***                          : Boolean;                    ***
;***                                                        ***
;***        Allocates a block of extended memory blockSize KB ***
;***        long that can be referenced via handle.          ***
;***                                                        ***
;***************************************************************

          .model   large,pascal

          include xmsdefs.asm

          extrn    errno:WORD
          extrn    xmsHandler:DWord


    ;
    ;   Define entry point
    ;
          public   XMS_XmBlk@allocXM

          .code

XMS_XmBlk@allocXM      proc    blockSize:Word, handle: Far Ptr Word

          mov      dx,blockSize      ; size in KB of block
          mov      ah,XMSAllocXM     ; Function code
          call     xmsHandler        ; call the guy

          or       ax,ax             ; AX=0 means error
          jz       errorReturn

          les      bx,handle
          mov      es:[bx],dx        ; new handle
```

```
        mov     ax,XMSErrOK              ; No error
        xor     dx,dx
        ret

errorReturn:
        mov     al,bl                    ; Move error code to AL
        xor     ah,ah                    ; Zero extend to 16 bits
        mov     errno,ax                 ; Copy to errno
        xor     dx,dx
        ret

XMS_XmBlk@allocXM       endp             ; end of procedure
        end
```

This source file presents the code to function XMS__XmBlk.allocXM(...). This function requests the XMS memory in kilobyte blocks and initializes the target XMS__XmBlk with the block's handle.

Xms__XmBlk.allocXM(...)

```
function   XMS__XmBlk.allocXM(
                    blockSize:   Word)
                  : Boolean;
```

where

blockSize   The number of kilobytes of XMS memory to allocate

Free an extended memory block

Figure 5-20 presents the source code listing to XMS0A.ASM.

5-20 The source code listing to XMS0A.ASM.

```
;******************************************************************
;***    XMS0A.ASM                                        ***
;***                                                     ***
;***    function        XMS_XmBlk.freeXM                 ***
;***                       : Boolean                     ***
;***                                                     ***
;***    Frees an extended memory block referred to by    ***
;***    handle.                                          ***
;***                                                     ***
;******************************************************************

        .model  large,pascal

        include xmsdefs.asm

        extrn   errno:WORD
        extrn   xmsHandler:DWord
```

```
;
;   Define entry point
;
        public  XMS_XmBlk@freeXM

        .code

XMS_XmBlk@freeXM      proc    handle:Far Ptr Word
        les     bx,handle
        mov     dx,es:[bx]              ; get the block's handle
        mov     ah,XMSFreeXM            ; Function code
        call    xmsHandler             ; call the guy

        or      ax,ax                  ; AX=0 means error
        jz      errorReturn

        mov     ax,XMSErrOK            ; No error
        ret

errorReturn:
        mov     al,bl                  ; Move error code to AL
        xor     ah,ah                  ; Zero extend to 16 bits
        mov     errno,ax               ; Copy to errno
        ret

XMS_XmBlk@freeXM      endp            ; end of procedure
        end
```

This source file presents the code to function XMS__Xms.freeXM(...). This function frees a previously allocated XMS memory referred to by the designated handle.

Function XMS__XmBlk.freeXM

```
function   XMS__XmBlk.freeXM
               : Boolean;
```

Copy an extended memory block

Figure 5-21 presents the source code listing to XMSOB.ASM.

5-21 The source code listing to XMSOB.ASM.

```
;*********************************************************
;***     XMSOB.ASM                                    ***
;***                                                  ***
;***     function        XMS_Xms.moveXM(              ***
;***                      var packet:     XMS_MovePacket) ***
;***                       : Boolean;                 ***
;***                                                  ***
;***     Moves an area of memory between or within XMS ***
;***     and/or conventional memory.                  ***
;***                                                  ***
;*********************************************************
;
```

```
        .model  large,pascal

        include xmsdefs.asm

        extrn   errno:WORD
        extrn   xmsHandler:DWord

;
;   Define entry point
;
        public  XMS_Xms@moveXM

        .code

XMS_Xms@moveXM      proc    packet:Far Ptr Word, self:DWord

    ;   We are required to pass the packet address in DS:SI.
    ;   As a result, we need to save DS. Further, we need to
    ;   copy DS to ES, so that we can find the address of the
    ;   xmsHandler when we need it.

        push    si                  ; Save SI

        push    ds                  ; Move DS to ES
        pop     es

        lds     si,packet           ; DS:SI gets packet address

        mov     ah,XMSMoveXM        ; Function code
        call    es:xmsHandler       ; call the guy

        push    es                  ; restore DS
        pop     ds

        or      ax,ax               ; AX=0 means error
        jz      errorReturn

        mov     ax,XMSErrOK         ; No error
        pop     si                  ; Restore SI
        ret

errorReturn:
        mov     al,bl               ; Move error code to AL
        xor     ah,ah               ; Zero extend to 16 bits
        mov     errno,ax            ; Copy to errno
        pop     si                  ; Restore SI
        ret

XMS_Xms@moveXM      endp            ; end of procedure
        end
```

This source file contains the code to function XMS_Xms.moveXM(...). This function attempts to transfer data from one location to another location. Although it is most commonly used to move memory between conventional memory and extended memory, it can also be used for memory moves within conventional memory or extended memory.

Function XMS__Xms.moveXM(...)

```
function   XMS__Xms.moveXM(
                    var packet:   XMS__MovePacket)
                    : Boolean;
```

where

packet   Points to an XMS__Xms.MovePacket structure (see __XMS.PAS,
FIG. 5-9, for the XMS__MovePacket structure)

Lock an extended memory block

Figure 5-22 presents the source code listing to XMS0C.ASM.

5-22 The source code listing to XMS0C.ASM.

```
;****************************************************************
;***      XMS0C.ASM                                         ***
;***                                                        ***
;***      function         XMS_XmBlk.lockXM(                ***
;***                        var physAddr:   DWord)          ***
;***                        : Boolean;                      ***
;***                                                        ***
;***      Locks an extended memory block, preventing it from ***
;***      moving in physical memory, and returns its        ***
;***      physical address.                                 ***
;***                                                        ***
;****************************************************************
;
          .model   large,pascal

          include xmsdefs.asm

          extrn    errno:WORD
          extrn    xmsHandler:DWord

;
;    Define entry point
;
          public   XMS_XmBlk@lockXM

          .code
XMS_XmBlk@lockXM        proc     physAddr: Far Ptr DWord, handle:Far Ptr Word
          les      bx,handle
          mov      dx,es:[bx]      ; handle of block to lock
          mov      ah,XMSLockXM    ; Function code
          call     xmsHandler      ; call the guy

          or       ax,ax           ; AX=0 means error
          jz       errorReturn

          mov      ax,bx           ; Save LSW of physical address
          les      bx,physAddr     ; Get addr of long return val
          mov      es:[bx],ax      ; LSW physical address
          mov      es:[bx+2],dx    ; MSW physical address

          mov      ax,XMSErrOK     ; No error
          ret
```

```
errorReturn:
        mov     al,bl               ; Move error code to AL
        xor     ah,ah               ; Zero extend to 16 bits
        mov     errno,ax            ; Copy to errno
        ret

XMS_XmBlk@lockXM        endp            ; end of procedure

        end
```

This source file presents the code to function XMS_XmBlk.lockXM(...). This function locks an extended memory block so that it cannot be moved in physical memory. The 32-bit physical address is returned.

Function XMS_XmBlk.lockXM(...)

```
function  XMS_XmBlk.lockXM(
                    var physAddr:   DWord)
              : Boolean;
```

where

physAddr   Receives the 32-bit base address of the XMS block

Unlock an extended memory block

Figure 5-23 presents the source code listing to XMS0D.ASM.

5-23 The source code listing to XMS0D.ASM.

```
;********************************************************
;***                                                 ***
;***     XMS0D.ASM                                   ***
;***                                                 ***
;***     function         XMS_XmBlk.unlockXM         ***
;***                      : Boolean;                 ***
;***                                                 ***
;***     Unlocks a previously locked memory block.   ***
;***                                                 ***
;********************************************************

        .model  large,pascal

        include xmsdefs.asm

        extrn   errno:WORD
        extrn   xmsHandler:DWord

;
;    Define entry point
;
        public  XMS_XmBlk@unlockXM

        .code
```

```
XMS_XmBlk@unlockXM  proc      handle:Far Ptr Word
        les     bx,handle
        mov     dx,es:[bx]            ; handle of block to lock
        mov     ah,XMSUnlockXM        ; Function code
        call    xmsHandler           ; call the guy

        or      ax,ax                ; AX=0 means error
        jz      errorReturn

        mov     ax,XMSErrOK          ; No error
        ret

errorReturn:
        mov     al,bl                ; Move error code to AL
        xor     ah,ah                ; Zero extend to 16 bits
        mov     errno,ax             ; Copy to errno
        ret

XMS_XmBlk@unlockXM  endp             ; end of procedure

        end
```

This source file presents the code to function XMS__Xms.unlockXM(...). This function unlocks an extended memory block so that it can be moved in physical memory.

Function XMS__XmBlk.unlockXM

```
function    XMS__XmBlk.unlockXM
                : Boolean;
```

Get extended memory block information

Figure 5-24 presents the source code listing to XMS0E.ASM.

5-24 The source code listing to XMS0E.ASM.

```
;***************************************************************
;***     XMS0E.ASM                                          ***
;***                                                        ***
;***     function       XMS_XmBlk.getHandInfo(              ***
;***                         var blockSize:  Word;          ***
;***                         var handlesLeft:Word;          ***
;***                         var lockCount:  Word)          ***
;***                         : Boolean;                     ***
;***                                                        ***
;***     Gets information about an allocated XM block.      ***
;***                                                        ***
;***************************************************************

        .model  large,pascal

        include xmsdefs.asm

        extrn   errno:WORD
        extrn   xmsHandler:DWord
```

5-24 Continued.

```
;
;    Define entry point
;
        public  XMS_XmBlk@getHandInfo
        .code
XMS_XmBlk@getHandInfo     proc     blSz:Far Ptr Word, nHand:Far Ptr Word,
                                   locks:Far Ptr Word, handle:Far Ptr Word
        les     bx,handle
        mov     dx,es:[bx]              ; get the handle
        mov     ah,XMSGetHandInfo       ; Function code
        call    xmsHandler              ; call the guy

        or      ax,ax                   ; AX=0 means error
        jz      errorReturn

;
;    Now return the values.
;
        mov     cx,bx                   ; save BH and BL contents
        les     bx,blSz                 ; Return the block size (KB)
        mov     es:[bx],dx

        les     bx,nHand                ; Return the number of free handles
        mov     al,cl                   ; Zero extend to 16 bits
        xor     ah,ah
        mov     es:[bx],ax

        les     bx,locks                ; Return the number of locks on block
        mov     al,ch                   ; Zero extend to 16 bits
        xor     ah,ah
        mov     es:[bx],ax

        mov     ax,XMSErrOK             ; No error
        ret
errorReturn:
        mov     al,bl                   ; Move error code to AL
        xor     ah,ah                   ; Zero extend to 16 bits
        mov     errno,ax                ; Copy to errno
        ret
XMS_XmBlk@getHandInfo     endp          ; end of procedure

        end
```

This source file contains the code to function XMS_Xms.getHandle Info(...). This function returns the block's lock count, the number of free extended memory block handles, and the block's length in kilobytes.

Function XMS_XmBlk.getHandleInfo(...)

```
function  XMS_XmBlk.getHandInfo(
                var blockSize:    Word;
                var handlesLeft:  Word;
                var lockCount:    Word)
                : Boolean;
```

where

> blockSize   Receives the extended memory block size in kilobytes
> handlesLeft Receives the number of free XMS handles
> lockCount   Receives block's lock count

Resize an extended memory block

Figure 5-25 presents the source code listing to XMSOF.ASM.

5-25 The source code listing to XMSOF.ASM.

```
;****************************************************************
;***      XMSOF.ASM                                      ***
;***                                                     ***
;***      function       XMS_XmBlk.resizeXM(             ***
;***                         newSize:       Word)        ***
;***                         : Boolean;                  ***
;***                                                     ***
;***      Changes the size of an already allocated block. ***
;***                                                     ***
;****************************************************************

        .model  large,pascal

        include xmsdefs.asm

        extrn   errno:WORD
        extrn   xmsHandler:DWord

;
;   Define entry point
;
        public  XMS_XmBlk@resizeXM

        .code
XMS_XmBlk@resizeXM  proc    newSize:Word, handle:Far Ptr Word

        les     bx,handle
        mov     dx,es:[bx]          ; get handle
        mov     bx,newSize          ; new block size
        mov     ah,XMSResizeXM      ; Function code
        call    xmsHandler          ; call the guy

        or      ax,ax               ; AX=0 means error
        jz      errorReturn

        mov     ax,XMSErrOK         ; No error
        ret

errorReturn:
        mov     al,bl               ; Move error code to AL
        xor     ah,ah               ; Zero extend to 16 bits
        mov     errno,ax            ; Copy to errno
        ret

XMS_XmBlk@resizeXM  endp            ; end of procedure

        end
```

This source file contains the code to function XMS__XmBlk.resizeXM(...). This function alters the size of a previously allocated extended memory block.

Function XMS__XmBlk.resizeXM(...)

```
function  XMS__XmBlk.resizeXM(
                    newSize:  Word)
                  : Boolean;
```

where

newSize Contains the new size for the extended memory block in kilo bytes

Allocate an Upper Memory Block (UMB)

Figure 5-26 presents the source code listing to XMS10.ASM.

5-26 The source code listing to XMS10.ASM.

```
;******************************************************************
;***      XMS10.ASM                                          ***
;***                                                         ***
;***      function         XMS_Xms.allocUM(                  ***
;***                           size:          Word;          ***
;***                           var address:   Pointer;       ***
;***                           var actualSize: Word)         ***
;***                           : Boolean;                    ***
;***                                                         ***
;***      Allocates a block of upper memory blockSize        ***
;***      paragraphs long. On successful return, address has ***
;***      the address of the block. If there is not enough   ***
;***      memory, actual size gives largest chunk available. ***
;***                                                         ***
;******************************************************************

        .model  large,pascal

        include xmsdefs.asm

        extrn   errno:WORD
        extrn   xmsHandler:DWord

;
;   Define entry point
;
        public  XMS_Xms@allocUM

        .code
XMS_Xms@allocUM     proc    blockSize:Word, address:Far Ptr DWord,
                            actual:Far Ptr Word, self:DWord

        mov     dx,blockSize        ; size in KB of block
        mov     ah,XMSAllocUM       ; Function code
        call    xmsHandler          ; call the guy
```

```
        or      ax,ax              ; AX=0 means error
        jz      errorReturn

        mov     ax,bx              ; Save returned segment #
        les     bx,address
        xor     cx,cx              ; Get a zero for the offset
        mov     es:[bx],cx         ; offset
        mov     es:[bx+2],ax       ; segment

        les     bx,actual          ; Return the actual size
        mov     es:[bx],dx

        mov     ax,XMSErrOK        ; No error
        ret

errorReturn:
        mov     al,bl              ; Move error code to AL
        xor     ah,ah              ; Zero extend to 16 bits
        mov     errno,ax           ; Copy to errno

        cmp     ax,XMSErrSmUMB     ; See if there's a smaller UMB
        je      errCommon          ; There is DX has its size

        xor     dx,dx              ; Indicate size is zero

errCommon:
        les     bx,actual          ; Return the largest block size
        mov     es:[bx],dx

        ret

XMS_Xms@allocUM     endp           ; end of procedure
        end
```

This source file contains the code to function XMS_Xms.allocUM(...). This function requests a free UMB (in 16-byte paragraphs) and returns a pointer to an upper memory block, and the actual size of the UMB is 16-byte paragraphs.

Function XMS_Xms.allocUM(...)

```
function   XMS_Xms.allocUM(
                size:              Word;
                var address:       Pointer;
                var actualSize:Word)
                : Boolean;
```

where

size   The amount of UM desired in 16-byte paragraphs
address   Receives a pointer to the allocated UMB
actualSize Receives the actual size of the allocated UMB in 16-byte paragraphs

Release an Upper Memory Block (UMB)

Figure 5-27 presents the source code listing to XMS11.ASM.

5-27 The source code listing to XMS11.ASM.

```
;***************************************************************
;***        XMS11.ASM                                       ***
;***                                                        ***
;***        function        XMS_Xms.freeUM(                 ***
;***                             address:        Pointer)   ***
;***                             : Boolean;                 ***
;***                                                        ***
;***        Frees a previously allocated Upper Memory Block ***
;***                                                        ***
;***************************************************************

        .model  large,pascal

        include xmsdefs.asm

        extrn   errno:WORD
        extrn   xmsHandler:DWord
;
;   Define entry point
;
        public  XMS_Xms@freeUM

        .code

XMS_Xms@freeUM  proc    addressHi:Word, addressLo:Word, self:DWord
        mov     ax,addressLo    ; Get offset
        or      ax,ax           ; See if it's zero (better be)
        jnz     offsetError     ; It's no good

        mov     dx,addressHi    ; Block segment address
        mov     ah,XMSFreeUM    ; Function code
        call    xmsHandler      ; call the guy

        or      ax,ax           ; AX=0 means error
        jz      errorReturn

        mov     ax,XMSErrOK     ; No error
        ret

offsetError:
        mov     bl,XMSErrUMBInv ; bogus UMB

errorReturn:
        mov     al,bl           ; Move error code to AL
        xor     ah,ah           ; Zero extend to 16 bits
        mov     errno,ax        ; Copy to errno

        ret

XMS_Xms@freeUM  endp            ; end of procedure

        end
```

This source file contains the code to function XMS__Xms.freeUM(...).
This function frees a previously allocated UMB. The pointer to the UMB
that is to be freed is passed as a parameter.

Function XMS__Xms.freeUM(...)

```
function  XMS__Xms.freeUM(
              address:  Pointer)
              : Boolean;
```

where

address   Points to the previously allocated UMB

Move raw XMS memory

Figure 5-28 presents the source code listing to XMSRAW.ASM.

5-28 The source code listing to XMSRAW.ASM.

```
;*******************************************************
;***    XMSRAW.ASM                                  ***
;***                                                ***
;***    function      XMS_Xms.rawMove(              ***
;***                      dest:       DWord;        ***
;***                      source:     DWord;        ***
;***                      length:     Word)         ***
;***                      : Boolean;                ***
;***                                                ***
;***    Move a block of XM from source to dest. This call ***
;***    uses physical addresses, and so the blocks must ***
;***    be locked.                                  ***
;***                                                ***
;*******************************************************

        .model  large,pascal

        include xmsdefs.asm

        extrn   errno:WORD
        extrn   xmsHandler:DWord

;
;   Define entry point
;
        public  XMS_Xms@rawMove

        .data

;
;   Define the raw move packet:
;
movePacket  dd  0,0,0,0
segLength1   dw  ?
sourceAddr   db  ?,?,?
             db  XMSBiosAccess
             dw  0
segLength2   dw  ?
destAddr     db  ?,?,?
             db  XMSBiosAccess
             dw  0,0,0,0,0,0,0,0
```

```
        .code
XMS_Xms@rawMove proc    destHi:Word, destLo:Word, sourceHi:Word, sourceLo:
WORD, xferLen:Word, self:DWord

        push    si                      ; Save SI

        mov     cx,xferLen              ; length in bytes of xfer
        mov     segLength1,cx
        mov     segLength2,cx

;
;       The bios call takes a number of words to move, so
;       we need to convert the byte count into a word count.
;       we give an error if the byte count was odd. We don't
;       want to round up, because this may be destructive.
;
        clc
        rcr     cx,1                    ; shift right into carry
        jc      oddLength               ; special error case

;
;       Transfer the three byte (24 bit) physical addresses:
;
        mov     ax,destLo               ; LSB 2 bytes of dest
        mov     Word Ptr destAddr,ax
        mov     ax,destHi               ; MSB byte of dest
        mov     destAddr+2,al

        mov     ax,sourceLo             ; LSB 2 bytes of source
        mov     Word Ptr sourceAddr,ax
        mov     ax,sourceHi             ; MSB byte of source
        mov     sourceAddr+2,al

;
;       We're ready to do the call:
;
        push    ds                      ; get ES:SI = packet
        pop     es
        lea     si,movePacket

        mov     ah,XMSBiosXMMove        ; Function code
        int     XMSBios

        jc      errorReturn             ; Carry means error occurred

        mov     ax,XMSErrOK             ; No error
        pop     si                      ; restore SI
        ret

oddLength:
        mov     ah,XMSErrLenInv         ; Invalid length

errorReturn:
        mov     al,ah                   ; Move error to AL
        xor     ah,ah                   ; Zero extend error
        mov     errno,ax                ; Save in errno
        pop     si                      ; Restore SI
        ret

XMS_Xms@rawMove endp                    ; end of procedure

        end
```

This file contains the code to function XMS_Xms.rawMove(...). This function moves memory by use of physical addresses. Note that the memory blocks must be locked.

Function XMS_Xms.RawMove(...)

```
function   XMS_Xms.rawMove(
                   dest:      DWord;
                   source:    DWord;
                   length:    Word)
                   : Boolean;
```

where

dest   Gives the physical address of destination buffer
source Gives the physical address of source buffer
length Gives the number of bytes to be moved

EMS function error reporting

The function XMS_Xms.errorText(...) allows the programmer to get the text message associated with an error code.

Function XMS_Xms.errorText(...)

```
function   XMS_Xms.errorText(
                   err:       Word)
                   : String;
```

where

err   Error holds the error code

Summary

Chapter 5 presented the XMS 2.0 interface, which facilitates the use of extended memory in your DOS real mode programs. Use the heavily documented XMS demonstration programs (FIGS. 5-1 through 5-8) as guides for understanding how the XMS related functions are used.

The XMS functions presented in this chapter are used as building blocks for the Virtual Memory Manager presented in Chapter 6.

6

The Virtual Memory Manager

This chapter begins with an overview of the Virtual Memory Manager. Once the Virtual Memory Manager has been described, the six simple-to-use VMM function prototypes for the applications programmer are presented. The VMM demonstration programs follow, and the chapter ends with the full source code for the VMM's internal operations.

The VMM presented in this last chapter is quite sophisticated in its operation. If you don't quite catch all the VMM concepts in the first reading, be patient. You'll catch on to what's happening in the VMM in time.

An overview of the Virtual Memory Manager

A Virtual Memory Manager (VMM) facilitates a program's use of all the available memory in its host computer system. For purposes of this chapter, "all the memory" means all the unallocated conventional memory, EMS, XMS, and hard disk space. This unallocated space will be referred to as the "memory pool."

The memory pool

Conventional memory
Unallocated EMS
Unallocated XMS
Unallocated hard disk

Let's say you need to work with 5M of data. It's pretty obvious that conventional memory will not fill the bill. Suppose your computer's memory pool is over 5M. Managing the way your 5M of data is dispersed in the memory pool can become quite nightmarish. What data is held in conventional memory? What data is held in EMS? What data is held in XMS? What data is held on disk?

The VMM isolates you from these hairy memory pool management requirements. It allows you to work with large amounts of data by using a few simple functions.

Overview of the VMM's architecture

The purpose of this overview is to give you a feel for the basic design principles of the VMM. This text is designed to help you visualize how the VMM system operates. The demonstration programs will show the simple VMM interface in use, and the heavily documented VMM source code will explain the nitty gritty of VMM system.

One of the first decisions that had to be made, centered on the size of the memory pages we were going to use in the VMM. The page is the basic unit of virtual memory. Although we considered using pages as small as 2K, ultimately we decided that 16K was our best choice, as it greatly simplified the building of the VMM. The 16K unit proves to be the least common multiple of EMS, XMS and disk page sizes.

VMM page size

16K page size

Once you have initialized the VMM, your next task is to allocate blocks of virtual memory (via a VMM function) where data can be stored. The VMM lets you wire virtual memory into conventional memory. Wiring an area of virtual memory means that you are bringing it into conventional memory where the data in the page is available to be read or written.

Unwiring a page makes it unavailable for reading or writing data and makes buffer space available for wiring other pages. If you want to write data to or read data from the unwired page, you must wire it again. An area of virtual memory may be wired and unwired an unlimited number of times.

When you request wiring an area, the pages which that area covers must be wired. Note that if even one byte of the area resides in a given page, that page must be wired.

Wiring a page

Imports a 16K page to memory where data may be read or written.

Unwiring a page

Making a page unavailable for reading or writing data.

If you attempt to wire a new area from your VMM allocated memory block and there is no room, one of the VMM unwired pages will be kicked out of the buffer. If there isn't enough buffer space to wire the area, you will receive an error.

For purposes of this chapter, conventional memory is called fast memory, while EMS and XMS are called slow memory. Disk memory is called slowest memory.

Memory access speed

Fast   → Conventional
Slow   → EMS, XMS
Slowest → Disk

The rule of thumb for 16K page location management is called the Least Recently Used (LRU) rule. When the VMM needs to throw an unwired page out of memory, it chooses the least recently used. The theory is that the less recently a page was used, the less likely it is to be used in the near future. If EMS and XMS are filled, then the LRU page in slow memory goes to disk and is replaced by the VMM allocated fast-memory block kicked-out page. Phew . . .

Least Recently Used (LRU) Principle

The less recently a 16K page was used, the higher the probability it will wind up in slowest memory. The more recently a 16K page was used, the higher the probability it will remain in fast memory.

The VMM keeps track of page status through an intricately crafted series of structures and linked lists. Fortunately for you, the entire page management scheme proves invisible to the programmer using the VMM. To use the VMM, you only need to use a few simple functions.

First, the prototypes for the VMM interface functions are presented and then the demonstration programs follow. The demonstration programs will help you see the VMM in action. After the demonstration programs are presented, you'll see the complete and heavily documented source code to the VMM. No secrets here!

One final note: the VMM uses an error reporting system in the same fashion as the EMS and XMS functions. An error is flagged by returning True from a function. When an error has occured, the error code can be found in the global variable errno, defined in __GLOBALS.PAS. Here is the VMM error code list:

Table 6-1 VMM error code list.

Name	Code	Meaning
VMErrOK	0	There is no error
VMErrEMS	1	There is an EMS-related error
VMErrXMS	2	There is an XMS-related error
VMErrDisk	3	There is a disk-related error
VMErrNoConv	4	No conventional memory is available
VMErrBadWire	5	There is a problem wiring a VMM area
VMErrNotWired	6	Attempted to unwire a page not wired
VMErrBounds	7	Tried to wire or unwire a page not in block

VMM interface functions

Initialize the VMM

Function VM__Vm.init(...) initializes the VMM. Looking at the function prototypes will help to facilitate its use in your programs. For detailed help,
see the heavily documented demonstration program source code.

Function VM__Vm.init(...)

```
function   VM__Vm.init(
                    maxSpace:   DWord)
                    : Boolean;
```

where

    maxSpace   The amount of conventional memory that the VMM is per-
mitted to use for buffer space

Shut down the VMM

Function VM__Vm.shutdown shuts down all VMM operations and frees up
the memory that had been allocated by the VMM initialization.

Function VM__Vm.shutdown

```
function   VM__Vm.shutdown
                    : Boolean;
```

Allocate a VMM block

Function VM__VmBlk.alloc(...) allocates a block of virtual memory. Physical
memory doesn't get allocated until you wire an area. The target VM__VmBlk
is initialized represent the new block.

Function VM__VmBlk.alloc(...)

```
function   VM__VmBlk.alloc(
                    size:       DWord)
                    : Boolean;
```

where

    size   Gives the amount of virtual memory desired in bytes

Free a previously allocated VMM block

Function VM__VmBlk.free frees up a previously allocated block.

Function VM__VmBlk.free

```
function   VM__VmBlk.free
                    : Boolean;
```

Wire a VMM area for reading and writing

Function VM__VmBlk.wire(...) allows you to make a specified amount of memory from a VMM block available for reading and writing.

Function VM__VmBlk.wire(...)

```
function   VM__VmBlk.wire(
                    areaOffset:         DWord;
                    areaSize:                    DWord;
                    var areaAddress:  Pointer)
                    : Boolean;
```

where

areaOffset	Gives, in bytes, the offset into the VMM block of the area that you want to access
areaSize	Gives, in bytes, the size of the VMM area you want to access
areaAddress	Receives a pointer to the conventional memory containing the wired area

Unwire a VMM page

Function VM__VmBlk.unwire(...) signals to the VMM that the specified area may be kicked out to slower memory if a new VMM area is to be wired and insufficient space is available. The buffer address returned by wiring the area becomes invalid after the area is unwired.

Function VM__VmBlk.unwire(...)

```
function   VM__VmBlk.unwire(
                    areaOffset:  DWord;
                    areaSize:              DWord;
                    dirty:          Boolean)
                    : Boolean;
```

where

areaOffset	Gives, in bytes, the offset into the VMM block of the area that you want released from conventional memory
areaSize	Gives, in bytes, the size of the VMM area you want released from conventional memory
dirty	A flag that tells the VMM system if the area has been modified since it was wired

VMM demonstration programs

This chapter presents two demonstration programs. Great care has been taken to document the VMM functions. By examining the source code, you'll be able to easily discern how the VMM functions are used.

Program PROG6-1.PAS demonstrates the following:

- initializing the VMM
- allocating a block of memory via a VMM function
- wiring a VMM page

Figure 6-1 presents the source code listing to PROG6-1.PAS.

6-1 The source code listing to PROG6-1.PAS.

```
(* * * * * * * * * * * * * * * * *
 *
 * prog6-1.pas --     VM demo
 *
 *       This test program demonstrates
 *             - vm intialization
 *             - allocation
 *             - wiring
 *
 * * * * * * * * * * * * * * * * * *)

program prog6_1;

uses    _globals,
        _vm;

label
    100;

var
    vm:                 VM_Vm;
    handle1:            VM_VmBlk;
    addr:               Pointer;

begin
    addr:= Nil;
    if vm.init(16384) then begin
        goto 100;
        end;

    if handle1.alloc(100000) then begin
        goto 100;
        end;

    (*
     *  Write some text to various places in the VM block
     *)
    if handle1.wire(54320, 80, addr) then begin
        goto 100;
        end;
    StrPtr(addr)^:= '       Americans are broad minded people. They''ll';
    if handle1.unwire(54320, 80, True) then begin
        goto 100;
        end;

    if handle1.wire(660, 80, addr) then begin
        goto 100;
        end;
    StrPtr(addr)^:= '       accept the fact that a person can be an alcoholic,';
    if handle1.unwire(660, 80, True) then begin
        goto 100;
        end;
```

```
if handle1.wire(9878, 80, addr) then begin
    goto 100;
    end;
StrPtr(addr)^:= '       a dope fiend, a wife beater, and even a newspaperman,';
if handle1.unwire(9878, 80, True) then begin
    goto 100;
    end;

if handle1.wire(76654, 80, addr) then begin
    goto 100;
    end;
StrPtr(addr)^:= '       but if a man doesn''t drive, there''s something wrong';
if handle1.unwire(76654, 80, True) then begin
    goto 100;
    end;

if handle1.wire(10, 80, addr) then begin
    goto 100;
    end;
StrPtr(addr)^:= '      with him.';
if handle1.unwire(10, 80, True) then begin
    goto 100;
    end;

if handle1.wire(24000, 80, addr) then begin
    goto 100;
    end;
StrPtr(addr)^:= '                          -- Art Buchwald';
if handle1.unwire(24000, 80, True) then begin
    goto 100;
    end;


(*
 *  Now let's recall the blocks.
 *)
if handle1.wire(54320, 80, addr) then begin
    goto 100;
    end;
writeln(StrPtr(addr)^);
if handle1.unwire(54320, 80, False) then begin
    goto 100;
    end;

if handle1.wire(660, 80, addr) then begin
    goto 100;
    end;
writeln(StrPtr(addr)^);
if handle1.unwire(660, 80, False) then begin
    goto 100;
    end;

if handle1.wire(9878, 80, addr) then begin
    goto 100;
    end;
writeln(StrPtr(addr)^);
if handle1.unwire(9878, 80, False) then begin
    goto 100;
    end;
```

```
    if handle1.wire(76654, 80, addr) then begin
        goto 100;
        end;
    writeln(StrPtr(addr)^);
    if handle1.unwire(76654, 80, False) then begin
        goto 100;
        end;

    if handle1.wire(10, 80, addr) then begin
        goto 100;
        end;
    writeln(StrPtr(addr)^);
    if handle1.unwire(10, 80, False) then begin
        goto 100;
        end;

    if handle1.wire(24000, 80, addr) then begin
        goto 100;
        end;
    writeln(StrPtr(addr)^);
    if handle1.unwire(24000, 80, False) then begin
        goto 100;
        end;

    if handle1.free then
        ;

    if vm.shutdown then
        ;

    Halt;
100:
    write('Died: Error #', errno);
end.
```

Program PROG6-2.PAS demonstrates the following:

- allocating two very large blocks of virtual memory
- running through them twice, first initializing them and then reading them (making sure they were correctly initialized).

Figure 6-2 presents the source code listing to PROG6-2.PAS.

6-2 The source code listing to PROG6-2.PAS.

```
(* * * * * * * * * * * * * * * * * *
 *
 * prog6-2.pas --     VM exerciser
 *
 *      This test program allocates two big blocks of virtual memory
 *      and runs through them twice, first initializing them and then
 *      reading them to make sure they were correctly initialized.
 *
 * * * * * * * * * * * * * * * * * * *)
```

```
program prog6_2;

uses    _globals,
        _vm;

label
    100;

type
    sixtyFourKB=          array[0..65519] of Byte;
    sixtyFourKBPtr=       ^sixtyFourKB;

var
    vm:                   VM_Vm;
    handle1:              VM_VmBlk;
    handle2:              VM_VmBlk;

    addr:                 sixtyFourKBPtr;

    i:                    DWord;
    j:                    DWord;

begin

    addr:= Nil;

    if vm.init(245760) then begin
        goto 100;
        end;

    if handle1.alloc(2113536) then begin
        goto 100;
        end;
    if handle2.alloc(2113536) then begin
        goto 100;
        end;

    for i:= 0 to 31 do begin
        (*
         * Wire a chunk of the first block and initialize it.
         *)
        if handle1.wire(i*65536, 65536, Pointer(addr)) then begin
            goto 100;
            end;
        writeln('--> ', i:2, ': wire #1, ',
                hex(Seg(addr^), 4), ':', hex(Ofs(addr^), 4));

        j:= 0;
        while j < 65534 do begin
            addr^[1]:= 0;
            addr^[16385]:= 1;
            addr^[32769]:= 2;
            addr^[49153]:= 3;
            if addr^[j] <> 0 then begin
                writeln('Error: handle1, i = ', i,
                        ', addr^[j] = ', addr^[j], ', j = ', j);
                end;
```

```
                addr^[j]:= i;

            j:= j + 8192;
            end;
        if handle1.unwire(i*65536, 65536, True) then begin
            goto 100;
            end;
        writeln('--> ', i:2, ': unwire #1');

        (*
         *  Wire a chunk of the second block and initialize it.
         *)
        if handle2.wire(i*65536, 65536, Pointer(addr)) then begin
            goto 100;
            end;
        writeln('--> ', i:2, ': wire #2, ',
                hex(Seg(addr^), 4), ':', hex(Ofs(addr^), 4));

        j:= 0;
        while j < 65534 do begin
            addr^[1]:- 0;
            addr^[16385]:= 1;
            addr^[32769]:= 2;
            addr^[49153]:= 3;
            if addr^[j] <> 0 then begin
                writeln('Error: handle2, i = ', i,
                        ', addr^[j] = ', addr^[j], ', j = ', j);
                end;
            addr^[j]:= i + 100;

            j:= j + 8192;
            end;
        if handle2.unwire(i*65536, 65536, True) then begin
            goto 100;
            end;
        writeln('--> ', i:2, ': unwire #2');
        end;

    for i:= 0 to 31 do begin
        (*
         *  Wire a chunk of the first block and make sure we get
         *  the values we expect.
         *)
        if handle1.wire(i*65536, 65536, Pointer(addr)) then begin
            goto 100;
            end;
        writeln('<-- ', i:2, ': wire #1, ',
                    hex(Seg(addr^), 4), ':', hex(Ofs(addr^), 4));
        writeln(
            addr^[1],
            addr^[16385],
            addr^[32769],
            addr^[49153]);
        j:= 0;
        while j < 65534 do begin
            if addr^[j] <> i then begin
```

```
                    writeln('Error: handle1, i = ', i,
                            ', addr^[j] = ', addr^[j],
                            ', j = ', j);
                end;

            j:= j + 8192;
            end;
        if handle1.unwire(i*65536, 65536, False) then begin
            goto 100;
            end;
        writeln('<-- ', i:2, ': unwire #1');

        (*
         *  Now validate a chunk of the second block.
         *)
        if handle2.wire(i*65536, 65536, Pointer(addr)) then begin
            goto 100;
            end;
        writeln('<-- ', i:2, ': wire #2, ',
                        hex(Seg(addr^), 4), ':', hex(Ofs(addr^), 4));
        writeln(
            addr^[1],
            addr^[16385],
            addr^[32769],
            addr^[49153]);
        j:= 0;
        while j < 65534 do begin
            if addr^[j] <> (i + 100) then begin
                writeln('Error: handle2, i = ', i,
                        ', addr^[j] = ', addr^[j],
                        ', j = ', j);
                end;

            j:= j + 8192;
            end;
        if handle2.unwire(i*65536, 65536, False) then begin
            goto 100;
            end;
        writeln('<-- ', i:2, ': unwire #2');

        end;


    if handle1.free then
        ;

    if handle2.free then
        ;


    if vm.shutdown then
        ;

    Halt;
100:
    writeln('Died: Error #', errno);
end.
```

The complete VMM source code listings

The VMM source code listing is broken up into five files. These files are heavily documented and might appear complex to those uninitiated in virtual memory management techniques. Take your time when exploring the source code. The real meat of the book resides in the source presented in this section of the book.

Figure 6-3 presents the __VM.PAS Turbo Pascal unit file listing for the VMM. This file defines all of the types objects and function prototypes for the VMM system. It also includes the other four files.

6-3 The source code listing to __VM.PAS.

```
(* * * * * * * * * * * * * * * * * * *
 *
 * _vm.pas
 *
 * External definitions for the virtual memory module
 *
 * * * * * * * * * * * * * * * * * * * *)

unit _vm;

INTERFACE

uses    _globals;

(*
 * Define some error codes
 *)
const
    VMErrOK=            0;
    VMErrEMS=           1;
    VMErrXMS=           2;
    VMErrDisk=          3;
    VMErrNoConv=        4;
    VMErrBadWire=       5;
    VMErrNotWired=      6;
    VMErrBounds=        7;


(*
 * Define the functions
 *)
type
    VM_Vm= object
        function        init(
                            maxSpace:       DWord)
                            : Boolean;
        function        shutdown
                            : Boolean;
        end;

    VM_VmBlk= object

        handle:         DWord;
```

```
        function        alloc(
                            size:           DWord)
                            : Boolean;
        function        free
                            : Boolean;
        function        wire(
                            areaOffset:     DWord;
                            areaSize:       DWord;
                            var areaAddress: Pointer)
                            : Boolean;
        function        unwire(
                            areaOffset:     DWord;
                            areaSize:       DWord;
                            dirty:          Boolean)
                            : Boolean;
        end;


IMPLEMENTATION

uses    _ems,
        _xms;

const
    (*
     * First let's define some important constants:
     *)
    VM_PAGE_SIZE=           16384;
    VM_PAGE_SHIFT=          14;
    VM_PAGE_OFFSET_MASK=    VM_PAGE_SIZE-1;
    VM_PAGE_NUM_MASK=       not VM_PAGE_OFFSET_MASK;

    VM_MAX_BUFF_SPACE=      131072;

type
    (*
     * Define the types of secondary memory
     *)
    VM_SecondaryKind= (
        VM_SEC_UNALLOCATED,
        VM_SEC_DISK,
        VM_SEC_XMS,
        VM_SEC_EMS);

    (*
     * Define the queues on which we might find a physical page.
     *)
    VM_SecondaryQueue= (
        VM_Q_FREE,
        VM_Q_LRU,
        VM_Q_WIRED);

    (*
     * Define all of the pointer types
     *)
    VM_QueueElemPtr=        ^VM_QueueELem;
    VM_FreeAreaPtr=         ^VM_FreeArea;
    VM_ConvBuffPtr=         ^VM_ConvBuff;
    VM_EmsBuffPtr=          ^VM_EmsBuff;
    VM_XmsBuffPtr=          ^VM_XmsBuff;
```

```
VM_EmsPagePtr=       ^VM_EmsPage;
VM_XmsPagePtr=       ^VM_XmsPage;
VM_DiskPagePtr=      ^VM_DiskPage;
VM_VmPagePtr=        ^VM_VmPage;
VM_VmBlockPtr=       ^VM_VmBlock;
VM_VmPageArrPtr=     ^VM_VmPageArr;
VM_PagePtr=          ^VM_Page;

(*
 *  Define what a virtual memory page is:
 *)
VM_Page=             array[0..VM_PAGE_SIZE-1] of Byte;

(*
 *  Define a generic queue element
 *)
VM_QueueElem= object
    next:           Pointer;
    prev:           Pointer;

    procedure       enqueTail(
                        head:       Pointer;
                        tail:       Pointer);
    procedure       enqueHead(
                        head:       Pointer;
                        tail:       Pointer);
    procedure       deque(
                        head:       Pointer;
                        tail:       Pointer);
    end;



(*
 *  Define a free area descriptor
 *)
VM_FreeArea= object (VM_QueueElem)
    handle:         DWord;          { EMS/XMS Buff addr (if appropriate) }
    start:          DWord;          { Start Address }
    size:           DWord;          { Size of Area  }
    end;



(*
 *  Define a conventional memory buffer descriptor.
 *)
VM_ConvBuff= object (VM_QueueElem)
    buffSize:       Word;           { Size in pages }
    address:        Pointer;        { Address of buffer }

    vmBlock:        VM_VmBlockPtr;  { Where the pages are from }
    startPage:      Word;           { First page in buffer }
    wiredPages:     Word;           { Number of wired pages }
    end;

(*
 *  Define an EMS buffer descriptor.
 *)
VM_EmsBuff= object (VM_QueueElem)
```

```
        buffSize:       Word;           { Size in pages }
        handle:         EMS_EmBlk;      { EMS handle }

        useCount:       Word;           { Number of pages in use }
        end;


(*
 *  Define an XMS buffer descriptor.
 *)
VM_XmsBuff= object (VM_QueueElem)

        buffSize:       Word;           { Size in pages }
        handle:         XMS_XmBlk;      { XMS handle }

        useCount:       Word;           { Number of pages in use }
        end;

(*
 *  Define the various secondary memory page descriptors
 *)
VM_EmsPage= object (VM_QueueElem)

        vmPage:         VM_VmPagePtr;   { Corresponding VM page }

        emsBuff:        VM_EmsBuffPtr;  { EMS buffer descriptor }
        pageNum:        Word;           { Page in buffer }

        secondaryQueue: VM_SecondaryQueue; { Queue page is on }
        end;

VM_XmsPage= object (VM_QueueElem)

        vmPage:         VM_VmPagePtr;   { Corresponding VM page }

        xmsBuff:        VM_XmsBuffPtr;  { XMS buffer descriptor }
        pageNum:        Word;           { Offset into buffer }

        secondaryQueue: VM_SecondaryQueue; { Queue page is on }
        end;


VM_DiskPage= object (VM_QueueElem)

        vmPage:         VM_VmPagePtr;   { Corresponding VM page }

        pageNum:        Word;           { Offset into file (in pages) }
        end;

(*
 *  Define a virtual memory page
 *)
VM_SecondaryPage= record
   case Word of
        1: (disk:       VM_DiskPagePtr;);{ Disk secondary page }
        2: (xms:        VM_XmsPagePtr;);{ XMS secondary page }
        3: (ems:        VM_EmsPagePtr;);{ EMS secondary page }
   end;
```

6-3 Continued.

```
VM_VmPage= record

    pageNum:          Word;                { Number of page in VM block }

    secondaryKind:    VM_SecondaryKind;    { Type of secondary }

    sec:              VM_SecondaryPage;{ Secondary Page }

    convBuff:         VM_ConvBuffPtr; { Conventional memory buffer }
    offset:           DWord;               { Offset in buffer }

    wired:            Word;                { Wire count }

    dirty:            Boolean;             { Page modified }
    end;

VM_VmPageArr=         array[0..0] of VM_VmPage;

(*
 *  Define a virtual memory block.
 *)
VM_VmBlock= object (VM_QueueElem)

    size:             Word;                { Size in pages }
    pages:            VM_VmPageArrPtr;{ Virtual pages }
    end;


(*
 *  Define the EMS Descriptor
 *)
VM_EmsDesc= record
    pageFrame:        EMS_PageFrame;  { Address of Page Frame }

    contents:         array [0..EMS_PAGE_FRAME_SIZE-1] of
                          VM_EmsPagePtr; { Pages in Page frame }

    mruPage:          VM_EmsPagePtr;  { Page LRU queue }
    lruPage:          VM_EmsPagePtr;

    firstWired:       VM_EmsPagePtr;  { Wired page list }
    lastWired:        VM_EmsPagePtr;

    firstFree:        VM_FreeAreaPtr; { Free page chain }
    lastFree:         VM_FreeAreaPtr;

    firstBuff:        VM_EmsBuffPtr;  { Buffer queue }
    lastBuff:         VM_EmsBuffPtr;

    pageBuffHandle: EMS_EmBlk;        { One page handle for buffering }

    emsBlockSize:     Word;           { Preferred block size }
    end;

(*
 *  Define the XMS descriptor.
 *)
VM_XmsDesc= record

    mruPage:          VM_XmsPagePtr;  { Page LRU queue }
    lruPage:          VM_XmsPagePtr;
```

```
            firstWired:        VM_XmsPagePtr;  { Wired page list }
            lastWired:         VM_XmsPagePtr;

            firstFree:         VM_FreeAreaPtr; { Free page chain }
            lastFree:          VM_FreeAreaPtr;

            firstBuff:         VM_XmsBuffPtr;  { Buffer queue }
            lastBuff:          VM_XmsBuffPtr;

            xmsBlockSize:      Word;           { Preferred block size }
            end;

       (*
        * Define the Disk descriptor.
        *)
       VM_DiskDesc=    record

            firstPage:         VM_DiskPagePtr; { Page queue }
            lastPage:          VM_DiskPagePtr;

            firstFree:         VM_FreeAreaPtr; { Free page chain }
            lastFree:          VM_FreeAreaPtr;

            channel:           File of VM_Page;{ File channel }

            fileSize:          DWord;          { Current size of file }
            end;

       (*
        * Define the conventional memory descriptor.
        *)
       VM_ConvDesc= record

            mruBuff:           VM_ConvBuffPtr; { Buffer LRU chain }
            lruBuff:           VM_ConvBuffPtr;

            firstWired:        VM_ConvBuffPtr; { Wired buffer list }
            lastWired:         VM_ConvBuffPtr;

            spaceAvail:        DWord;          { maxSpace - Memory allocated for buffers }
            end;
const
    PFABUFF: VM_ConvBuffPtr=      (VM_ConvBuffPtr(-1));

(*
 * Declare some extern functions
 *)
procedure       vm_addFree(
                    handle:            DWord;
                    start:             DWord;
                    size:              DWord;
                    var head:          VM_FreeAreaPtr;
                    var tail:          VM_FreeAreaPtr);
                    forward;

procedure       vm_freeVmPage(
                    vmPage:            VM_VmPagePtr);
                    forward;
```

6-3 Continued.

```
procedure        vm_freeEmsPage(
                    emsPage:          VM_EmsPagePtr);
                 forward;

procedure        vm_freeXmsPage(
                    xmsPage:          VM_XmsPagePtr);
                 forward;

procedure        vm_freeDiskPage(
                    diskPage:         VM_DiskPagePtr);
                 forward;

procedure        vm_freeConvBuff(
                    convBuff:         VM_ConvBuffPtr);
                 forward;

procedure        vm_freeEmsBuff(
                    emsBuff:          VM_EmsBuffPtr);
                 forward;

procedure        vm_freeXmsBuff(
                    XmsBuff:          VM_XmsBuffPtr);
                 forward;

function         vm_faultInPages(
                    var vmBlock:      VM_VmBlock;
                    startPage:        Word;
                    endPage:          Word)
                    : Boolean;
                 forward;

function         vm_faultToEMS(
                    var vmBlock:      VM_VmBlock;
                    startPage:        Word;
                    endPage:          Word)
                    : Boolean;
                 forward;

function         vm_faultToXMS(
                    var vmBlock:      VM_VmBlock;
                    startPage:        Word;
                    endPage:          Word)
                    : Boolean;
                 forward;

function         vm_faultToDisk(
                    var vmBlock:      VM_VmBlock;
                    startPage:        Word;
                    endPage:          Word)
                    : Boolean;
                 forward;

function         vm_tryMapPFA(
                    var vmBlock:      VM_VmBlock;
                    startPage:        Word;
                    endPage:          Word)
                    : Boolean;
                 forward;

function         vm_tryMapConv(
                    var vmBlock:      VM_VmBlock;
                    startPage:        Word;
                    endPage:          Word)
                    : Boolean;
                 forward;
```

```
procedure          vm_getEMSPages(
                       number:              Word;
                       var chain:           VM_EmsPagePtr);
                       forward;

procedure          vm_getXMSPages(
                       number:              Word;
                       var chain:           VM_XmsPagePtr);
                       forward;

procedure          vm_getDiskPages(
                       number:              Word;
                       var chain:           VM_DiskPagePtr);
                       forward;

procedure          vm_promoteToEMS(
                       var vmPage:          VM_VmPage;
                       var emsPage:         VM_EmsPage);
                       forward;

procedure          vm_promoteToXMS(
                       var vmPage:          VM_VmPage;
                       var xmsPage:         VM_XmsPage);
                       forward;

procedure          vm_promoteToDisk(
                       var vmPage:          VM_VmPage;
                       var diskPage:        VM_DiskPage);
                       forward;

procedure          vm_demoteFromEMS(
                       var emsPage:         VM_EmsPage);
                       forward;

procedure          vm_demoteFromXMS(
                       var xmsPage:         VM_XmsPage);
                       forward;

procedure          vm_flushVmPage(
                       var vmPage:          VM_VmPage);
                       forward;

procedure          vm_loadVmPage(
                       var vmPage:          VM_VmPage;
                       var convBuff:        VM_ConvBuff);
                       forward;

function           vm_freeLRUConvBuff
                       : Boolean;
                       forward;

procedure          vm_moveSecPageToWired(
                       var vmPage:          VM_VmPage);
                       forward;

procedure          vm_dequeSecPage(
                       var vmPage:          VM_VmPage);
                       forward;

procedure          vm_fatal(
                       errorMsg:            String);
                       forward;
```

```
(*
 *  Now declare global data
 *)
var
    ems:                EMS_Ems;
    xms:                Xms_Xms;
    em:                 VM_EmsDesc;
    xm:                 VM_XmsDesc;
    disk:               VM_DiskDesc;
    conv:               VM_ConvDesc;

    firstVmBlock:       VM_VmBlockPtr;
    lastVmBlock:        VM_VmBlockPtr;

    emsPresent:         Boolean;
    xmsPresent:         Boolean;

    logFile:            Text;
{$I VMINIT}
{$I VMALLOC}
{$I VMWTRF}
{$I VMUTIL}

begin
    Assign(logFile, 'logfile');
    ReWrite(logFile);
end.
```

Figure 6-4 presents the source code listing to VMINIT.PAS. This source file contains the code to functions that initialize the VMM's data structures.

6-4 The source code listing to VMINIT.PAS.

```
(* * * * * * * * * * * * * * * * *
 *
 *  vminit.pas --      VM initialization
 *
 *       Initialization and termination of VM module
 *
 * * * * * * * * * * * * * * * * * *)

function VM_Vm.init(maxSpace: DWord) : Boolean;

var
    i:                  Integer;
    numHandles:         Word;
    totalPages:         Word;
    freePages:          Word;
    activeHandles:      Word;
    freeKXM:            Word;
    contiguousKXM:      Word;
    xmsHandle:          XMS_XmBlk;
    .blockSize:         Word;
    lockCount:          Word;
```

```
begin

    (*
     *  First look into initializing EMS
     *)
    em.mruPage:= Nil;
    em.lruPage:= Nil;
    em.firstWired:= Nil;
    em.lastWired:= Nil;
    em.firstFree:= Nil;
    em.lastFree:= Nil;
    em.firstBuff:= Nil;
    em.lastBuff:= Nil;

    emsPresent:= False;
    if (not ems.init) and (not ems.getStatus) then begin
        emsPresent:= True;

        (*
         *  Get the page frame address
         *)
        if ems.getPFA(em.pageFrame) then begin
            errno:= VMErrEMS;
            init:= True;
            Exit;
            end;

        (*
         *  Indicate that the page frame area is empty
         *)
        for i:= 0 to EMS_PAGE_FRAME_SIZE-1 do begin
            em.contents[i]:= Nil;
            end;


        (*
         *  Allocate a one page buffer that we will use for
         *  reading and writing pages between XMS and DISK.
         *
         *  This is to avoid spending valuable conventional memory on
         *  the buffer.
         *)
        if em.pageBuffHandle.allocEM(1) then begin
            em.pageBuffHandle.handle:= 0;
            end;

        (*
         *  Let's figure out how big blocks we should allocate.
         *  We do this by dividing the total available pages by the
         *  total available handles.
         *)
        if ems.getTotalHandles40(numHandles) then begin
            (*
             *  Probably not 4.0 EMS. Just assume 64 handles.
             *)
            numHandles:= 64;
            end;
        if ems.getNumActiveHandles(activeHandles) then begin
            vm_fatal('EMS_Ems.getNumActiveHandles');
            end;
```

```
      if ems.getFreeEM(totalPages, freePages) then begin
          vm_fatal('EMS_Ems.getFreeEM');
          end;

      em.emsBlockSize:= (freePages + numHandles - 1) div
                        (numHandles - activeHandles);

      em.emsBlockSize:= max(em.emsBlockSize, 8);
      end;

(*
 *  Now let's look at XMS.
 *)
xm.mruPage:= Nil;
xm.lruPage:= Nil;
xm.firstWired:= Nil;
xm.lastWired:= Nil;

xm.firstFree:= Nil;
xm.lastFree:= Nil;

xm.firstBuff:= Nil;
xm.lastBuff:= Nil;

xmsPresent:= False;
if not xms.init then begin
    xmsPresent:= True;

    (*
     *  Let's figure out how big blocks we should allocate.
     *  We do this by dividing the total available pages by the
     *  total available handles.
     *
     *  Start by just getting a handle.
     *)
    if xms.getFreeXM(freeKXM, contiguousKXM) then begin
        if errno = XMSErrNoXMLeft then begin
            freeKXM:= 0;
            end
        else begin
            vm_fatal('XMS_Xms.getFreeXM');
            end;
        end;

    if freeKXM <> 0 then begin
        if xmsHandle.allocXM(1) then begin
            vm_fatal('XMS_XmBlk.allocXM');
            end;
        if xmsHandle.getHandInfo(blockSize, numHandles, lockCount) then begin
            vm_fatal('XMS_Xms.getHandleInfo');
            end;

        freePages:= freeKXM div (VM_PAGE_SIZE div XMS_PAGE_SIZE);
        xm.xmsBlockSize:= (freePages + numHandles - 1) div numHandles;

        xm.xmsBlockSize:= max(xm.xmsBlockSize, 8);

        if xmsHandle.freeXM then begin
            vm_fatal('XMS_XmBlk.freeXM');
            end;
        end
```

```
            else begin
                xm.xmsBlockSize:= 8;
                end;
            end;

        (*
         *  Now initialize the disk
         *)
        disk.firstPage:= Nil;
        disk.lastPage:= Nil;
        disk.firstFree:= Nil;
        disk.lastFree:= Nil;
        disk.fileSize:= 0;

        assign(disk.channel, 'TMPFILE');
        rewrite(disk.channel);
(*      if disk.channel = Nil then begin
            return VMErrDisk;
            end;
 *)

        (*
         *  Initialize conventional memory descriptor:
         *)
        conv.mruBuff:= Nil;
        conv.lruBuff:= Nil;
        conv.firstWired:= Nil;
        conv.lastWired:= Nil;
        conv.spaceAvail:= maxSpace;

        (*
         *  Now initialize the VM block queue
         *)
        firstVmBlock:= Nil;
        lastVmBlock:= Nil;

        errno:= VMErrOK;
        init:= False;
end;

function VM_Vm.shutdown : Boolean;

var
    i:                  Word;

    currFreeArea:       VM_FreeAreaPtr;
    nextFreeArea:       VM_FreeAreaPtr;

    currConvBuff:       VM_ConvBuffPtr;
    nextConvBuff:       VM_ConvBuffPtr;

    currEmsBuff:        VM_EmsBuffPtr;
    nextEmsBuff:        VM_EmsBuffPtr;

    currXmsBuff:        VM_XmsBuffPtr;
    nextXmsBuff:        VM_XmsBuffPtr;

    currVmPage:         VM_VmPagePtr;

    currVmBlock:        VM_VmBlockPtr;
    nextVmBlock:        VM_VmBlockPtr;
```

```
begin
    (*
     *  Start by going through the VM blocks.
     *)
    currVmBlock:= firstVmBlock;
    while currVmBlock <> Nil do begin
        nextVmBlock:= currVmBlock^.next;

        (*
         *  Now go through the pages for the block
         *)
        for i:= 0 to currVmBlock^.size - 1 do begin
            currVmPage:= @currVmBlock^.pages^[i];

            if currVmPage^.secondaryKind <> VM_SEC_UNALLOCATED then begin
                Dispose(currVmPage^.sec.disk);
                end;
            end;
        FreeMem(currVmBlock^.pages,
                    sizeof(VM_VmPage) * currVmBlock^.size);
        Dispose(currVmBlock);

        currVmBlock:= nextVmBlock;
        end;


    (*
     *  Now free up the various buffers and buffer descriptors
     *)
    currConvBuff:= conv.mruBuff;
    while currConvBuff <> Nil do begin
        nextConvBuff:= currConvBuff^.next;

        (*
         *  Free the actual buffer
         *)
        FreeMem(currConvBuff^.address,
                currConvBuff^.buffSize * VM_PAGE_SIZE);

        (*
         *  Free the buffer descriptor
         *)
        Dispose(currConvBuff);

        currConvBuff:= nextConvBuff;
        end;

    currEmsBuff:= em.firstBuff;
    while currEmsBuff <> Nil do begin
        nextEmsBuff:= currEmsBuff^.next;

        (*
         *  Free the actual buffer
         *)
        if currEmsBuff^.handle.freeEM then begin
            writeln('VM: Fatal Error: ',
                        ems.errorText(errno), ' EMS Handle #',
                                            currEmsBuff^.handle.handle);
            Halt;
            end;
```

```
(*
 *  Free the buffer descriptor
 *)
Dispose(currEmsBuff);

currEmsBuff:= nextEmsBuff;
end;

currXmsBuff:= xm.firstBuff;
while currXmsBuff <> Nil do begin
    nextXmsBuff:= currXmsBuff^.next;

    (*
     *  Free the actual buffer
     *)
    if currXmsBuff^.handle.freeXM then begin
        writeln('VM: Fatal Error: ',
                  xms.errorText(errno), ' XMS Handle #',
                               currXmsBuff^.handle.handle);
        Halt;
        end;

    (*
     *  Free the buffer descriptor
     *)
    Dispose(currXmsBuff);

    currXmsBuff:= nextXmsBuff;
    end;

(*
 *  Now free various free chains.
 *)
currFreeArea:= em.firstFree;
while currFreeArea <> Nil do begin
    nextFreeArea:= currFreeArea^.next;
    Dispose(currFreeArea);

    currFreeArea:= nextFreeArea;
    end;

currFreeArea:= xm.firstFree;
while currFreeArea <> Nil do begin
    nextFreeArea:= currFreeArea^.next;
    Dispose(currFreeArea);

    currFreeArea:= nextFreeArea;
    end;

currFreeArea:= disk.firstFree;
while currFreeArea <> Nil do begin
    nextFreeArea:= currFreeArea^.next;
    Dispose(currFreeArea);

    currFreeArea:= nextFreeArea;
    end;

(*
 *  Free up the one page EMS buffer
 *)
```

6-4 Continued.

```
    if emsPresent then begin
        if em.pageBuffHandle.freeEM then begin
            vm_fatal('EMS_EmBlock.freeEM');
            end;
        end;

    (*
     *  Now close the temp file and delete it.
     *)
    Close(disk.channel);
    Erase(disk.channel);

    (*
     *  All done.
     *)
    shutdown:= False;
end;
```

Figure 6-5 presents the source code listing to VMUTIL.PAS. This source file contains the code to functions that maintain the linked lists that keep track of where pages are located.

6-5 The source code listing to VMUTIL.PAS.

```
(* * * * * * * * * * * * * * * * * *
 *
 * vmutil.pas    -- Some utility functions for VM
 *
 *      Defines routines for queue handling and free
 * area handling. Also defines the vm_fatal routine.
 *
 * * * * * * * * * * * * * * * * * *)
procedure VM_QueueElem.enqueTail(
    head:               Pointer;
    tail:               Pointer);

var
    qHead:              ^VM_QueueElemPtr;
    qTail:              ^VM_QueueElemPtr;

begin
    qHead:= head;
    qTail:= tail;

    prev:= qTail^;
    next:= Nil;
    if qTail^ <> Nil then begin
        qTail^^.next:= @self;
        end
    else begin
        qHead^:= @self;
        end;
    qTail^:= @self;
end;
```

```
procedure VM_QueueElem.enqueHead(
    head:               Pointer;
    tail:               Pointer);

var
    qHead:              ^VM_QueueElemPtr;
    qTail:              ^VM_QueueElemPtr;

begin
    qHead:= head;
    qTail:= tail;

    next:= qHead^;
    prev:= Nil;
    if qHead^ <> Nil then begin
        qHead^^.prev:= @self;
        end
    else begin
        qTail^:= @self;
        end;
    qHead^:= @self;
end;


procedure VM_QueueElem.deque(
    head:               Pointer;
    tail:               Pointer);
var
    qHead:              ^VM_QueueElemPtr;
    qTail:              ^VM_QueueElemPtr;

begin
    qHead:= head;
    qTail:= tail;

    (*
     *  DEQUEing an element from a list that isn't on the list
     *  can cause all kinds of problems. Let's do a sanity check.
     *)
    if prev = Nil then begin
        if qHead^ <> @self then begin
            vm_fatal('deque error');
            end;
        end
    else begin
        if VM_QueueElemPtr(prev)^.next <> @self then begin
            vm_fatal('deque error');
            end;
        end;

    if next = Nil then begin
        if qTail^ <> @self then begin
            vm_fatal('deque error');
            end;
        end
    else begin
        if VM_QueueElemPtr(next)^.prev <> @self then begin
            vm_fatal('deque error');
            end;
        end;
```

```
        if prev = Nil then begin
            qHead^:= next;
            end
        else begin
            VM_QueueElemPtr(prev)^.next:= next;
            end;
        if next = Nil then begin
            qTail^:= prev;
            end
        else begin
            VM_QueueElemPtr(next)^.prev:= prev;
            end;

end;

procedure vm_addFree(
    handle:             DWord;
    start:              DWord;
    size:               DWord;
    var head:           VM_FreeAreaPtr;
    var tail:           VM_FreeAreaPtr);

label
    100;

var

    nextArea:           VM_FreeAreaPtr;
    prevArea:           VM_FreeAreaPtr;
    newArea:            VM_FreeAreaPtr;

begin
    (*
     *  Find the right place to insert it.
     *)
    prevArea:= NIl;
    nextArea:= head;
    while nextArea <> Nil do begin
        if (nextArea^.handle > handle) or
                (nextArea^.handle = handle) and
                    (nextArea^.start >= start + size) then begin
            goto 100;
            end;
        prevArea:= nextArea;
        nextArea:= nextArea^.next;
        end;

100:
    (*
     *  See if we merge with previous area
     *)
    if (prevArea <> Nil) and
            (prevArea^.handle = handle) and
            (prevArea^.start + prevArea^.size = start) then begin
        (*
         *  See if we merge with next area
         *)
        if (nextArea <> Nil) and
                (nextArea^.handle = handle) and
                (start + size = nextArea^.start) then begin
```

```
                    (*
                     *   New area is sandwiched between prev and next.
                     *   Merge them all into prev.
                     *)
                    prevArea^.size:= prevArea^.size + size + nextArea^.size;
                    nextArea^.deque(@head, @tail);
                    Dispose(nextArea);
                    end
                else begin
                    (*
                     *   Merge with previous area
                     *)
                    prevArea^.size:= prevArea^.size + size;
                    end;
                end
            else begin
                (*
                 *   See if we merge with next area
                 *)
                if (nextArea <> Nil) and
                        (nextArea^.handle = handle) and
                        (start + size = nextArea^.start) then begin
                    (*
                     *   We merge with next area.
                     *)
                    nextArea^.start:= start;
                    nextArea^.size:= size + nextArea^.size;
                    end
                else begin
                    (*
                     *   No merging. We need to insert a new element.
                     *)
                    New(newArea);
                    newArea^.handle:= handle;
                    newArea^.start:= start;
                    newArea^.size:= size;
                    newArea^.next:= nextArea;
                    newArea^.prev:= prevArea;
                    if prevArea <> Nil then begin
                        prevArea^.next:= newArea;
                        end
                    else begin
                        head:= newArea;
                        end;
                    if nextArea <> Nil then begin
                        nextArea^.prev:= newArea;
                        end
                    else begin
                        tail:= newArea;
                        end;
                    end;
                end;
end;

procedure vm_fatal(errorMsg: String);

begin
    writeln('Fatal error: ', errorMsg, ', ', errno);
    Halt;
end;
```

Figure 6-6 presents the source code listing to VMALLOC.PAS. This source file contains the code to functions that allocate and free VM blocks.

6-6 The source code listing to VMALLOC.PAS.

```
(* * * * * * * * * * * * * * * * * *
 *
 * vmalloc.pas  --      Allocate and Free VM blocks
 *
 *      Defines routines for allocating and freeing VM blocks
 *
 * * * * * * * * * * * * * * * * * * *)

function VM_VmBlk.alloc(size: DWord) : Boolean;

var
    newVmBlock:         VM_VmBlockPtr;
    page:               VM_VmPagePtr;
    i:                  Word;

    numPages:           Word;

begin
    (*
     *  Get a new VM_VmBlock structure:
     *)
    New(newVmBlock);

    (*
     *  Start by changing size to number of pages
     *)
    numPages:= Word((size + VM_PAGE_OFFSET_MASK) shr VM_PAGE_SHIFT);

    (*
     *  Allocate the vm block and pages
     *)
    newVmBlock^.size:= numPages;
    GetMem(newVmBlock^.pages, sizeof(VM_VmPage) * numPages);

    for i:= 0 to numPages-1 do begin
        page:= @newVmBlock^.pages^[i];

        page^.pageNum:= i;
        page^.secondaryKind:= VM_SEC_UNALLOCATED;
        page^.sec.disk:= Nil;
        page^.convBuff:= Nil;
        page^.offset:= 0;
        page^.wired:= 0;
        page^.dirty:= False;
        end;

    (*
     *  Link it into the list of blocks
     *)
    newVmBlock^.enqueHead(@firstVmBlock, @lastVmBlock);
```

```
(*
 * Finally return the handle
 *)
handle:= DWord(newVmBlock);

(*
 * Indicate that there was no error
 *)
errno:= VMErrOK;
alloc:= False;

end;


function VM_VmBlk.free : Boolean;

var

    i:                 Integer;

    vmBlock:           VM_VmBlockPtr;

begin

    vmBlock:= VM_VmBlockPtr(handle);

    (*
     * One by one, free up the pages.
     *)
    for i:= 0 to vmBlock^.size-1 do begin
        vm_freeVmPage(@vmBlock^.pages^[i]);
        end;

    (*
     * Free the page array
     *)
    FreeMem(vmBlock^.pages, sizeof(VM_VmPage) * vmBlock^.size);

    (*
     * Unlink the block
     *)
    vmBlock^.deque(@firstVmBlock, @lastVmBlock);

    (*
     * Finally, free it up
     *)
    Dispose(vmBlock);

    (*
     * Give no error
     *)
    errno:= VMErrOK;
    free:= False;

end;


procedure vm_freeVmPage(vmPage: VM_VmPagePtr);
```

6-6 Continued.

```
begin

    (*
     *  First free the secondary memory page
     *)
    case vmPage^.secondaryKind of
    VM_SEC_UNALLOCATED:
        ;

    VM_SEC_DISK:
        vm_freeDiskPage(vmPage^.sec.disk);

    VM_SEC_EMS:
        vm_freeEmsPage(vmPage^.sec.ems);

    VM_SEC_XMS:
        vm_freeXmsPage(vmPage^.sec.xms);
        end;

    (*
     *  Now free the primary memory page (if it's in memory)
     *)
    if (vmPage^.convBuff <> Nil) and (vmPage^.convBuff <> PFABUFF) then begin
        vm_freeConvBuff(vmPage^.convBuff);
        end;

end;


procedure vm_freeDiskPage(diskPage: VM_DiskPagePtr);

begin

    (*
     *  First remove it from the list of disk pages.
     *)
    diskPage^.deque(@disk.firstPage, @disk.lastPage);

    (*
     *  Now add the space to the free list
     *)
    vm_addFree(0, diskPage^.pageNum, 1,
                    disk.firstFree, disk.lastFree);

    (*
     *  Finally free the actual memory.
     *)
    Dispose(diskPage);

end;

procedure vm_freeEmsPage(emsPage: VM_EmsPagePtr);

begin

    (*
     *  First remove it from the list of disk pages.
     *)
    if emsPage^.vmPage^.wired <> 0 then begin
        emsPage^.deque(@em.firstWired, @em.lastWired);
        end
```

```
        else begin
            emsPage^.deque(@em.mruPage, @em.lruPage);
            end;

    (*
     *  Now add the space to the free list
     *)
    vm_addFree(DWord(emsPage^.emsBuff),
                emsPage^.pageNum,
                1,
                em.firstFree,
                em.lastFree);
    emsPage^.emsBuff^.useCount:= emsPage^.emsBuff^.useCount;

    (*
     *  This might have emptied the buffer. If so, free the buffer.
     *)
    if emsPage^.emsBuff^.useCount = 0 then begin
        vm_freeEmsBuff(emsPage^.emsBuff);
        end;

    (*
     *  Finally free the actual memory.
     *)
    Dispose(emsPage);

end;

procedure vm_freeXmsPage(xmsPage: VM_XmsPagePtr);

begin

    (*
     *  First remove it from the list of disk pages.
     *)
    if xmsPage^.vmPage^.wired <> 0 then begin
        xmsPage^.deque(@xm.firstWired, @xm.lastWired);
        end
    else begin
        xmsPage^.deque(@xm.mruPage, @xm.lruPage);
        end;

    (*
     *  Now add the space to the free list
     *)
    vm_addFree(DWord(xmsPage^.xmsBuff),
                xmsPage^.pageNum,
                1,
                xm.firstFree,
                xm.lastFree);
    xmsPage^.xmsBuff^.useCount:= xmsPage^.xmsBuff^.useCount - 1;

    (*
     *  This might have emptied the buffer. If so, free the buffer.
     *)
    if xmsPage^.xmsBuff^.useCount = 0 then begin
        vm_freeXmsBuff(xmsPage^.xmsBuff);
        end;
```

6-6 Continued.

```
    (*
     *   Finally free the actual memory.
     *)
    Dispose(xmsPage);

end;

procedure vm_freeConvBuff(convBuff: VM_ConvBuffPtr);

var
    i:                  DWord;
    pageNum:            Word;

begin

    (*
     *   First go through all of the pages in the buffer
     *   removing references to this buffer.
     *)
    pageNum:= convBuff^.startPage;
    for i:= 0 to convBuff^.buffSize - 1 do begin
        convBuff^.vmBlock^.pages^[pageNum].convBuff:= Nil;
        convBuff^.vmBlock^.pages^[pageNum].offset:= 0;

        pageNum:= pageNum + 1;
        end;

    (*
     *   Remove the buffer from the buffer list
     *)
    convBuff^.deque(@conv.mruBuff, @conv.lruBuff);

    (*
     *   Free the buffer memory
     *)
    FreeMem(convBuff^.address, convBuff^.buffSize * VM_PAGE_SIZE);

    (*
     *   Finally, free the descriptor itself
     *)
    Dispose(convBuff);

end;

procedure vm_freeEmsBuff(emsBuff: VM_EmsBuffPtr);

var
    currFreeArea:       VM_FreeAreaPtr;
    nextFreeArea:       VM_FreeAreaPtr;

begin

    (*
     *   First remove it from the ems buffer list
     *)
    emsBuff^.deque(@em.firstBuff, @em.lastBuff);

    (*
     *   Now release the EMS memory
     *)
```

```
    if emsBuff^.handle.freeEM then begin
        vm_fatal('EMS_EmBlk.freeEM');
        end;

    (*
     *  Now go through the free memory chain removing any references
     *  to this buffer
     *)
    currFreeArea:= em.firstFree;
    while currFreeArea <> Nil do begin
        nextFreeArea:= currFreeArea^.next;

        if currFreeArea^.handle = DWord(emsBuff) then begin
            currFreeArea^.deque(@em.firstFree, @em.lastFree);
            Dispose(currFreeArea);
            end;

        currFreeArea:= nextFreeArea;
        end;

    (*
     *  Now release the buffer descriptor
     *)
    Dispose(emsBuff);

end;

procedure vm_freeXmsBuff(xmsBuff: VM_XmsBuffPtr);

var
    currFreeArea:       VM_FreeAreaPtr;
    nextFreeArea:       VM_FreeAreaPtr;

begin

    (*
     *  First remove it from the xms buffer list
     *)
    xmsBuff^.deque(@xm.firstBuff, @xm.lastBuff);

    (*
     *  Now release the XMS memory
     *)
    if xmsBuff^.handle.freeXM then begin
        vm_fatal('XMS_Xms.freeXM');
        end;

    (*
     *  Now go through the free memory chain removing any references
     *  to this buffer
     *)
    currFreeArea:= xm.firstFree;
    while currFreeArea <> Nil do begin
        nextFreeArea:= currFreeArea^.next;

        if currFreeArea^.handle = DWord(xmsBuff) then begin
            currFreeArea^.deque(@xm.firstFree, @xm.lastFree);
            Dispose(currFreeArea);
            end;
```

```
        currFreeArea:= nextFreeArea;
        end;

    (*
     *  Now release the buffer descriptor
     *)
    Dispose(xmsBuff);

end;
```

Figure 6-7 presents the source code listing to VMWIRE.PAS. This source file contains the code to functions that permit the wiring and unwiring of VMM pages.

6-7 The source code listing to VMWIRE.PAS.

```
(* * * * * * * * * * * * * * * * * *
 *
 * vmwire.pas -- Wire and unwire VM pages
 *
 *      Defines routines for wiring and unwiring VM pages.
 * Wiring a page makes it accessable to a program. Unwiring
 * indicates that the page will not be needed until it is
 * wired again.
 *
 * * * * * * * * * * * * * * * * * * *)

function VM_VmBlk.wire(areaOffset: DWord;
            areaSize: DWord;
            var areaAddress: Pointer): Boolean;

label
    100;

var

    startPage:          Word;
    endPage:            Word;
    pageNum:            Word;
    offset:             Word;

    blockBuffer:        VM_ConvBuffPtr;

    vmBlock:            VM_VmBlockPtr;
    vmPage:             VM_VmPagePtr;

    error:              Integer;
    contiguous:         Boolean;
    pageWired:          Boolean;
    resident:           Boolean;

    tmpEmsPage:         VM_EmsPagePtr;
```

```
begin
    (*
     * Start by casting the handle into an appropriate pointer.
     *)
    vmBlock:= VM_VmBlockPtr(handle);

    (*
     * Let's translate the offset and size into page
     * values.
     * The offset is truncated to a page number, and the
     * size is rounded up to a page number.
     *)
    startPage:= Word(areaOffset shr VM_PAGE_SHIFT);
    endPage:= Word((areaOffset + areaSize - 1) shr VM_PAGE_SHIFT);
    offset:= Word(areaOffset and VM_PAGE_OFFSET_MASK);

    (*
     * Make sure the pages are within the bounds of the block:
     *)
    if endPage >= vmBlock^.size then begin
        errno:= VMErrBounds;
        wire:= True;
        end;

    (*
     * We need to see whether the pages are wired or resident already.
     * If there is an already wired page in the set, it cannot be moved.
     * Otherwise, we would invalidate the address returned to the caller
     * who wired it. Since it cannot be moved, we must have room in its
     * buffer for all of the other pages that we are loading. If there
     * is room in the buffer, then the other pages we are mapping will
     * be there, because we do not replace individual pages in a buffer.
     * This, though, does not hold true for the PFA, so we make an
     * exception.
     *)

    (*
     * blockBuffer will hold the convBuff address for the resident
     * pages. Contiguous will flag whether all of the resident pages
     * are in the same buffer. If there is a wired page, they must
     * be.
     *)
    contiguous:= True;
    resident:= True;
    pageWired:= False;
    blockBuffer:= vmBlock^.pages^[startPage].convBuff;
    for pageNum:= startPage to endPage do begin
        vmPage:= @vmBlock^.pages^[pageNum];

        if vmPage^.convBuff = Nil then begin
            resident:= False;
            end;

        if vmPage^.wired <> 0 then begin
            if not contiguous then begin
                goto 100;
                end;
            pageWired:= True;
            end;
```

```
        if vmPage^.convBuff <> blockBuffer then begin
            if pageWired then begin
                goto 100;
                end;
            contiguous:= False;
            end;
        end;

(*
 *  OK, we're good. Either we already have the pages in a
 *  contiguous block, or none of them are wired.
 *  blockBuffer tells us which is the case.
 *)
if not resident or not contiguous then begin
        (*
         *  Oh well, we have to do some work. I hate it when that happens.
         *
         *  Where to begin, where to begin?  I know, let's call another
         *  routine to do the mapping. This will give the appearance of
         *  progress.
         *)
        if vm_faultInPages(vmBlock^, startPage, endPage) then begin
            wire:= True;
            Exit;
            end;
        end
    else begin
        (*
         *  We need to move stuff from the LRU queues to
         *  the wired queues.
         *)
        if vmBlock^.pages^[startPage].convBuff^.wiredPages = 0 then begin
            vmBlock^.pages^[startPage].convBuff^.deque(
                            @conv.mruBuff,
                            @conv.lruBuff);
            vmBlock^.pages^[startPage].convBuff^.enqueTail(
                            @conv.firstWired,
                            @conv.lastWired);
            end;

        end;

(*
 *  Everythings resident. Let's go through, upping the
 *  wire counts, and then return the address of the first page
 *)
for pageNum:= startPage to endPage do begin
        if (vmBlock^.pages^[pageNum].wired = 0) and
                (vmBlock^.pages^[pageNum].convBuff <> PFABUFF) then begin
            vmBlock^.pages^[pageNum].convBuff^.wiredPages:=
                    vmBlock^.pages^[pageNum].convBuff^.wiredPages + 1;
            end;

        vmBlock^.pages^[pageNum].wired:= vmBlock^.pages^[pageNum].wired + 1;

        vm_moveSecPageToWired(vmBlock^.pages^[pageNum]);
        end;

(*
 *  We're set, let's return the address.
 *)
```

```
    vmPage:= @vmBlock^.pages^[startPage];
    if vmPage^.convBuff = PFABUFF then begin
        areaAddress:= Pointer(DWord(em.pageFrame)
                              + Word(vmPage^.offset) + offset);
        end
    else begin
        areaAddress:= Pointer(DWord(vmPage^.convBuff^.address) +
                                    vmPage^.offset + offset);
        end;

    errno:= VMErrOK;
    wire:= False;

    Exit;
100:
    errno:= VMErrBadWire;
    wire:= True;
end;

function vm_faultInPages(var vmBlock: VM_VMBlock;
                    startPage: Word; endPage: Word): Boolean;

var
    toss:                   Boolean;

begin

    (*
     *  Let's promote these pages to EMS or XMS (if possible and
     *  necessary).
     *  This achieves two purposes. First, we get the pages into
     *  EMS if possible so that we can map them into the PFA, which
     *  is our fastest mapping method. Second, if the pages are on
     *  disk, they are promoted to EMS or XMS so that we maintain
     *  the most recently used pages in EMS or XMS as opposed to disk.
     *
     *  We'll try EMS; if that fails, for example, because the system
     *  has no EMS, we'll try XMS. If that fails, then OK, we'll get
     *  the pages from disk. The only real reason for vm_faultToDisk
     *  is to handle the possibility that the pages are unallocated.
     *)
    if vm_faultToEMS(vmBlock, startPage, endPage) then begin
        if vm_faultToXMS(vmBlock, startPage, endPage) then begin
            toss:= vm_faultToDisk(vmBlock, startPage, endPage);
            end;
        end;

    (*
     *  OK, the pages are in the best secondary memory we have.
     *  Let's see if we can map them into the EMS PFA
     *)
    if not vm_tryMapPFA(vmBlock, startPage, endPage) then begin
        errno:= VMErrOK;
        vm_faultInPages:= False;
        Exit;
        end;

    (*
     *  That didn't work. Let's put it into a normal buffer
     *)
```

```
    if not vm_tryMapConv(vmBlock, startPage, endPage) then begin
        errno:= VMErrOK;
        vm_faultInPages:= False;
        Exit;
        end;

    (*
     *  That didn't work either. We're out of luck.
     *)
    vm_faultInPages:= True;

end;

function vm_faultToEMS(var vmBlock: VM_VMBlock;
                startPage: Word; endPage: Word): Boolean;

label
    100;

var

    emsPage:            VM_EmsPagePtr;
    nextEmsPage:        VM_FmsPagePtr;
    emsPageChain:       VM_EmsPagePtr;

    vmPage:             VM_VmPagePtr;

    pageNum:            Word;
    nonEMSPages:        Integer;

begin

    if not emsPresent then begin
        (*
         *  We don't even have EMS. Let's give an error
         *)
        vm_faultToEMS:= True;
        Exit;
        end;


    (*
     *  First go through and see how many pages are not in EMS.
     *  Pages that _are_ in EMS must be put onto the wired queue,
     *  lest they be booted out to make way for other pages in this wire.
     *)
    nonEMSPages:= 0;
    for pageNum:= startPage to endPage do begin
        if vmBlock.pages^[pageNum].secondaryKind < VM_SEC_EMS then begin
            nonEMSPages:= nonEMSPages + 1;
            end
        else begin
            vm_moveSecPageToWired(vmBlock.pages^[pageNum]);
            end;
        end;

    (*
     *  Now let's get as many pages as we can. This will include
     *  swapping older pages from EMS to disk.
     *)
    vm_getEMSPages(nonEMSPages, emsPageChain);
```

```
(*
 *  Let's promote as many pages as possible.
 *)
pageNum:= startPage;
emsPage:= emsPageChain;
pageNum:= startPage;
while pageNum <= endPage do begin

    vmPage:= @vmBlock.pages^[pageNum];

    (*
     *  If this is one of the nonEMS pages, we need to take
     *  an emsPage and promote it.
     *)

    if vmPage^.secondaryKind < VM_SEC_EMS then begin
        (*
         *  Before anything else, let's see if there's a
         *  page left.
         *)

        if emsPage = Nil then begin

            goto 100;
            end;

        (*
         *  Promotion will enque the page, so we need to get
         *  its 'next' pointer now.
         *)
        nextEmsPage:= emsPage^.next;

        vm_promoteToEMS(vmPage^, emsPage^);

        emsPage:= nextEmsPage;
        end;

    pageNum:= pageNum + 1;
    end;

100:
    if pageNum <= endPage then begin
        (*
         *  We weren't able to promote all of the pages. Return
         *  a flag to that effect.
         *)
        vm_faultToEMS:= True;
        Exit;
        end;

    vm_faultToEMS:= False;

end;


function vm_faultToXMS(var vmBlock: VM_VMBlock;
                    startPage: Word; endPage: Word): Boolean;

label
    100;
```

```
var
    xmsPage:            VM_XmsPagePtr;
    nextXmsPage:        VM_XmsPagePtr;
    xmsPageChain:       VM_XmsPagePtr;

    vmPage:             VM_VmPagePtr;

    pageNum:            Word;
    nonXMSPages:        Integer;

begin
    if not xmsPresent then begin
        (*
         *  We don't even have XMS. Let's give an error
         *)
        vm_faultToXMS:= True;
        Exit;
        end;


    (*
     *  First go through and see how many pages are not in XMS
     *)
    nonXMSPages:= 0;
    for pageNum:= startPage to endPage do begin
        if vmBlock.pages^[pageNum].secondaryKind < VM_SEC_XMS then begin
            nonXMSPages:= nonXMSPages + 1;
            end
        else if vmBlock.pages^[pageNum].secondaryKind = VM_SEC_XMS then begin
            vm_moveSecPageToWired(vmBlock.pages^[pageNum]);
            end;
        end;

    (*
     *  Now let's get as many pages as we can. This will include
     *  swapping older pages from XMS to disk.
     *)
    vm_getXMSPages(nonXMSPages, xmsPageChain);

    (*
     *  Let's promote as many pages as possible.
     *)
    pageNum:= startPage;
    xmsPage:= xmsPageChain;
    pageNum:= startPage;
    while pageNum <= endPage do begin

        vmPage:= @vmBlock.pages^[pageNum];

        (*
         *  If this is one of the nonXMS pages, we need to take
         *  an emsPage and promote it.
         *)
        if vmPage^.secondaryKind < VM_SEC_XMS then begin
            (*
             *  Before anything else, let's see if there's a
             *  page left.
             *)
            if xmsPage = Nil then begin
                goto 100;
                end;
```

```
            (*
            *   Promotion will enque the page, so we need to get
            *   its 'next' pointer now.
            *)
            nextXmsPage:= xmsPage^.next;

            vm_promoteToXMS(vmPage^, xmsPage^);

            xmsPage:= nextXmsPage;
            end;

        pageNum:= pageNum + 1;
        end;

100:
    if pageNum <= endPage then begin
        (*
        *   We weren't able to promote all of the pages. Return
        *   a flag to that effect.
        *)
        vm_faultToXMS:= True;
        Exit;
        end;

    vm_faultToXMS:= False;

end;

function vm_faultToDisk(var vmBlock: VM_VMBlock;
                    startPage: Word; endPage: Word): Boolean;

label
    100;

var
    diskPage:           VM_DiskPagePtr;
    nextDiskPage:       VM_DiskPagePtr;
    diskPageChain:      VM_DiskPagePtr;

    pageNum:            Word;
    nonDiskPages:       Integer;

begin

    (*
    *   First go through and see how many pages are not allocated
    *)
    nonDiskPages:= 0;
    for pageNum:= startPage to endPage do begin
        if vmBlock.pages^[pageNum].secondaryKind < VM_SEC_DISK then begin
            nonDiskPages:= nonDiskPages + 1;
            end;
        end;

    (*
    *   Now let's get as many pages as we can. This will include
    *   swapping older pages from Disk to disk.
    *)
    vm_getDiskPages(nonDiskPages, diskPageChain);
```

```
    (*
    *   Let's promote as many pages as possible.
    *)
    pageNum:= startPage;
    diskPage:= diskPageChain;
    while diskPage <> Nil do begin
        (*
        *   If this is one of the non Disk pages, we need to take
        *   a diskPage and promote it.
        *)
        if vmBlock.pages^[pageNum].secondaryKind < VM_SEC_DISK then begin
            (*
            *   Promotion will enque the Disk page, so we need to
            *   get the 'next' pointer now.
            *)
            nextDiskPage:= diskPage^.next;

            vm_promoteToDisk(vmBlock.pages^[pageNum], diskPage^);

            diskPage:= nextDiskPage;
            end;

        pageNum:= pageNum + 1;
        end;

    if pageNum <= endPage then begin
        (*
        *   We weren't able to promote all of the pages. Return
        *   a flag to that effect.
        *)
        vm_faultToDisk:= True;
        end;

    vm_faultToDisk:= False;

end;

procedure    vm_getEMSPages(number: Word; var chain: VM_EmsPagePtr);

var

    newEmsPage:         VM_EmsPagePtr;
    tmpEmsPage:         VM_EmsPagePtr;
    newEmsBuff:         VM_EmsBuffPtr;

    freePages:          Word;
    totalPages:         Word;
    requestNum:         Word;
    pageHandle:         EMS_EmBlk;

    tmpFreeArea:        VM_FreeAreaPtr;

begin

    (*
    *   Start by making the return chain empty.
    *)
    chain:= Nil;
```

```
(*
 *  Now try to get pages as we can up to the number requested.
 *)
while number <> 0 do begin

    if em.firstFree <> Nil then begin
        (*
         *  We've got some free pages.
         *  Create an EmsPage and fill it in.
         *)
        New(newEmsPage);
        newEmsPage^.emsBuff:= VM_EmsBuffPtr(em.firstFree^.handle);
        newEmsPage^.pageNum:= Word(em.firstFree^.start);
        newEmsPage^.secondaryQueue:= VM_Q_FREE;

        (*
         *  Bump the buffer's use count.
         *)
        newEmsPage^.emsBuff^.useCount:= newEmsPage^.emsBuff^.useCount + 1;

        (*
         *  Remove the page from the free chain.
         *)
        em.firstFree^.size:= em.firstFree^.size - 1;
        em.firstFree^.start:= em.firstFree^.start + 1;
        if em.firstFree^.size = 0 then begin
            tmpFreeArea:= em.firstFree;
            tmpFreeArea^.deque(@em.firstFree, @em.lastFree);
            Dispose(tmpFreeArea);
            end;

        (*
         *  Add our new page to the return list.
         *)
        newEmsPage^.next:= chain;
        chain:= newEmsPage;

        (*
         *  We've added a page. Decrement 'number';
         *)
        number:= number - 1;
        end
    else begin
        (*
         *  Nothing on the free chain. Look into EMS from the
         *  EMS manager.
         *)
        if ems.getFreeEM(totalPages, freePages) then begin
            ems_demoError('EMS_Ems.getNumPages');
            end;

        if freePages <> 0 then begin
            (*
             *  We've got some EMS left.
             *  Allocate a block of EMS. We've computed this size
             *  so that we can use all of EMS with the available
             *  handles.
             *)
            requestNum:= min(em.emsBlockSize, freePages);
            if pageHandle.allocEM(requestNum) then begin
                ems_demoError('EMS_Ems.allocEM');
                end;
```

```
            New(newEmsBuff);
            newEmsBuff^.buffSize:= requestNum;
            newEmsBuff^.handle:= pageHandle;
            newEmsBuff^.useCount:= 0;
            newEmsBuff^.enqueHead(@em.firstBuff, @em.lastBuff);

            (*
             *  Put the pages on the free chain.
             *)
            vm_addFree(DWord(newEmsBuff), 0,
                            requestNum, em.firstFree, em.lastFree);

            (*
             *  We haven't actually returned a page, so
             *  we don't decrement 'number'
             *)
            end
        else begin

            (*
             *  We've got no EMS. Let's start throwing stuff out.
             *)
            if em.lruPage <> Nil then begin

                (*
                 *  Pull the least recently used page.
                 *)
                tmpEmsPage:= em.lruPage;
                tmpEmsPage^.deque(@em.mruPage, @em.lruPage);
                tmpEmsPage^.secondaryQueue:= VM_Q_FREE;

                (*
                 *  Demote it to XMS or disk.
                 *)
                vm_demoteFromEMS(tmpEmsPage^);

                (*
                 *  Enque the newly available page to the return chain.
                 *)
                tmpEmsPage^.next:= chain;
                chain:= tmpEmsPage;

                number:= number - 1;
                end
            else begin

                (*
                 *  We're totally out of EMS. Let's just return.
                 *  We've done the best we could.
                 *)
                Exit;
                end;
            end;
        end;
    end;

end;

procedure vm_getXMSPages(number: Word; var chain: VM_XmsPagePtr);
```

```
var

    newXmsPage:          VM_XmsPagePtr;
    tmpXmsPage:          VM_XmsPagePtr;
    newXmsBuff:          VM_XmsBuffPtr;

    freePages:           Word;
    contiguousPages:     Word;
    requestNum:          Word;
    pageHandle:          XMS_XmBlk;

    tmpFreeArea:         VM_FreeAreaPtr;

begin
    (*
     * Start by making the return chain empty.
     *)
    chain:= Nil;

    (*
     * Now try to get pages as we can up to the number requested.
     *)
    while number <> 0 do begin
        if xm.firstFree <> Nil then begin
            (*
             * We've got some free pages.
             * Create an XmsPage and fill it in.
             *)
            New(newXmsPage);
            newXmsPage^.xmsBuff:= VM_XmsBuffPtr(xm.firstFree^.handle);
            newXmsPage^.pageNum:= Word(xm.firstFree^.start);
            newXmsPage^.secondaryQueue:= VM_Q_FREE;

            (*
             * Bump the buffer's use count.
             *)
            newXmsPage^.xmsBuff^.useCount:= newXmsPage^.xmsBuff^.useCount + 1;

            (*
             * Remove the page from the free chain.
             *)
            xm.firstFree^.size:= xm.firstFree^.size - 1;
            xm.firstFree^.start:= xm.firstFree^.start + 1;
            if xm.firstFree^.size = 0 then begin
                tmpFreeArea:= xm.firstFree;
                tmpFreeArea^.deque(@xm.firstFree, @xm.lastFree);
                Dispose(tmpFreeArea);
                end;

            (*
             * Add our new page to the return list.
             *)
            newXmsPage^.next:= chain;
            chain:= newXmsPage;

            (*
             * We've added a page. Decrement 'number';
             *)
            number:= number - 1;
            end
```

```
else begin
    (*
     *  Nothing on the free chain. Look into XMS from the
     *  XMS manager.
     *)
    if xms.getFreeXM(freePages, contiguousPages) then begin
        if errno = XMSErrNoXMLeft then begin
            contiguousPages:= 0;
            end
        else begin
            xms_demoError('XMS_Xms.getFreeXM');
            end;
        end;
    contiguousPages:= contiguousPages
            div (VM_PAGE_SIZE div XMS_PAGE_SIZE);

    if contiguousPages <> 0 then begin
        (*
         *  We've got some XMS left.
         *  Try to allocate as much as we can to satisfy
         *  our needs.
         *)
        requestNum:= min(xm.xmsBlockSize, contiguousPages);
        if pageHandle.allocXM(requestNum *
                (VM_PAGE_SIZE div XMS_PAGE_SIZE)) then begin
            xms_demoError('xms_allocXM');
            end;

        New(newXmsBuff);
        newXmsBuff^.buffSize:= requestNum;
        newXmsBuff^.handle:= pageHandle;
        newXmsBuff^.useCount:= 0;
        newXmsBuff^.enqueHead(@xm.firstBuff, @xm.lastBuff);

        (*
         *  Put the pages on the free chain.
         *)
        vm_addFree(DWord(newXmsBuff), 0,
                    requestNum, xm.firstFree, xm.lastFree);

        (*
         *  We haven't actually returned a page, so
         *  we don't decrement 'number'
         *)
        end
    else begin
        (*
         *  We've got no XMS. Let's start throwing stuff out.
         *)
        if xm.lruPage <> Nil then begin
            (*
             *  Pull the least recently used page.
             *)
            tmpXmsPage:= xm.lruPage;
            tmpXmsPage^.deque(@xm.mruPage, @xm.lruPage);
            tmpXmsPage^.secondaryQueue:= VM_Q_FREE;

            (*
             *  Demote it to disk.
             *)
            vm_demoteFromXMS(tmpXmsPage^);
```

```
                        (*
                         *  Enque the newly available page to the return chain.
                         *)
                        tmpXmsPage^.next:= chain;
                        chain:= tmpXmsPage;

                        number:= number - 1;
                        end
                    else begin
                        (*
                         *  We're totally out of XMS. Let's just return.
                         *  We've done the best we could.
                         *)
                        Exit;
                        end;
                end;
            end;
        end;

end;

procedure vm_getDiskPages(number: Word; var chain: VM_DiskPagePtr);

var
    newDiskPage:        VM_DiskPagePtr;
    lastDiskPage:       VM_DiskPagePtr;

    tmpFreeArea:        VM_FreeAreaPtr;

begin
    (*
     *  Start by making the return chain empty.
     *)
    chain:= Nil;
    lastDiskPage:= Nil;

    (*
     *  Now try to get as many pages as we can up to the number requested.
     *  We enque pages in order rather than in reverse order as in
     *  the getXMS and getEMS functions because we want to write
     *  pages in order to minimize disk access if we're extending EOF.
     *)
    while number <> 0 do begin
        if disk.firstFree <> Nil then begin
            (*
             *  We've got some free pages.
             *  Create a DiskPage and fill it in.
             *)
            New(newDiskPage);
            newDiskPage^.pageNum:= Word(disk.firstFree^.start);

            (*
             *  Remove the page from the free chain.
             *)
            disk.firstFree^.size:= disk.firstFree^.size - 1;
            disk.firstFree^.start:= disk.firstFree^.start + 1;
            if disk.firstFree^.size = 0 then begin
                tmpFreeArea:= disk.firstFree;
                tmpFreeArea^.deque(@disk.firstFree, @disk.lastFree);
                Dispose(tmpFreeArea);
                end;
```

```
            (*
             *  Add our new page to the return list.
             *)
            newDiskPage^.next:= Nil;
            if lastDiskPage <> Nil then begin
                lastDiskPage^.next:= newDiskPage;
                end
            else begin
                chain:= newDiskPage;
                end;
            lastDiskPage:= newDiskPage;

            (*
             *  We've added a page. Decrement 'number';
             *)
            number:= number - 1;
            end
        else begin
            (*
             *  Put an appropriate number of pages on the free chain
             *  starting at the current end of file.
             *)
            vm_addFree(0, disk.fileSize,
                            number, disk.firstFree, disk.lastFree);

            (*
             *  Advance the EOF marker.
             *)
            disk.fileSize:= disk.fileSize + number;

            (*
             *  We haven't actually returned a page, so
             *  we don't decrement 'number'
             *)
            end;
        end;

end;

procedure vm_promoteToEMS(var vmPage: VM_VmPage; var emsPage: VM_EmsPage);

var
    xmsMovePk:              XMS_MovePacket;

begin

    (*
     *  First off, let's see if the page is already in EMS. If so
     *  we're done.
     *)
    if vmPage.secondaryKind = VM_SEC_EMS then begin
        Exit;
        end;

    (*
     *  We need to save the page map (pages in PFA), map the page, and then
     *  xfer the data to the mapped page, then restore the page map.
     *)
```

```
(*
 *  Save the current state of the PFA
 *)
if emsPage.emsBuff^.handle.savePageMap then begin
    ems_demoError('EMS_Ems.savePageMap');
    end;

(*
 *  Map the EMS page into the first page of the PFA
 *)
if emsPage.emsBuff^.handle.mapPage(0, emsPage.pageNum) then begin
    ems_demoError('EMS_EmBlk.mapPage');
    end;

(*
 *  Let's do the xfer:
 *)
case vmPage.secondaryKind of
VM_SEC_UNALLOCATED:
    (*
     *  The page is as yet unallocated. Zero it out.
     *)
    memset(@em.pageFrame^[0], 0, VM_PAGE_SIZE);

VM_SEC_DISK: begin
    (*
     *  The page is on disk. Read it in.
     *)
    Seek(disk.channel, DWord(vmPage.sec.disk^.pageNum));
    Read(disk.channel, VM_Page(em.pageFrame^[0]));

    (*
     *  Free the disk page.
     *)
    vm_addFree(0, vmPage.sec.disk^.pageNum, 1,
                    disk.firstFree, disk.lastFree);

    (*
     *  Release the disk page descriptor.
     *)
    vm_dequeSecPage(vmPage);
    Dispose(vmPage.sec.disk);
    end;

VM_SEC_XMS: begin
    (*
     *  The page is in XMS. Let's xfer it in.
     *)
    xmsMovePk.length:= VM_PAGE_SIZE;
    xmsMovePk.srcHandle:= vmPage.sec.xms^.xmsBuff^.handle.handle;
    xmsMovePk.srcOffset:= DWord(vmPage.sec.xms^.pageNum) *
                            VM_PAGE_SIZE;
    xmsMovePk.destHandle:=0;
    xmsMovePk.destOffset:=DWord(@em.pageFrame^[0]);
    if xms.moveXM(xmsMovePk) then begin
        xms_demoError('XMS_Xms.moveXM');
        end;

    (*
     *  Free the xms page.
     *)
```

```
            vm_addFree(DWord(vmPage.sec.xms^.xmsBuff),
                       vmPage.sec.xms^.pageNum, 1,
                       xm.firstFree, xm.lastFree);

        (*
         *  Release the xms page descriptor.
         *)
        vm_dequeSecPage(vmPage);
        Dispose(vmPage.sec.xms);
        end;

    else
        vm_fatal('Bogus vmPage.secondaryKind');
        end;

    (*
     *  Set up the EMS page descriptor.
     *)
    emsPage.vmPage:= @vmPage;
    vmPage.secondaryKind:= VM_SEC_EMS;
    vmPage.sec.ems:= @emsPage;

    (*
     *  Let's just restore the PFA map.
     *)
    if emsPage.emsBuff^.handle.restorePageMap then begin
        ems_demoError('EMS_Ems.restorePageMap');
        end;

end;

procedure vm_promoteToXMS(var vmPage: VM_VmPage; var xmsPage: VM_XmsPage);

var

    pageBuff:          VM_PagePtr;
    xmsMovePk:         XMS_MovePacket;

begin

    (*
     *  If EMS is initialized, we have a page of EMS to use as
     *  a buffer. Otherwise we need to use conventional memory.
     *)
    if emsPresent and (em.pageBuffHandle.handle <> 0) then begin
        (*
         *  Save the current page frame map.
         *)
        if em.pageBuffHandle.savePageMap then begin
            ems_demoError('EMS_EmBlk.savePageMap');
            end;

        (*
         *  Map the EMS page into the first page of the PFA
         *)
        if em.pageBuffHandle.mapPage(0, 0) then begin
            ems_demoError('EMS_EmBlk.mapPage');
            end;

        pageBuff:= @em.pageFrame^[0];
        end
```

```
else begin
    (*
     *  No EMS, we need to use conventional memory.
     *)
    New(pageBuff);
    end;

(*
 *  Let's do the xfer:
 *)
case vmPage.secondaryKind of
VM_SEC_UNALLOCATED: begin
    (*
     *  The page is as yet unallocated. Zero it out.
     *)
    memset(pageBuff, 0, VM_PAGE_SIZE);
    end;

VM_SEC_DISK: begin
    (*
     *  The page is on disk. Read it in.
     *)
    Seek(disk.channel, vmPage.sec.disk^.pageNum);
    Read(disk.channel, pageBuff^);

    (*
     *  Free the disk page.
     *)
    vm_addFree(0, vmPage.sec.disk^.pageNum, 1,
                    disk.firstFree, disk.lastFree);

    (*
     *  Release the disk page descriptor.
     *)
    vm_dequeSecPage(vmPage);
    Dispose(vmPage.sec.disk);

    end;

else
    vm_fatal('Bogus vmPage.secondaryKind');
    end;

(*
 *  We have the page in memory. Let's transfer it to
 *  XMS now.
 *)
xmsMovePk.length:= VM_PAGE_SIZE;
xmsMovePk.srcHandle:= 0;
xmsMovePk.srcOffset:= DWord(pageBuff);
xmsMovePk.destHandle:= xmsPage.xmsBuff^.handle.handle;
xmsMovePk.destOffset:= DWord(xmsPage.pageNum) * VM_PAGE_SIZE;
if xms.moveXM(xmsMovePk) then begin
    xms_demoError('XMS_Xms.moveXM');
    end;

(*
 *  Set up the XMS page descriptor.
 *)
xmsPage.vmPage:= @vmPage;
vmPage.secondaryKind:= VM_SEC_XMS;
vmPage.sec.xms:= @xmsPage;
```

```
(*
 *  Now release the buffer
 *)
if emsPresent and (em.pageBuffHandle.handle <> 0) then begin
    (*
     *  Let's just restore the PFA map.
     *)
    if em.pageBuffHandle.restorePageMap then begin
        ems_demoError('EMS_EmBlk.restorePageMap');
        end;
    end
else begin
    (*
     *  Free the conventional memory buffer
     *)
    Dispose(pageBuff);
    end;


end;

procedure vm_promoteToDisk(var vmPage: VM_VmPage; var diskPage:
VM_DiskPage);

var
    pageBuff:           VM_PagePtr;

begin

    (*
     *  If EMS is initialized, we have a page of EMS to use as
     *  a buffer. Otherwise we need to use conventional memory.
     *)
    if emsPresent and (em.pageBuffHandle.handle <> 0) then begin
        (*
         *  Save the current page frame map.
         *)
        if em.pageBuffHandle.savePageMap then begin
            ems_demoError('EMS_EmBlk.savePageMap');
            end;

        (*
         *  Map the EMS page into the first page of the PFA
         *)
        if em.pageBuffHandle.mapPage(0, 0) then begin
            ems_demoError('EMS_EmBlk.mapPage');
            end;

        pageBuff:= @em.pageFrame^[0];
        end
    else begin
        (*
         *  No EMS, we need to use conventional memory.
         *)
        New(pageBuff);
        end;

    (*
     *  Let's do the xfer:
     *)
    case vmPage.secondaryKind of
```

```
VM_SEC_UNALLOCATED: begin
    (*
     *  The page is as yet unallocated. Zero it out.
     *)
    memset(pageBuff, 0, VM_PAGE_SIZE);
    end;

else
    vm_fatal('Bogus vmPage.secondaryKind');
    end;

(*
 *  Let's write the thing to disk now.
 *)
Seek(disk.channel, diskPage.pageNum);
Write(disk.channel, pageBuff^);

(*
 *  Set up the Disk page descriptor.
 *)
diskPage.vmPage:= @vmPage;
vmPage.secondaryKind:= VM_SEC_DISK;
vmPage.sec.disk:= @diskPage;

(*
 *  Enque to the list of pages
 *)
diskPage.enqueTail(@disk.firstPage, @disk.lastPage);

(*
 *  Now release the buffer
 *)
if emsPresent and (em.pageBuffHandle.handle <> 0) then begin
    (*
     *  Let's just restore the PFA map.
     *)
    if em.pageBuffHandle.restorePageMap then begin
        ems_demoError('EMS_EmBlk.restorePageMap');
        end;
    end
else begin
    (*
     *  Free the conventional memory buffer
     *)
    Dispose(pageBuff);
    end;

end;

procedure vm_demoteFromEMS(var emsPage: VM_EmsPage);

var
    vmPage:             VM_VmPagePtr;
    xmsPage:            VM_XmsPagePtr;
    diskPage:           VM_DiskPagePtr;

    pageType:           VM_SecondaryKind;
    xmsMovePk:          XMS_MovePacket;
```

```
begin
    (*
     *  Just get a handy pointer to the VM page
     *)
    vmPage:= emsPage.vmPage;

    (*
     *  This page could possibly be in the PFA. If so we need to
     *  remove it.
     *)
    if vmPage^.convBuff = PFABUFF then begin
        (*
         *  OK. It's in the PFA. It's OK to leave the EMS page there,
         *  because we're going to need it anyway. However, we want
         *  to indicate that the virtual page is no longer there, because
         *  it is being disconnected from the EMS page.
         *)
        vmPage^.convBuff:= Nil;
        vmPage^.offset:= 0;
        end;


    (*
     *  The first thing we need to do is to try to find a
     *  page to go to. We first try XMS, if that fails, we
     *  go to Disk.
     *)
    vm_getXMSPages(1, xmsPage);
    pageType:= VM_SEC_XMS;
    if xmsPage = Nil then begin
        vm_getDiskPages(1, diskPage);
        pageType:= VM_SEC_DISK;
        end;


    (*
     *  We need to map the page. We'll save the current page map
     *  so we can restore it later.
     *)

    (*
     *  Save the current page frame map.
     *)
    if emsPage.emsBuff^.handle.savePageMap then begin
        ems_demoError('EMS_EmBlk.savePageMap');
        end;

    (*
     *  Map the EMS page into the first page of the PFA
     *)
    if emsPage.emsBuff^.handle.mapPage(0, emsPage.pageNum) then begin
        ems_demoError('EMS_EmBlk.mapPage');
        end;

    (*
     *  Let's do the xfer:
     *)
    case pageType of
    VM_SEC_DISK: begin
```

```
        (*
         *  We're demoting to disk. Write the page out.
         *)
        Seek(disk.channel, diskPage^.pageNum);
        Write(disk.channel, VM_Page(em.pageFrame^[0]));

        (*
         *  Update the VM page, etc.
         *)
        diskPage^.vmPage:= vmPage;
        vmPage^.secondaryKind:= VM_SEC_DISK;
        vmPage^.sec.disk:= diskPage;

        (*
         *  Enque the disk page. Note that it will be the most
         *  recently used on disk.
         *)
        diskPage^.enqueHead(@disk.firstPage, @disk.lastPage);

        end;

    VM_SEC_XMS: begin
        (*
         *  We're demoting to XMS, let's move it on out.
         *)
        xmsMovePk.length:= VM_PAGE_SIZE;
        xmsMovePk.srcHandle:= 0;
        xmsMovePk.srcOffset:= DWord(@em.pageFrame^[0]);
        xmsMovePk.destHandle:= xmsPage^.xmsBuff^.handle.handle;
        xmsMovePk.destOffset:= DWord(xmsPage^.pageNum) * VM_PAGE_SIZE;
        if xms.moveXM(xmsMovePk) then begin
            xms_demoError('XMS_Xms.moveXM');
            end;

        (*
         *  Update the VM page, etc.
         *)
        xmsPage^.vmPage:= vmPage;
        vmPage^.secondaryKind:= VM_SEC_XMS;
        vmPage^.sec.xms:= xmsPage;

        (*
         *  Enque the XMS page. Note that it will be the most
         *  recently used on XMS.
         *)
        xmsPage^.enqueHead(@xm.mruPage, @xm.lruPage);
        xmsPage^.secondaryQueue:= VM_Q_LRU;

        end;

    else
        vm_fatal('Bogus vmPage.secondaryKind');
        end;
    (*
     *  Let's just restore the PFA map.
     *)
    if emsPage.emsBuff^.handle.restorePageMap then begin
        ems_demoError('EMS_EmBlk.savePageMap');
        end;

end;
```

```
procedure vm_demoteFromXMS(var xmsPage: VM_XmsPage);

var
    vmPage:                 VM_VmPagePtr;
    diskPage:               VM_DiskPagePtr;

    xmsMovePk:              XMS_MovePacket;

    pageBuff:               VM_PagePtr;

begin
    (*
     *  Just get a handy pointer to the VM page
     *)
    vmPage:= xmsPage.vmPage;

    (*
     *  The first thing we need to do is to try to find a
     *  page to go to.
     *)
    vm_getDiskPages(1, diskPage);


    (*
     *  If EMS is initialized, we have a page of EMS to use as
     *  a buffer. Otherwise we need to use conventional memory.
     *)
    if emsPresent and (em.pageBuffHandle.handle <> 0) then begin
        (*
         *  Save the current page frame map.
         *)
        if em.pageBuffHandle.savePageMap then begin
            ems_demoError('EMS_EmBlk.savePageMap');
            end;

        (*
         *  Map the EMS page into the first page of the PFA
         *)
        if em.pageBuffHandle.mapPage(0, 0) then begin
            ems_demoError('EMS_EmBlk.mapPage');
            end;

        pageBuff:= @em.pageFrame^[0];
        end
    else begin
        (*
         *  No EMS, we need to use conventional memory.
         *)
        New(pageBuff);
        end;

    (*
     *  First let's transfer from the XMS page to the
     *  buffer.
     *)
    xmsMovePk.length:= VM_PAGE_SIZE;
    xmsMovePk.srcHandle:= xmsPage.xmsBuff^.handle.handle;
    xmsMovePk.srcOffset:= DWord(xmsPage.pageNum) * VM_PAGE_SIZE;
    xmsMovePk.destHandle:= 0;
    xmsMovePk.destOffset:= DWord(pageBuff);
```

```
    if xms.moveXM(xmsMovePk) then begin
        xms_demoError('XMS_Xms.moveXM');
        end;

    (*
     *  Now transfer the page to disk
     *)
    Seek(disk.channel, diskPage^.pageNum);
    Write(disk.channel, pageBuff^);

    (*
     *  Update the VM page, etc.
     *)
    diskPage^.vmPage:= vmPage;
    vmPage^.secondaryKind:= VM_SEC_DISK;
    vmPage^.sec.disk:= diskPage;

    (*
     *  Enque the disk page. Note that it will be the most
     *  recently used on disk.
     *)
    diskPage^.enqueHead(@disk.firstPage, @disk.lastPage);


    (*
     *  Now release the buffer
     *)
    if emsPresent and (em.pageBuffHandle.handle <> 0) then begin
        (*
         *  Let's just restore the PFA map.
         *)
        if em.pageBuffHandle.restorePageMap then begin
            ems_demoError('EMS_EmBlk.restorePageMap');
            end;
        end
    else begin
        (*
         *  Free the conventional memory buffer
         *)
        Dispose(pageBuff);
        end;



end;

function vm_tryMapPFA(
        var vmBlock:    VM_VmBlock;
        startPage:      Word;
        endPage:        Word)
        : Boolean;

label
    100;

var
    emsPage:            VM_EmsPagePtr;

    pageCount:          Word;
    pageNum:            Word;
```

```
    freeString:         Word;
    offset:             Word;
    i:                  Word;

begin
    (*
     *  First, let's make a couple of quick checks:
     *      Can the pages fit in the PFA ?
     *      Are the pages all in EMS ?
     *)
    pageCount:= endPage - startPage + 1;
    if pageCount > EMS_PAGE_FRAME_SIZE then begin

        errno:= VMErrNoConv;
        vm_tryMapPFA:= True;
        Exit;
        end;

    for pageNum:= startPage to endPage do begin
        if vmBlock.pages^[pageNum].secondaryKind <> VM_SEC_EMS then begin

            errno:= VMErrNoConv;
            vm_tryMapPFA:= True;
            Exit;
            end;
        end;

    (*
     *  OK, the initial checks have passed. Let's see whether we
     *  actually have a block of pages in the PFA which we can use.
     *
     *  Note that we do not concern ourselves with lru-ness. Mapping
     *  pages is too fast to worry about it, since there is no
     *  data movement.
     *)
    freeString:= 0;
    offset:= 0;
    while offset < EMS_PAGE_FRAME_SIZE do begin
        if (em.contents[offset] = Nil) or
                (em.contents[offset]^.vmPage^.wired = 0) then begin
            freeString:= freeString + 1;
            end
        else begin
            freeString:= 0;
            end;

        if freeString >= pageCount then begin
            offset:= offset - freeString + 1;
            goto 100;
            end;

        offset:= offset + 1;
        end;

100:
    (*
     *  If offset isn't in the PFA, we can't do anything.
     *)
    if offset >= EMS_PAGE_FRAME_SIZE then begin
```

6-7 Continued.

```
          errno:= VMErrNoConv;
          vm_tryMapPFA:= False;
          Exit;
          end;

    (*
     *  Now we need to take any pages out of conventional memory
     *  buffers and flush them back to EMS.
     *)
    for pageNum:= startPage to endPage do begin
        vm_flushVmPage(vmBlock.pages^[pageNum]);
        end;

    (*
     *  Now let's mark the pages we're replacing as history.
     *)
    pageNum:= offset;
    for i:= 0 to pageCount-1 do begin
        if em.contents[pageNum] <> Nil then begin
            em.contents[pageNum]^.vmPage^.convBuff:= Nil;
            em.contents[pageNum]^.vmPage^.offset:= 0;
            end;

        pageNum:= pageNum + 1;
        end;

    (*
     *  We're finally ready to map the pages.
     *)
    for pageNum:= startPage to endPage do begin
        emsPage:= vmBlock.pages^[pageNum].sec.ems;
        if emsPage^.emsBuff^.handle.mapPage(
                        offset+(pageNum-startPage),
                        emsPage^.pageNum) then begin
            ems_demoError('EMS_EmBlk.mapPage');
            end;

        (*
         *  Note where we've mapped them.
         *)
        em.contents[offset+(pageNum-startPage)]:= emsPage;
        emsPage^.vmPage^.convBuff:= PFABUFF;
        emsPage^.vmPage^.offset:= (offset+(pageNum-startPage)) *
VM_PAGE_SIZE;
        end;

    errno:= VMErrOK;
    vm_tryMapPFA:= False;


end;

function vm_tryMapConv(
    var vmBlock:        VM_VmBlock;
    startPage:          Word;
    endPage:            Word): Boolean;

var

    newConvBuff:        VM_ConvBuffPtr;
```

```
    pageNum:            Word;
    pageCount:          Word;
    memNeeded:          DWord;

    newBuffSpace:       Pointer;

begin
    (*
     *  Get the number of pages.
     *)
    pageCount:= endPage - startPage + 1;

    (*
     *  Free up buffers till we can get the buffer space.
     *)
    memNeeded:= DWord(pageCount) * VM_PAGE_SIZE;
    while memNeeded > conv.spaceAvail do begin
        if vm_freeLRUConvBuff then begin
            errno:= VMErrNoConv;
            vm_tryMapConv:= True;
            Exit;
            end;
        end;
    GetBigMem(newBuffSpace, memNeeded);
    conv.spaceAvail:= conv.spaceAvail - memNeeded;

    (*
     *  We've got memory for the buffer. Let's create a buffer header.
     *)
    New(newConvBuff);
    newConvBuff^.buffSize:= pageCount;
    newConvBuff^.address:= newBuffSpace;
    newConvBuff^.vmBlock:= @vmBlock;
    newConvBuff^.startPage:= startPage;
    newConvBuff^.wiredPages:= 0;
    newConvBuff^.enqueTail(@conv.firstWired, @conv.lastWired);

    (*
     *  OK, we've got a buffer. Let's bring in the pages.
     *)
    for pageNum:= startPage to endPage do begin
        vm_loadVmPage(vmBlock.pages^[pageNum], newConvBuff^);
        end;

    errno:= VMErrOK;
    vm_tryMapConv:= False;


end;

procedure vm_flushVmPage(var vmPage: VM_VmPage);

var
    xmsMovePk:          XMS_MovePacket;
    emsPage:            VM_EmsPagePtr;

    pageAddr:           Pointer;
```

```
begin

    (*
    *   If the page is dirty, and resident, write it to secondary
    *)
    if vmPage.dirty and (vmPage.convBuff <> nil) and
                (vmPage.convBuff <> PFABUFF) then begin

        pageAddr:= Pointer(DWord(vmPage.convBuff^.address) + vmPage.offset);

        case vmPage.secondaryKind of
        VM_SEC_UNALLOCATED: begin
            (*
            *   The page is as yet unallocated. This is a NOP
            *)
            end;

        VM_SEC_DISK: begin
            (*
            *   The page is on disk. Write it out
            *)
            Seek(disk.channel, vmPage.sec.disk^.pageNum);
            Write(disk.channel, VM_Page(pageAddr^));
            end;

        VM_SEC_XMS: begin
            (*
            *   The page is in XMS. Let's xfer it out.
            *)
            xmsMovePk.length:= VM_PAGE_SIZE;
            xmsMovePk.srcHandle:= 0;
            xmsMovePk.srcOffset:= DWord(pageAddr);
            xmsMovePk.destHandle:= vmPage.sec.xms^.xmsBuff^.handle.handle;
            xmsMovePk.destOffset:= DWord(vmPage.sec.xms^.pageNum) *
VM_PAGE_SIZE;
            if xms.moveXM(xmsMovePk) then begin
                xms_demoError('XMS_Xms.moveXM');
                end;

            end;

        VM_SEC_EMS: begin
            (*
            *   Get and convenient handle on the emsPage.
            *)
            emsPage:= vmPage.sec.ems;

            (*
            *   We need to save the PFA for a bit.
            *)
            if emsPage^.emsBuff^.handle.savePageMap then begin
                ems_demoError('EMS_EmBlk.savePageMap');
                end;

            (*
            *   Map the EMS page in.
            *)
            if emsPage^.emsBuff^.handle.mapPage(0, emsPage^.pageNum) then
```

```
                 begin
                 ems_demoError('EMS_EmBlk.mapPage');
                 end;

          (*
           *  Copy the memory.
           *)
          VM_Page(em.pageFrame^[0]):= VM_Page(pageAddr^);

          (*
           *  Restore the page map.
           *)
          if emsPage^.emsBuff^.handle.restorePageMap then begin
              ems_demoError('EMS_EmBlk.restorePageMap');
              end;

          end;

      else
          vm_fatal('Bogus vmPage.secondaryKind');
          end;
      end;


end;

procedure vm_loadVmPage(
    var vmPage:      VM_VmPage;
    var convBuff:    VM_ConvBuff);

var

    xmsMovePk:       XMS_MovePacket;
    emsPage:         VM_EmsPagePtr;

    pageAddr:        Pointer;

begin

    (*
     *  First figure out the address of the buffer.
     *)
    vmPage.convBuff:= @convBuff;
    vmPage.offset:= DWord(vmPage.pageNum - convBuff.startPage) *
VM_PAGE_SIZE;
    pageAddr:= Pointer(DWord(vmPage.convBuff^.address) + vmPage.offset);

    case vmPage.secondaryKind of
    VM_SEC_DISK: begin
        (*
         *  The page is on disk. Read it in.
         *)

        Seek(disk.channel, vmPage.sec.disk^.pageNum);
        Read(disk.channel, VM_Page(pageAddr^));
        end;

    VM_SEC_XMS: begin
        (*
         *  The page is in XMS. Let's xfer it in.
         *)
```

```
                xmsMovePk.length:= VM_PAGE_SIZE;
                xmsMovePk.srcHandle:= vmPage.sec.xms^.xmsBuff^.handle.handle;
                xmsMovePk.srcOffset:= DWord(vmPage.sec.xms^.pageNum) * VM_PAGE_SIZE;
                xmsMovePk.destHandle:= 0;
                xmsMovePk.destOffset:= DWord(pageAddr);
                if xms.moveXM(xmsMovePk) then begin
                    xms_demoError('XMS_Xms.moveXM');
                    end;
            end;

        VM_SEC_EMS: begin
            (*
             *  Get and convenient handle on the emsPage.
             *)
            emsPage:= vmPage.sec.ems;

            (*
             *  We need to save the PFA for a bit.
             *)
            if emsPage^.emsBuff^.handle.savePageMap then begin
                ems_demoError('EMS_EmBlk.savePageMap');
                end;

            (*
             *  Map the EMS page in.
             *)
            if emsPage^.emsBuff^.handle.mapPage(0, emsPage^.pageNum) then begin
                ems_demoError('EMS_EmBlk.mapPage');
                end;

            (*
             *  Copy the memory.
             *)

            VM_Page(pageAddr^):= VM_Page(em.pageFrame^[0]);

            (*
             *  Restore the page map.
             *)
            if emsPage^.emsBuff^.handle.restorePageMap then begin
                ems_demoError('EMS_EmBlk.restorePageMap');
                end;

            end;

    else
        vm_fatal('Bogus vmPage.secondaryKind');
        end;

end;


function vm_freeLRUConvBuff: Boolean;

var

    convBuff:           VM_ConvBuffPtr;
    vmBlock:            VM_VmBlockPtr;

    pageNum:            Word;
    i:                  Word;
```

```
begin

    (*
     *  First, see if there is an unwired buffer, otherwise we're
     *  out of luck.
     *)
    if conv.lruBuff = Nil then begin
        errno:= VMErrNoConv;
        vm_freeLRUConvBuff:= True;
        Exit;
        end;

    (*
     *  O.K, let's get rid of the LRU buffer.
     *)
    convBuff:= conv.lruBuff;
    convBuff^.deque(@conv.mruBuff, @conv.lruBuff);

    (*
     *  Flush, and mark the virtual pages as gone.
     *)
    vmBlock:= convBuff^.vmBlock;
    pageNum:= convBuff^.startPage;
    for i:= 0 to convBuff^.buffSize-1 do begin
        vm_flushVmPage(vmBlock^.pages^[pageNum]);

        vmBlock^.pages^[pageNum].convBuff:= Nil;
        vmBlock^.pages^[pageNum].offset:= 0;

        pageNum:= pageNum + 1;
        end;

    (*
     *  Free up the memory.
     *)
    FreeBigMem(convBuff^.address, DWord(convBuff^.buffSize) *
VM_PAGE_SIZE);

    conv.spaceAvail:= conv.spaceAvail +
            DWord(convBuff^.buffSize) * VM_PAGE_SIZE;
    Dispose(convBuff);

    errno:= VMErrOK;
    vm_freeLRUConvBuff:= False;
end;

function VM_VmBlk.unwire(
    areaOffset:         DWord;
    areaSize:           DWord;
    dirty:              Boolean): Boolean;

var

    startPage:          Word;
    endPage:            Word;
    pageNum:            Word;

    vmBlock:            VM_VmBlockPtr;
    vmPage:             VM_VmPagePtr;

    tmpEmsPage:         VM_EmsPagePtr;
```

6-7 Continued.

```
begin
    (*
     *  Start by casting the handle into an appropriate pointer.
     *)
    vmBlock:= VM_VmBlockPtr(handle);

    (*
     *  Let's translate the offset and size into page
     *  values.
     *  The offset is truncated to a page number, and the
     *  size is rounded up to a page number.
     *)
    startPage:= Word(areaOffset shr VM_PAGE_SHIFT);
    endPage:= Word((areaOffset + areaSize - 1) shr VM_PAGE_SHIFT);

    (*
     *  Make sure the pages are within the bounds of the block:
     *)
    if endPage >= vmBlock^.size then begin
        errno:= VMErrBounds;
        unwire:= True;
        Exit;
        end;

    (*
     *  Now let's go through and make sure they're wired.
     *)
    for pageNum:= startPage to endPage do begin
        if not (vmBlock^.pages^[pageNum].wired <> 0) then begin
            errno:= VMErrNotWired;
            unwire:= True;
            Exit;
            end;
        end;

    (*
     *  OK, all of the pages are wired. Let's unwire the pages and
     *  mark them dirty as necessary.
     *  If a buffer becomes totally unwired, we move it to the LRU
     *  queue.
     *)
    for pageNum:= startPage to endPage do begin
        vmPage:= @vmBlock^.pages^[pageNum];

        vmPage^.dirty:= vmPage^.dirty or dirty;

        vmPage^.wired:= vmPage^.wired - 1;
        if (vmPage^.wired = 0) and (vmPage^.convBuff <> PFABUFF) then begin
            vmPage^.convBuff^.wiredPages:= vmPage^.convBuff^.wiredPages - 1;
            if vmPage^.convBuff^.wiredPages = 0 then begin
                (*
                 *  Move the buffer to the LRU.
                 *)
                vmPage^.convBuff^.deque(@conv.firstWired, @conv.lastWired);
                vmPage^.convBuff^.enqueHead(@conv.mruBuff, @conv.lruBuff);
                end;
            end;
```

```
            (*
             *  If the page is in EMS or XMS, move it from the wired
             *  queue to the LRU chain.
             *)
            case vmPage^.secondaryKind of
            VM_SEC_EMS: begin
                vmPage^.sec.ems^.deque(@em.firstWired, @em.lastWired);
                vmPage^.sec.ems^.enqueHead(@em.mruPage, @em.lruPage);
                vmPage^.sec.ems^.secondaryQueue:= VM_Q_LRU;
                end;
            VM_SEC_XMS: begin
                vmPage^.sec.xms^.deque(@xm.firstWired, @xm.lastWired);
                vmPage^.sec.xms^.enqueHead(@xm.mruPage, @xm.lruPage);
                vmPage^.sec.xms^.secondaryQueue:= VM_Q_LRU;
                end;
            else
                ;
                end;
            end;

    errno:= VMErrOK;
    unwire:= False;

end;

procedure vm_moveSecPageToWired(
    var vmPage:            VM_VmPage);

begin

    case vmPage.secondaryKind of
    VM_SEC_EMS: begin
        if vmPage.sec.ems^.secondaryQueue = VM_Q_LRU then begin
            vmPage.sec.ems^.deque(@em.mruPage, @em.lruPage);
            end;
        if vmPage.sec.ems^.secondaryQueue <> VM_Q_WIRED then begin
            vmPage.sec.ems^.enqueTail(@em.firstWired, @em.lastWired);
            end;
        vmPage.sec.ems^.secondaryQueue:= VM_Q_WIRED;
        end;
    VM_SEC_XMS: begin
        if vmPage.sec.xms^.secondaryQueue = VM_Q_LRU then begin
            vmPage.sec.xms^.deque(@xm.mruPage, @xm.lruPage);
            end;
        if vmPage.sec.xms^.secondaryQueue <> VM_Q_WIRED then begin
            vmPage.sec.xms^.enqueTail(@xm.firstWired, @xm.lastWired);
            end;
        vmPage.sec.xms^.secondaryQueue:= VM_Q_WIRED;
        end;
    else
        ;
        end;

end;

procedure vm_dequeSecPage(
    var vmPage:            VM_VmPage);
```

```
begin

    case vmPage.secondaryKind of
    VM_SEC_EMS: begin
        if vmPage.sec.ems^.secondaryQueue = VM_Q_LRU then begin
            vmPage.sec.ems^.deque(@em.mruPage, @em.lruPage);
            end
        else if vmPage.sec.ems^.secondaryQueue = VM_Q_WIRED then begin
            vmPage.sec.ems^.deque(@em.firstWired, @em.lastWired);
            end;
        vmPage.sec.ems^.secondaryQueue:= VM_Q_FREE;
        end;
    VM_SEC_XMS: begin
        if vmPage.sec.xms^.secondaryQueue = VM_Q_LRU then begin
            vmPage.sec.xms^.deque(@xm.mruPage, @xm.lruPage);
            end
        else if vmPage.sec.xms^.secondaryQueue = VM_Q_WIRED then begin
            vmPage.sec.xms^.deque(@xm.firstWired, @xm.lastWired);
            end;
        vmPage.sec.xms^.secondaryQueue:= VM_Q_FREE;
        end;
    VM_SEC_DISK: begin
        vmPage.sec.disk^.deque(@disk.firstPage, @disk.lastPage);
        end;
    else
        ;
        end;

end;
```

Summary

In a very real sense the VMM is the crown jewel of this book because its foundation lies in the EMS and XMS functions presented earlier. Standard library I/O disk functions were used as a last resort when there wasn't enough EMS and XMS memory available to meet the needs of the program's VMM requests.

The Virtual Memory Manager (VMM) allows you to allocate and use blocks of memory far beyond the normal size associated with standard DOS-based memory allocation functions. The VMM pools EMS, XMS, and disk memory to meet the needs of the VMM block size request. The beauty of the VMM lies in the fact that it makes the complex task of tracking which data is held in EMS, XMS, and on disk invisible to the applications programmer.

Epilogue

Please feel free to use the memory management functions presented in the book in your personal and commercial code. We hope that you had as much enjoyment from reading this book as we had in writing it.

We're always interested in how readers may use or react to the code presented in our books. Feel free to write us via the publisher if you have any comments or code you'd like to share with us. We'll try our best to write back as time permits.

Namaste',
Len and Marc

Index

Other Bestsellers of Related Interest

**FOXPRO® PROGRAMMING—2nd Edition
—Les Pinter, Foreword by Walter
Kennamer, COO, Fox Software**

If you've been looking for a book that concentrates entirely on the FoxPro language and not on the production itself, then look no further! This book is a gold mine of fully-tested techniques, ready-to-run source code, and application templates to use as is or build upon in your own programs. You'll get complete programming models for creating FoxPro report generators, screens, menus, spreadsheets, multiuser interfaces, network support, and much more. 384 pages, 150 illustrations. Book No. 4057, $22.95 paperback only

**MAINTAIN AND REPAIR YOUR COMPUTER PRINTER AND SAVE A BUNDLE
—Stephen J. Bigelow**

A few basic tools are all you need to fix many of the most common printer problems quickly and easily. You may even be able to avoid printer hangups altogether by following a regular routine of cleaning, lubrication, and adjustment. Why pay a repairman a bundle when you don't need to? With this time- and money-saving book on your printer stand, repair bills will be a thing of the past! 240 pages, 160 illustrations. Book No. 3922, $16.95 paperback, $26.95 hardcover

**CONVERTING C TO TURBO C++
—Len Dorfman**

Discover how to move existing C applications into the OOP/GUI environment—often without changing a single line of code! This book explains the principles of OOP and outlines the procedures you should follow to develop commercial-quality graphical interfaces with C++. You'll develop C++ class libraries for all functions—display, window, keyboard, sound, and mouse—of software development and a complete object-oriented user interface. 352 pages, 100 illustrations. Book No. 4084, $29.95 paperback, $39.95 hardcover

**VISUAL BASIC: Easy Windows™
Programming
—Namir C. Shammas**

Enter the exciting new world of visual object-oriented programming for the Windows environment. This guide is chock-full of screen dumps, program listings, and illustrations to give you a clear picture of how your code should come together. You'll find yourself referring to its tables, listings, and quick-reference section long after your master Visual Basic. As a bonus, the book is packaged with a 3.5-inch disk filled with all the working Visual Basic application programs discussed in the text. 480 pages, 249 illustrations. Book No. 4086, $29.95 paperback only

**ONLINE INFORMATION HUNTING
—Nahum Goldmann**

Cut down dramatically on your time and money spent online, and increase your online productivity with this helpful book. It will give you systematic instruction on developing cost-effective techniques for large-scale information networks. You'll also get detailed coverage of the latest online services, new hardware and software, and recent advances that have affected online research. 256 pages, 125 illustrations. Book No. 3943, $19.95 paperback, $29.95 hardcover

**BUSINESS APPLICATIONS SHAREWARE
—PC-SIG, Inc.**

Shareware allows you to evaluate hundreds of dollars worth of software before buying it. Once you decide, you simply register the shareware you want at a fraction of the cost of buying commercially marketed packages. This resource shows you a wide variety of these programs including: PC Payroll, Bill Power Plus, Painless Accounting, Graphtime, PC Inventory Plus, Formgen, and more. 312 pages, 81 illustrations. Book No. 3920, $29.95 paperback only

MACINTOSH HARD DISK MANAGEMENT
—Bob Brant

Keep your hard drive healthy. This comprehensive guide takes a close look at the disk itself—how it works, how to keep it running properly, and how to fix it if it breaks down. In addition, you'll explore how to make the most of your Mac hard drive's storage capacity and capabilities. Several utilities, such as ADB Probe, Connectix Mode 32, RAM Check, system Picker, DisKeeper, Speedometer, and Layout, are included on an accompanying 3.5″ disk! 344 pages, 150 illustrations, 3.5″ disk. Book No. 4087, $29.95 paperback only

BUILD YOUR OWN 386/386SX COMPATIBLE AND SAVE A BUNDLE—2nd Edition
—Aubrey Pilgrim

Assemble an 80386 microcomputer at home using mail-order parts that cost a lot less today than they did several years ago. Absolutely no special technical know-how is required—only a pair of pliers, a couple of screwdrivers, and this detailed, easy-to-follow guide. 248 pages, 79 illustrations. Book No. 4089. $18.95 paperback, $29.95 hardcover

HIGH-PERFORMANCE C GRAPHICS PROGRAMMING FOR WINDOWS®
—Lee Adams

Take advantage of the explosive popularity of Windows with the help of computer graphics ace Lee Adams. He offers you an introduction to a wide range of C graphics programming topics that have interactive and commercial applications. From software prototypes to finished applications, this toolkit not only explores graphics programming, but also gives you many examples of working source code. 528 pages, 224 illustrations. Includes coupon for supplementary C graphics for Windows programming disk. Book No. 4103, $24.95 paperback, $34.95 hardcover

THE INFORMATION BROKER'S HANDBOOK
—Sue Rugge and Alfred Glossbrenner

Start and run a profitable information brokerage. You'll examine all of the search and retrieval options today's successful information brokers use, everything from conventional library research to online databases, special interest groups, CD-ROMs, and bulletin board systems. No successful information brokers should be without this valuable reference tool for his or her office. 408 pages, 100 illustrations, 5.25″ disk. Book No. 4104, $29.95 paperback, $39.95 hardcover

EASY PC MAINTENANCE AND REPAIR
—Phil Laplante

Keep your PC running flawlessly—and save hundreds of dollars in professional service fees! This money-saving guide will show you how. It provides all the step-by-step instructions and troubleshooting guidance you need to maintain your IBM PC-XT, 286, 386, or 486 compatible computer. If you have a screwdriver, a pair of pliers, and a basic understanding of how PCs function, you're ready to go to work. 152 pages, 68 illustrations. Book No. 4143, $14.95 paperback, $22.95 hardcover

BUILD YOUR OWN MACINTOSH AND SAVE A BUNDLE—2nd Edition
—Bob Brant

Assemble an affordable Mac with inexpensive, easy-to-obtain mail-order parts. This helpful book includes all-new illustrated instructions for building the Mac Classic, Mac portable, and new 68040-based machines (LC, IIci, and Quadra 700). It also provides valuable tips for using System 7, outlines ways you can breathe new life into older Macs with a variety of upgrade options, and updates prices on all peripherals, expansion boards, and memory upgrades. 368 pages, Illustrated. Book No. 4156, $19.95 paperback, $29.95 hardcover

MICROSOFT® MONEY MANAGEMENT
—Jean E. Gutmann

Written especially for first-time Windows users, this is a complete guide to effective financial recordkeeping with Microsoft Money—the new money management software for Windows that's perfect for individuals and small businesses that don't need a full-fledged, double-entry accounting package. With this user-friendly guide, you'll become a pro in no time as you take advantage of the expert hints and proven techniques not found in software manuals. 272 pages, 132 illustrations. Book No. 4172, $17.95 paperback only

BATCH FILES TO GO: A Programmer's Library
—Ronny Richardson

Ronny Richardson, respected research analyst and programmer, has assembled this collection of ready-to-use batch files featuring over 80 exclusive keystroke-saving programs. These fully developed programs—all available on disk for instant access—can be used as they are, or altered to handle virtually any file management task. 352 pages, 100 illustrations, 5.25″ disk. Book No. 4165, $34.95 paperback only

Prices Subject to Change Without Notice.

Look for These and Other TAB Books at Your Local Bookstore

To Order Call Toll Free 1-800-822-8158
(24-hour telephone service available.)

or write to TAB Books, Blue Ridge Summit, PA 17294-0840.

Title	Product No.	Quantity	Price

☐ Check or money order made payable to TAB Books

Charge my ☐ VISA ☐ MasterCard ☐ American Express

Acct. No. _____ Exp. _____

Signature: _____

Name: _____

Address: _____

City: _____

State: _____ Zip: _____

Subtotal	$ _____
Postage and Handling ($3.00 in U.S., $5.00 outside U.S.)	$ _____
Add applicable state and local sales tax	$ _____
TOTAL	$ _____

TAB Books catalog free with purchase; otherwise send $1.00 in check or money order and receive $1.00 credit on your next purchase.

Orders outside U.S. must pay with international money in U.S. dollars drawn on a U.S. bank.

TAB Guarantee: If for any reason you are not satisfied with the book(s) you order, simply return it (them) within 15 days and receive a full refund.

BC

Order Form for Readers
Requiring a Single 5.25" Disk

This Windcrest/McGraw-Hill software product is also available on a 5.25"/1.2Mb disk. If you need the software in 5.25" format, simply follow these instructions:

- Complete the order form below. Be sure to include the exact title of the Windcrest/McGraw-Hill book for which you are requesting a replacement disk.

- Make check or money order made payable to *Glossbrenner's Choice*. The cost is **$5.00 ($8.00** for shipments outside the U.S.) to cover media, postage, and handling. Pennsylvania residents, please add 6% sales tax.

- Foreign orders: please send an international money order or a check drawn on a bank with a U.S. clearing branch. We cannot accept foreign checks.

- Mail order form and payment to:

  Glossbrenner's Choice
  Attn: Windcrest/McGraw-Hill Disk Replacement
  699 River Road
  Yardley, PA 19067-1965

Your disks will be shipped via First Class Mail. Please allow one to two weeks for delivery.

Windcrest/McGraw-Hill Disk Replacement

Please send me a replacement disk in 5.25"/1.2Mb format for the following Windcrest/McGraw-Hill book:

Book Title _____

Name _____

Address _____

City/State/ZIP _____

If you need help
with the enclosed disk . . .

The disk included in this book contains codes and programs appearing in *Turbo Pascal Memory Management Techniques* (Book #4193), © 1993 by Len Dorfman and Marc J. Neuberger.

You might find it more convenient to have these files on your hard drive. To create a subdirectory to place these files in, type

    MKDIR *directory-name*

at your hard drive prompt, where *directory-name* is what you want to name the subdirectory.

Some of these files have been compacted into five files in order to fit them all on the disk. The five compacted files are as follows:

    EXE.EXE   ASM.EXE
    OBJ.EXE   PAS.EXE
    TPU.EXE

To unzip these files so that you can use them, place your 3.5" disk in the disk drive (probably letter B) and type

    B:*filename* C:*directory-name*

The files will all be unzipped into your newly created subdirectory.

For any other questions or specifics about the code, simply read the book.